Life's Too Short To Cry

The Compelling Memoir of a Battle of Britain Ace

Tim Vigors

ISIS

LARGE PRINT

Oxford

Copyright © Tim and Diana Vigors

First published in Great Britain 2006
by
Grub Street

Published in Large Print 2007 by ISIS Publishing Ltd.,
7 Centremead, Osney Mead, Oxford OX2 0ES
by arrangement with
Grub Street

British Library Cataloguing in Publication Data
Vigors, Tim
    Life's too short to cry: the compelling memoir of a
    Battle of Britain ace. – Large print ed.
    (Isis reminiscence series)
    1. Vigors, Tim
    2. Great Britain. Royal Air Force. Squadron, 222
    3. Great Britain. Royal Air Force – Officers –
    Biography
    4. Fighter pilots – Great Britain – Biography
    5. World War, 1939–1945 – Aerial operations, British
    6. World War, 1939–1945 – Personal narratives,
    British
    7. Large type books
    I. Title
    940.5'44941'092

        ISBN 978–0–7531–9452–2 (hb)
        ISBN 978–0–7531–9453–9 (pb)

Contents

When you have risked your neck and nearly lost it
  Battling with an enemy in the sky
Built a bridge of dreams and nearly crossed it
  You soon will learn that life's too short to cry

If you have diced with death and thrown two sixes
  And the best that he could throw was double five
Breakfasted with goblins, dined with pixies
  You'll wake up feeling life's too short to cry

When you have lost one love and found another
  Who gives you joy the Gods cannot deny
Lost friends, in losing found a brother
  You'll start to find that life's too short to cry

On the front nine you've made blunder after blunder
  And the stakes for which you play are far too high
You grit your teeth and shoot the back side in one
under
  You'll be happy that you never stopped to cry

On your colt you've grabbed a large slice of the action
  After six the whole damned field has passed him by
He battles back and gets his nose up by a fraction
  In a horse race there is never time to cry

Straight running fox, lean hounds, just twenty couple
   Green fields, stout fences and a scent breast high
Soft rain, far hills, fast horses brave and supple
   It's just hounds who have the right to sound full cry

Now when you've made your fortune all by working
   And blown it in the twinkling of an eye
Yet stumbled on new ground where gold was lurking
   You'll dig my son that life's too short to cry

The day you missed your plane by just one minute
   Heard later that you're lucky not to die
It crashed! Killed everybody in it
   You sure will know that life's too short to cry

When finally the stream of life has passed you
   And the time has come to look God in the eye
You see laughter through eternity to last you
   You'll realise life and death are both too short to cry!

TIM VIGORS 1997

CHAPTER
ONE

Penang, and Johore
Hospital

Fire can be frightening. Particularly if you are in the middle of it. Even more frightening when the cause of the fire is one hundred and fifty gallons of aviation fuel exploding under your feet. And even more mind blowing when the blaze is about 10,000 feet up in the sky. Yes, fire can be frightening.

December 12th 1941. Earlier that year I had reached the ripe old age of twenty years. For the past three months I had been commanding officer of a squadron of Brewster Buffalo aircraft, flying from airfields in Malaya. The Buffalo single-seat fighters, which the RAF had inherited from the Americans as part of the Churchill/Roosevelt Lease Lend agreement, were chubby little aircraft which had first flown in the mid-1930s. They had arrived with us in Singapore packed in large wooden crates, rather like the cartons in which came those toy aircraft I used to buy as a boy.

Four days earlier the Japanese had launched their attack on the mainland of Malaya. A few days earlier they had struck a body blow to the Allied cause by sinking two famous British battleships, *Prince of Wales* and *Repulse*. I had brought the squadron up from Singapore to Kuala Lumpur the previous afternoon and, that morning, had been ordered to take six aircraft to Butterworth. On landing I could see a hut and some petrol tankers. As I climbed down from my Buffalo, I was met by the officer commanding the airfield.

"Mighty glad to see you Tim! The Japs are very active and we have been strafed several times in the last twenty-four hours. They normally dive in from the north but there's very little warning. The only radar we have is that man there." He pointed to an airman standing on the roof of the hut. "When he starts waving his red flag it means he's spotted them and you'd better get off the ground, quick!"

I cast an eye towards the hut and sure enough there was the man. I was about to look away when I saw him raise the flag he had been holding by his side and begin to brandish it wildly from side to side above his head. It took a couple of seconds for the penny to drop but then I was yelling at my boys, telling them to get back into their aircraft and scramble. As I started my engine I saw three Japanese aircraft diving on the field from the north. That sharp stab of fear with which I had grown so familiar over the past twelve months, shot through me. "Here we go again," I thought.

With my No.2 taxiing beside me, I swung my aircraft northwards and pushed open the throttle. As we left the ground a stream of tracer streaked over us as we passed beneath the oncoming enemy. Turning sharply I saw behind me one of the Buffalos explode in a ball of flame. But the other three were off the ground safely and were climbing towards me. Glancing upwards I saw a large formation of what could only be enemy aircraft heading towards Penang. They looked to be flying at about 10,000 feet and there appeared to be at least twenty of them.

I yelled over the intercom to my three pilots, telling them to go after the Japs who had attacked the airfield while my No.2 followed me. We two climbed at full throttle to intercept the enemy formation heading for Penang. Broken fluffy clouds gave plenty of cover as we clawed for height, making for the classic attacking position, up sun and above the opponents. To my surprise I identified the Japanese aircraft as Army 97 fighters, old-fashioned and slow compared with the Messerschmitt 109s with which I had been tangling so often the previous year over England. I could not believe my luck. Here was Tim Vigors, the hardened Battle of Britain fighter ace, about to show these bloody little Japs in their antique fixed undercarriage toy planes how the Luftwaffe had been brought to its knees. I called my No.2. "OK, let's attack these little bastards and knock them all out of the sky!"

Did somebody say that pride comes before a fall? Well, I was certainly full of pride but I was about to learn in the next few minutes that there was indeed a long way to fall. Four guns blazing, I tore into the attack only to experience a rude shock; it was obvious that the Army 97 was not only the most manoeuvrable fighter with which I had fought but was also being flown by pilots who knew how to fight and fly. Black

3

smoke billowed from the aircraft in front of me and I knew I'd got the first one. But I had another one on my tail. Out of the corner of my eye I saw my No.2 in dire trouble as he tangled with two of the enemy and I hauled even harder on the stick to try to come to his assistance. I could sense by the closeness of the tracer whistling past my wing tip that my opponent was turning inside me. I wrenched the nose of my Buffalo downwards and for a moment managed to escape his attention. At the same time I got another of his friends in my sights. More black smoke and I yelled with glee out loud, "That's two of the bastards!"

My joy was shortlived. In the Brewster Buffalo the petrol tank was located almost exactly beneath the pilot's seat. The shock of having even a half tank of petrol explode underneath one is, to say the least, traumatic. It causes one hell of a big bang! A bang in fact so big that it stuns. Something had gone wrong and it took me a couple of seconds to realise that I was sitting in the middle of a bonfire. I thought, "Well old fellow, it's happened at last!" It just seemed too much of an effort to do anything about it. I even thought quickly of all the many good friends who had gone the same way over the last two years. Then, suddenly, the will to survive rose in me.

A long held habit of mine had been always to slide open the cockpit hood of any aircraft I flew in action. This habit had become ingrained, though sometimes it could be a less than pleasurable experience, such as when flying at extreme heights. On this morning with fire all around me it wasn't the cold I was worrying about, though. Pulling the pin to release my shoulder harness I placed my right foot on the stick and kicked it. Although an unorthodox way of leaving an aircraft, it is certainly a quick way.

Kicking the control column of an aircraft flying at some 250 mph creates a catapult effect which throws a human body about 200 feet into space. This was to ensure the fast exit I was looking for that morning, but it also led to the mistake which was to cause me nearly as much pain for the next few days as any of my other injuries. A falling human body has a terminal velocity of 112 mph. The drill for parachuting from an aircraft in those days was to allow time for one's body to slow down after exiting and before pulling the ripcord to release the parachute. I must have had other things on my mind because, on leaving the aircraft, I pulled the ripcord almost immediately.

Whether this over-quick reaction was caused by curiosity to see whether the thing would open or whether it was just natural impatience I don't know. But I was quickly to find out: when a parachute deploys it will abruptly stop a body which is travelling at 250 mph. The jerk of the harness between the legs is something not to be thought about — even decades later! At that time of my life I had not thought much about reproducing. But the blinding pain flashed a warning that, whatever else happened in the next few minutes, that part of my life might well be over forever!

I had not parachuted before and my first reaction was one of relief that the 'chute had opened. My second, on looking below me, was satisfaction to see that I was smack over the middle of Penang Island and not over the sea. I have always been a bad swimmer and I certainly didn't want a dip that morning. For the second time that day my relief was shortlived. Hanging in the parachute I suddenly became conscious that one of the Japanese fighters was flying straight towards me. My immediate reaction was that he was just coming to have a close look at his victim and, as we had done so often with the Germans the year before, wave a friendly salute. I was just about to raise a hand in acknowledgement when the Jap pilot opened fire. That was the worst moment of my life. I just couldn't believe what was happening. I was powerless and petrified. This then was death. Now I knew for real what the victim must feel like when he faces the firing squad. Bullets tore near me and I felt a sharp pain in my left leg but as the aircraft roared past I realised that, miraculously, I was still alive. However, I could see that the aircraft was turning to renew the attack. I knew I couldn't be as lucky a second time. A sensation of naked vulnerability gripped me. The worst was that there was nothing I could do to defend myself. Or was there?

People have said that when you know you are going to die your past life flashes by you. But I saw no ponies, dogs or horses, or foxhunting, fishing or shooting scenes, nor even my family or my lovely girl friends. Instead, a forgotten conversation came suddenly to mind. One afternoon in June 1940 I was at Ringway Airport in Manchester. At that time, Ringway was being used for the training of parachutists. That evening in the Officers' Mess the scene was a pretty good shambles with empty glasses, burnt out cigarette stubs and a few fellow officers lying around in drunken slumber. My only other fully conscious companion was an army captain. Our conversation turned to parachuting.

"Tim, my friend," said the captain, rising unsteadily to his feet, "let me get you one for the road and give you some good advice." The drinks poured, the lecture began. I can thank the good God for blessing me with an extra strong head when it comes to consuming large quantities of alcohol. If I had been in a slumber like my fellow officers I certainly would not have been alive to tell my tale.

"You probably know that during the fighting in France earlier this year there were quite a few incidents of the Jerries shooting at your fellows after they had bailed out. In nearly every case your friends were killed. Now let me tell you something. If this ever happens to you there is still a chance to survive if you know what to do."

The captain took another swig and kept going. "As your enemy comes in to attack, climb up one side of the parachute's rigging lines. After you've taken two or three good handfuls the parachute will collapse and you will drop like a stone. Once he has finished firing let go of the rigging lines, you will drop and the parachute will re-open normally. If he attacks again put off his aim by repeating the procedure."

More out of politeness than any real interest, I asked, "How many times can you collapse the damn thing before it fails to open?" He thought for a moment. "No set rules, but maybe four times out of five or, if you're lucky, nine times out of ten!" We downed our drinks and retired for the night. I never thought of his words again until that fateful moment when I found myself hanging helpless over Penang Island.

There are different grades of fear. During the past eighteen months I had experienced most of them. Until that morning I had never encountered grade 10, that stark naked terror which had gripped me the first time the Japanese pilot opened fire. Now he had turned and was diving again. But this time the surge of terror which rose inside me was only grade 9. However remote the chances, I now realised that there was something I could do about it. Reaching upwards I grasped the parachute rigging lines. Until that moment I had been unaware that there was no skin left on the palms of my hands. I learnt that day that fear can be positive — it helps to kill pain.

Hand over hand I went up those rigging lines. Just as the Jap opened fire I felt the parachute collapse and, as guaranteed by my captain friend, I did indeed drop like a stone. Tracer tore through the sky above me. Thank God for the captain! It had worked and I could fight back. Now for the crucial test. I let go of the rigging lines and swung free.

The parachute billowed out above me and my rapid descent slowed causing me considerable pain once again in the nether regions, but also infinite relief. But the aircraft once again was approaching and once more I repeated the process. Again it worked; bullets passed above me and once more the parachute opened. But this time I noticed that, as it was opening, some of the rigging lines became entangled and threatened to collapse the canopy.

I muttered to myself, "Don't leave it collapsed for too long." To my dismay I saw that my torturer had now been joined by one of his pals who had come to take part in the fun, attacking from a different direction. Once more I did the dropping act but bullets from one or both of the Japanese ripped through the parachute silk. Yet again, the canopy deployed as soon as I let go of the rigging lines. Looking down I estimated I was 2,000 feet above the jungle below.

"Only room for one more drop." For what I hoped was the last time I began to climb the rigging lines. But I had left it late. Bullets whistled round me and I felt some graze my clothing. By a miracle none of them hit me. Pressing home his attack the pilot looked as though he was going to ram me. Thinking of the ground so close below I let go of the rigging lines. His aircraft roared over me and now trees were rushing up from below. In desperation I searched for a clear spot. A clearing in the trees on my left appeared, but could I steer myself there? Gingerly, I pulled the rigging lines on the left side and found myself slipping towards the clearing. The ground rose, fast, and I braced myself. When I hit, the impact was more than anticipated but I rolled on the blessed earth with a surge of relief. But my ordeal was not over. The Japs were still intent on killing me. I staggered to my feet and ran for cover. But my parachute harness anchored me.

I reached down for the release knob to free myself. In those days the parachute webbing was gathered into the harness and fastened by a big round serrated metal knob. For safety's sake it was designed to be stiff to turn. The idea was that one just banged the metal knob to be free of the harness. Did I say that fear killed pain? Gripping and turning that cold metal in my raw hands was a sensation which will live with me forever. But fear makes you braver and, bullets spattering around me, I grasped the knob, turned and banged it, staggered a few paces, and collapsed into the undergrowth.

Fear may delay pain but the moment fear goes pain begins. From the time I had catapulted myself out of my blazing Buffalo the only intense pain I had felt was when the 'chute first opened and when I had tried to turn that terrible release knob. Now, as the roar of the Japanese engines faded away, I surveyed my sorry state. My khaki short-sleeved shirt and my trousers were scorched black, the trousers pretty much burnt away. My arms, which a short time ago had been strong, sunburnt and covered in bleached blond hair, were now a livid red and covered in blisters the size of grapefruit. Long strips of burnt skin hung from them as they did from my hands and fingers. My legs, only to some extent protected by my trousers, were in much the same state.

However, it was then that I noticed that blood was gushing from a large hole in the back of my left thigh. Closer inspection revealed that a bullet had entered the top of my thigh and passed straight through. The pain, which I was to live with for many days, really began at

10

this point. I took in my surroundings. The clearing in which I had landed was pretty much on top of the mountain which overlooks the centre of Penang Island. Jungle covered the slopes all round me but I could see the city of Penang itself on the seashore far below. "The quicker I start getting off this mountain," I thought, "the more chance I have of getting to the bottom without running out of blood."

My wounded thigh seemed to bear my weight so the bone was obviously still intact. With one last look at the parachute which had saved my life I started to wend my way gingerly through the trees doing my best to avoid contact with the undergrowth. About 300 yards down the mountain, I stumbled onto a rough path. The going on the path was difficult and my left leg was becoming weaker and weaker. Some fifteen minutes later I realised I was not going to make it, as I was losing blood at a hell of a rate and had a swimming feeling in my head. I longed to rest but I knew that to stop was fatal. I struggled on but another five minutes of drunken progress saw me collapsed in a heap. My burns hurt so much and I was so utterly tired that I felt hopeless and just did not care any more. I passed out.

Cold water poured onto burnt flesh feels like boiling oil! As I had drifted down on my burning parachute, my helmet, oxygen mask and goggles had protected most of my face from the flames. But a narrow strip of flesh between goggles and helmet had been exposed. The cold water on this raw strip woke me up with a jerk. Two small Malayans stood above me and one of them was pouring water on my head from a wooden bowl. They backed off when I tried to sit up, obviously scared that this weird looking, half-burnt, blood-stained animal was going to attack them.

"English! English!" I spluttered, hoping to reassure them. They seemed to understand and advanced cautiously towards me. Using sign language, mixed with pidgin English and a smattering of Malayan, which I had picked up over the previous six months, I managed to explain the cause of my predicament. The men appeared to be father and son, and the younger one filled the bowl again from a stream nearby and held it out for me to drink. I showed him my hands and he held it to my mouth.

Blood was still gushing from the hole in my thigh. The cold water had helped to revive me and now I started to think of priorities. To stem this flow of blood was top of the list. I managed to get this across to my rescuers and, with the aid of a piece of cord which one of them was using as a makeshift belt, and a small branch of a tree, we managed to construct a rough tourniquet. They tightened this on the top of my thigh. To my surprise and relief the flow of blood slowed down immediately. Next, using two branches from a tree, my Mae West, their own shirts and even one of their trousers, the Malays put together a makeshift stretcher. Then they helped me to roll onto the stretcher and, with an effort, lifted my thirteen and a half stone off the ground.

And so we set off on the long haul down the mountain. May God bless those two Malayans! They could only bear my weight for about 200 yards at a time and so it was a journey of many starts, stops and jolts. Sometime during the early afternoon a heavy thunderstorm struck. The raindrops hitting my hands and arms felt like red hot pins. But one comfort on that long and painful journey, accompanied by shattering skies and torrential rain, was that my leg appeared to have pretty much stopped bleeding. My fears of dying from loss of blood eased a little.

During one of our halts I got my helpers to lift me to my feet and, with one supporting me on each side, tried to walk. But my left leg simply would not work. With relief I sunk back onto the stretcher. The rain had stopped and the sun was sinking behind the mountain and it was sometime around then that I heard the sound of traffic. We realised we were getting nearer to civilisation. The tropical twilight came quickly and darkness fell. We emerged onto a narrow tarmac road and all three of us gave a croaking cheer. Another short rest and my brave saviours lifted me up one more time and started at what was almost a jog down the road.

A little later on we could hear a vehicle approaching. As it came round a bend we were caught in the headlights and it drew to a halt. It proved to be some sort of military jeep and was driven by another Malayan. After some quick exchanges I was lifted up into the back and, with my two friends beside me, we jolted off towards the city.

Fifteen minutes later we drew up outside a hospital. With care I was carried inside and met by an English-speaking nurse. I quickly told her my story. My friends wanted to come into the hospital with me but the doorman stopped them. As I was carried inside I shouted my thanks to them and at the same time asked the nurse to get their names. I was really sad to see them go. They had become so close to me during that long day and I vowed that before I left Penang I would somehow find them and reward them. After all I owed them my life. I did not know then that I was never to see them again.

The next period of my life is a blur in which there is only one constant memory — pain! Pain admittedly dulled from time to time by painkilling drugs but nevertheless, to one degree or another, constant. The first injection very soon after my arrival in the hospital brought instant, blessed, relief.

The treatment for severe burns in those days was the application of a dressing known as Tanic acid. This not only was a quick healer but also took away a lot of the discomfort caused by burns. The down side was that if it was applied to hands and fingers it just about seized up the joints of the hand being treated and left the patient, for ever after, with a stiff claw. Luckily for me this new treatment had not yet reached Penang Hospital. The treatment administered to me consisted of dipping the burnt parts of my anatomy in warm water, heavily laced with salt. Despite the painkiller administered earlier, this treatment really hurt badly but proved to be a marvellous healer. Even more important it left me with practically the full use of my finger joints. From that day on, when any of my family or friends accidentally burnt themselves I immediately made them pop the affected part into salt and water!

Of the next couple of days I only remember a few moments of complete coherency. One night a nurse told me that the Japs were preparing to invade Penang Island from the mainland and that all the patients in the hospital were to be evacuated early the next morning. As it turned out it was the following evening that we were carried on stretchers to waiting ambulances and trucks and driven down to the harbour. I remember, distinctly, lying on the quayside for hours before being loaded onto the deck of a tugboat alongside a number of wounded service personnel and civilians. Eventually the boat got going but, due to the fact that no lights were being used, the captain lost his way and ended up on the mainland but in the wrong river mouth. It was dawn before we found the right landing place and a long time later that we were removed from the tugboat and placed on a train. During this time only a minimum of medical attention was possible. I was not the only one who was in a pretty bad way.

We wounded were laid on the floor of what appeared to be some sort of mail van. But a doctor arrived and did his best to alleviate discomfort. Eventually the train jerked into motion and we were on our way south. Every few hours the train would stop and we were told that enemy aircraft were in the vicinity. However, we were never attacked and the next morning arrived in Kuala Lumpur where ambulances took us to the military hospital and our wounds were dressed. The people in Penang had written on the label around my neck "saline baths", so, without delay, I found myself

15

with arms and legs immersed in a strong solution of salt and water. No sooner had this been completed, and my leg wound dressed, than the wounded were once again loaded on the ambulances and taken back to the railway station. This time our stretchers were hung on poles across the mail van, which proved to be a great deal more comfortable than the floor.

On the following rail journey we had nurses and several doctors to administer to our needs. Despite this I had soon reached a stage of weakness of mind and body so that, no matter how hard I tried, I could not stop moaning aloud. I felt unhappy and ashamed about what this noise must be doing to my fellow passengers and when an Indian doctor passed my stretcher I begged him to give me something to make me unconscious.

From a bag he produced an enormous syringe and filled it with a black looking liquid. Pain is comparative and on a normal occasion I would have yelled as he injected into the top of my arm, where the bandages stopped. However, as soon as the liquid entered my bloodstream a feeling of euphoria began to creep over me. By the time the syringe was empty I was in a glorious haze of nothingness and I sank back into a cocoon of the softest cottonwool imaginable. Here at last was peace. Peace free from pain, free from worry, peace full of comfort and a strange happiness and almost excitement.

To this day, I do not know what liquid the Indian doctor stuck into me. Some form of extra strong morphine I can only guess. But whatever it was I spent the next twelve hours in a wonderful dream. All I loved most in my life was part of it and all that I wanted in life came true. I rode in steeplechases culminating in the Grand National, which I won on my own horse with crowds of my Irish friends yelling encouragement. I had wonderful hunts over big banks and ditches, always close to hounds with a game fox running true and straight in front up to the blue hills in the distance. I took beautiful girls in my arms giving them and myself the utmost in excitement and pleasure. Does the heroin addict experience this utopia of sensation? If he has suffered as much discomfort and pain as I then experienced I cannot say I blame him for taking his dose.

The descent from this high was slow but painful. Gradually my beautiful dream began to fade. Reality was unpleasant. It was a jolting train rushing through the Malayan jungle in sweltering heat, tired and pain-racked occupants swinging on stretchers inside it. It was the raw flesh on my arms grating against bandages and that stinging ache in my left thigh. It was a descent from Heaven into Hell.

Nonetheless, during the hours of my euphoria we had made good progress and a nurse said we would be arriving in Johore shortly. This was to be our final destination. My Indian doctor did not appear again but should he ever read these words I would like to thank him for that glorious twelve hours of release he gave me with his big needle.

Lying in a clean bed again was wonderful and the constant attention of kind, and sometimes pretty, nurses day and night provided consolation for the discomfort we wounded still felt. However, I could see from the expression in the eyes of those doctors and nurses who attended me that they were worried about my general condition. The lack of medical attention on the long journey down the peninsula had done my wounds no good at all. The screen put round my bed seemed to me to be ominous. I could get no satisfactory explanation for this isolation from the nurses. One morning a clergyman was ushered into my private compartment and, although I was somewhat delirious at the time, I knew him straight away. He had travelled out on the same boat with me from England. He started muttering some sort of blessing. I stopped him immediately.

"If you think I'm going to die Padre," I croaked, "you've got it wrong! And if you think those bloody Japs can knock off Tim Vigors where the Germans failed you can start thinking again!"

"But you're not Tim Vigors." He stared more closely at my bandaged face. "I buried Tim Vigors on Penang Island nearly a week ago."

"For God's sake, of course I'm Tim Vigors," I almost yelled. "Ask the nurses! Look at the name on the end of my bed! Look at me!"

Gradually the truth began to dawn on him. "Well, there must have been some mistake," he stuttered. "I was shown the big body of some poor burnt pilot which had been picked up out of the sea off Penang. I was told by an RAF officer that it was Tim Vigors. His face was unrecognisable from burns and he looked the same build as you so I took it for granted it was you. He had no identification tab on him so I went ahead and buried him. I'm sorry Tim but may God rest his soul. Anyway I'm glad to see you're alive." He withdrew behind my screens and I could hear him muttering to the nurses. "Goddamit Padre," I yelled, "I'm not going to die, so stop bothering God about me!"

In a funny kind of way I think this incident acted as a tonic. I had started to wallow in a bog of self-pity and the news that my No.2 in the fight over Penang had been killed made me very sad. I hadn't known him well as he had only just joined the squadron but he was a good flier and a brave fighter. His death, in a manner which I had so nearly suffered myself, brought me up short. Instead of feeling sorry for myself I realised how incredibly lucky I was to be alive.

Soon, my condition began to improve. The screens were removed from around my bed and my burns hurt less. But when burns stop hurting they start itching and although it's not as bad as the pain it drives you mad for a couple of days, especially when your hands are in bandages and you can't use them to scratch.

My leg was much better too. I was soon on my feet and for the first time able to wobble my way to the lavatory. What a blessed relief that was after a long time on my back. The indignity of having to be helped with your natural needs is something I never could stand. But soon I was wandering round the ward and talking to my companions, quite a few of whom I knew, although there were none from my own squadron. We began to catch up with the progress of the war and the

19

news was all bad. The Japanese, trained for months in jungle fighting, were outstripping and out manoeuvring our forces and were advancing rapidly down the mainland of Malaya. It became evident that unless the Army could put up one hell of a stand the Japs were going to be on top of Johore and Singapore in the very near future. Thoughts began as to what one was to do when they arrived on the doorstep.

Although my arms and hands were almost covered in bandages the pain had practically disappeared and the itching was getting less. My fingernails, on both hands, had fallen off but now were showing signs of growing again. One morning I looked at myself in a full-length mirror and what an emaciated looking object I was. I got on the scales to see how much weight I had lost and was astounded to see the needle stop at nine stone seven pounds. My immediate reaction was that the scales must be wrong. There was no way that I could have lost four stone. Although big-boned I had never carried an ounce of fat on my large frame. But on checking I found the scales were right. The thought crossed my mind that for the first time in my adult life I would be light enough to ride in races. I would like to have sent a cable to my father in Ireland asking him whether he had a horse ready for me to ride in the Grand National! Such a cable would certainly give him a shock. By this time, he would have been informed by the Air Ministry that I was missing believed killed.

And so a period of utter boredom set in. I wanted to get up and leave the hospital and get on with my life, but I was still too weak to walk more than the length of the ward. So for the first time in my life I started to think of the past in more than just brief snatches. I started to think of my first pony . . .

CHAPTER
TWO

Early Days and Beaudesert

Some people say that they learnt to swim or ski or ride or whatever before they could walk. I was put on the back of a pony before I can remember. In fact my first memories are of clutching a pony's back with my mother's supporting arm holding me in the saddle as we proceeded down the cinder path leading from the stables to the house. Not very long after I was making the journey without the support of my mother's arm and soon after that I was coming down the path from the stables without anybody holding the pony's bridle. In fact I had gone solo!

At the time of this momentous occasion in my life I had just turned two. The year was 1923 and my Irish father, who had survived the First World War as an officer in the British Army, was now a partner in the well-known London stockbroking firm of Cazenove & Akroyd. Both he and my mother were crazy about horses and everything to do with them so they chose to live in a charming old farmhouse near the village of Wookey Hole in Somerset. Here, in the middle of the famous Mendip fox hunting country, they had every opportunity to pursue their first love.

My elder brother, Terence, two years older than myself, had already been taken out hunting on a leading rein by the time I had completed my first solo. As is the way with younger brothers, I was quick to catch up and I think I was still only three years old when I first attended a meet of the foxhounds in the saddle.

The passion for fox hunting is very hard to explain to the majority of those who do not share it. It was described by Oscar Wilde as "the unspeakable in pursuit of the uneatable" or, more accurately, "the very image of war without its guilt and only twenty-five per cent of its danger"! Suffice to say that hunting has been an overriding passion in my life.

Why is this? What has drawn me, and many others like me, to this extraordinary, thrilling, character-building, challenging, dangerous, beautiful and totally useless and time wasting, pastime? It is certainly not any desire to kill a fox. In fact I love them and am fascinated by their wily ways, cunning intelligence, and speed, stamina and courage.

"How then," you will say, "can you go out with forty dogs and chase a poor fox across country until such time he is so tired that he is pulled down by your dogs and torn to pieces?" Again, I look to Oscar Wilde who (I think) once wrote "All men kill the things they love."

Fox hunting people go to endless lengths and some expense to protect foxes. Without the protection afforded to them by fox hunting they would be subjected to the fate of all other vermin, for that is what foxes are. But the fox is an animal that the fox hunter finds very difficult to get close enough to when using a gun. As a result, for every ten which are shot at, five probably escape unscathed and at least four will be mortally wounded and left to crawl away to die slowly, alone and in agony. When they are chased by hounds only about one in twenty are killed and those which do meet their deaths are virtually all killed instantaneously. They are long dead before they are torn to pieces.

Now for the fox hunter. What does he get out of this strange sport? He gets long days in the fresh air in all sorts of weather. He gets hours of riding along lanes or standing beside woods waiting for the first cry of hounds to signify that somewhere in that wood there is a fox afoot. He gets that wild thrill when he hears the whipper-in, stationed at the end of the wood, let out a blood curdling yell to signify that the fox has broken for the open country. He gets the excitement of the first cavalry charge in the direction of where the fox has gone. He gets the mental exercise of his mind going into top gear to assess the weather, the lie of the land, even the habits of the foxes in that area, and in which direction this particular fox will run. He gets the gambler's anticipation as he turns his horse away from the rest of his companions and strikes out on a line of his own which he believes will take him directly to where the fox is heading. He uses his skill and knowledge to pick out where to jump the fences which confront him and, while his horse rises to take the jump, to search quickly for where to jump out of the field he will land in. He feels the wild pleasure of a good horse galloping underneath him and taking hold of the bit. Then suddenly he sees hounds gathered together on top of each other in the corner of the field baying and digging at the bank in front of them. The fox has found its earth and gone to ground.

I do have a hazy memory of my first meet. It took place with the Mendip Foxhounds, several miles from our home, so I was taken in a car and once arrived scrambled onto my pony with the aid of our young groom whose job it was to care for the various horses and ponies belonging to my father and mother. My father, mother and brother had ridden from home and were already mounted and mingling with all the other hunting people preparing for their day's sport. I remember being led on a leading rein by the groom walking beside me as the hounds were taken off down the road by the huntsman towards the first covert.

It still gives me a thrill now to remember the first cry of the hounds as they scented the presence of a fox in the covert. I can recall the loud "Holloa" of the whipper-in as he saw the fox leaving the covert and can re-live the excitement of the first cavalry charge towards the direction of where hounds were leaving behind their quarry. I can still remember my frustration at being anchored by a leading rein to the groom running alongside me and everybody else galloping after hounds. And the bitter disappointment at the sound of hounds, horses and people fading away into the distance. And that was the end of my first day's hunting.

The following year I was still on the leading rein but this time I was being led by my mother who herself was riding one of her more placid horses. Skilfully led by her across the fields through gates and along lanes, I started to partake in the hunt and feel the real excitement of what was going on around me.

Then came the great day when I was allowed to attend a meet unrestricted by a leading rein, free under the guidance of my mother, to make my own way across the country. The fields of the Mendip hills are divided not by ordinary fences or banks but by stone walls. Some of these are over five foot high but in many cases are much lower than this. Even in the high walls there is nearly always a place where stones have been knocked from the top of the wall making a smaller obstacle. To start off with it was to these lower parts of the walls which my mother guided me, jumping first herself and then turning to watch me safely over. By having to divert to these smaller obstacles we inevitably lost ground on those people who were galloping straight after hounds and taking the walls as they met them. But very often we managed to make up for this. Since that day, I have met and hunted with many women who could cross the country as well as and better than most men. But in all my life I never met a greater woman to ride to hounds than my mother. Above this she seemed to possess a natural instinct as to which way the fox was going to turn and, using this instinct, in addition to her wonderful eye for the lie of the land, we managed on many occasions to stay remarkably close to the hounds.

My brother and I used to count our falls. My father promised a prize of two shillings and sixpence to the one who got to a hundred first. We were neck and neck in this race and both coming close to the magic number one fine morning when we were all out for a ride on the top of a gorse-covered hillock, above Ebor Wood. My pony swerved in mid-air when jumping one of these bushes and despite desperately clinging onto her mane, I crashed to the ground. Picking myself up, bruised but unhurt, I suddenly realised that I had reached the figure of ninety-nine. Retrieving my pony I jumped on her back and made for where my mother and father were sitting on their horses watching our antics. As I cantered past them I let loose a yell of triumph and flung myself over my pony's side, landing in a heap at my parents' feet.

"That makes the hundred!" I shouted triumphantly. "I want my two and sixpence!" And I immediately got it!

In those days my brother Terence (nicknamed "Tel") and I were very close. However, the day came when he was sent off to a preparatory school near Stroud called Beaudesert Park. The term time was lonely without Tel.

It was during that season's hunting, when I was just rising eight years old, that I had my first serious fall. Galloping fast in pursuit of hounds I faced my pony at an extra large wall which loomed up at me. She just failed to clear it and I shot over her head as we hit the ground together. Unfortunately my face landed on a loose stone lying in the grass and, at that moment, the pony rolled on me. As a result my mouth was a bloody mess. I had acquired only a few of my permanent teeth but one of these, my pride and joy, was an enormous tooth which, along with the rest of my front teeth, was knocked out.

Before anyone could come to my assistance I remounted my pony and off we dashed in pursuit of hounds. When I caught up with the rest of the hunt, the hounds had checked and the huntsman was casting them in a wide semi-circle to pick up the line. My mother turned and saw me and with an appalled look rushed over to inspect the damage. The car, driven by our groom, was on the road nearby and, protesting, I was bustled into it and driven to the local doctor for repairs. As a result of this accident I sported a large gap in the front of my mouth until I had a capping job done years later.

At the end of the Easter holidays, 1929, I was sent off to join Tel at Beaudesert. I recall to this day the feeling of utter misery which engulfed me when, waking up at school the first morning, I realised that I was confined and was no longer my own master. My life up until this time had been one of glorious freedom and I was totally unprepared for the restriction which any school must of necessity enforce on its young inmates. I just could not get my mind to accept that this restriction applied to me. As I looked out of my dormitory window that morning I expected every moment to see my mother driving up the road to the school on her way to rescue me from the indignity to which I had, obviously mistakenly, been subjected. When no mother in car materialised I started to bawl like a baby and hardly let up for the next forty-eight hours. But time is a great healer and gradually that awful feeling of homesickness started to fade and little by little, I became adjusted to the routine of school life.

My first weekend at Beaudesert was to change the course of my life. On Sunday afternoons the entire school, about eighty boys between the age of eight and thirteen, were allowed complete freedom on the large grass field which lay in the woods below the school building. There each boy could do his own thing for a couple of hours either singularly or collectively. Although I had been at school for nearly a week I had not yet made any close contacts with my fellow pupils. Wallowing in my personal misery I had refrained from trying to make friends and now found myself too shy to intrude on any of the groups. Sadly I wandered across the field and sat down by myself under a tree. It was then that I spotted a lean dark-haired boy of about my own age launching into the air what was evidently a model aeroplane.

My only direct contact with aeroplanes up to then had been when Teddy Tiarks, a nephew of Herman Tiarks who was Master of the Mendip Foxhounds, had flown a Tiger Moth through some telegraph wires. He was showing off to some of his friends, including my father and mother. I remember very clearly the impact as the little aeroplane hit the ground and crumpled up. Strangely it didn't burn. But when Teddy was dragged from the wreckage he was dead.

With these morbid memories I watched with only a vague interest as the boy launched his flimsy wooden and canvas contraption into the air. Its propeller was driven by a large elastic band and once aloft it could achieve about twenty yards of powered flight before the band had fully unwound and it glided, powerless, to the grass. On the first couple of attempts its wing tip hit the ground first and it cartwheeled to a stop bringing back vivid memories to me of Teddy. But the third time the boy made some minor adjustment to the tail and, when the propeller stopped, it glided to a perfect landing.

"Did you ever see a smoother landing than that?", the boy said turning to me. The next time he flew the aircraft he allowed me to pick it up. As I held it I felt an unaccountable shiver run through me. I could suddenly imagine myself sitting behind those wings and soaring into the sky.

"What's it called?

"A Warnford Monoplane", he replied. "Look, you can adjust the elevator and the rudder and the ailerons! Not like the old one I had. I believe I can make this fly away and turn in a circle and come right back to me."

"What's your name?"

"Tim Vigors," I replied. "What's yours?"

"Henry Maudslay," he said. "I'm a new boy, are you?" I told him how I hated it.

"Oh, it's not so bad", he said, "particularly if you have a friend." And so started one of the closest friendships of my life. We shared an interest in aeroplanes which was to absorb us both for the next nine years and, later, one dark night over Germany, was to kill Henry. An interest that so often nearly killed me too.

Memories of school days come back in flashes. Rugger, wielding a cricket bat for the first time and with very little natural talent, more difficult lessons, flying aeroplanes with Henry, and our first experience of parade drill under a fierce old Irishman, Sergeant Major Miller the school PT master, singing at the school concert and receiving an unexpectedly warm ovation, yet more difficult lessons, running truant through the woods down to the village in the valley below the school to buy chocolate, flying bigger and better aeroplanes with Henry, croquet on the lawn in front of the school, winning the school junior long jump and the pride of being presented with a tiny silver cup — the only cup I've ever won — and endless difficult lessons.

Being of Irish descent I had a natural affinity with Sergeant Major Miller. He nearly made me rich for life. Through his connections the Sergeant Major had managed to obtain a book of tickets in the Irish Hospital Sweepstake. In the England of that time betting on such sweepstakes was illegal, but one day he told me that he had just one ticket left and asked me if I'd like to buy it. Henry agreed, somewhat grudgingly, to go halves with me and we set out to raise the necessary five shillings.

Each week boys were allowed to draw their own money from the school bank, presided over by our kindly yet fearsome headmaster, Mr Richardson. "How much do you want this week, Maudslay?" Mr Richardson asked. Henry stepped forward and asked for five shillings.

"What do you want it for? Buying another aeroplane?"

"No, sir," replied Henry. "I'm buying a ticket in the Irish Sweep with Vigors."

The headmaster turned purple.

We were threatened with all sorts of punishment, but in the end we were allowed to go. "You were a silly bloody fool to tell Richardson about the ticket," I raged at Henry, "but thank goodness you didn't split on the Sergeant Major, he'd have lost his job." Henry mumbled apologies and we went off to tell my friend that we had changed our minds about buying the ticket.

The Sergeant Major subsequently sold the ticket to an old lady in the village. She drew a horse named Tipperary Tim who proceeded to win the Grand National. The old lady won twenty-five thousand pounds. Sergeant Major Miller got a prize of five hundred pounds for selling the winning ticket. I heard later that the old lady drank herself to death. Maybe Henry and I would have gone down the same path!

Soon after I went to Beaudesert my brother and I started spending the whole of the month of August each year with my Uncle Edward at Burgage, the family home in County Carlow in the middle of the south of Ireland. My mother would accompany us on these visits and my father would travel over for weekends. Burgage was originally built by one of my ancestors about 300 years previously when, as a Huguenot, he had been hounded from his estate near the town of Caen in Normandy.

That ancestor of mine certainly knew how to choose a site for a house. Situated on a grassy slope above the

River Barrow it looks out across rolling country to the beautifully moulded shape of Mount Leinster. Since it was built Burgage has twice been partially destroyed by fire, once intentionally during "The Troubles" and once unintentionally by one of my ancestors who after a good dinner went to sleep in his armchair smoking a large cigar. The house is approached from the main road by an undulating, winding drive which is bordered by great oak and beech trees and opens onto a wide gravel sweep in front of the steps leading up to the front door. Behind the house lies the spectacular view over the River Barrow to Mount Leinster.

It was during one of our summer visits to Burgage at the ripe age of nine years that I fell head over heels in love for the first time. I was totally unprepared. I had no sisters and the only cousins with whom I had close contact were all boys. I must have met girls at children's parties but I have absolutely no memory of them up to that time.

The object of my affections was the same age as myself. She was of medium height, had beautiful light blue eyes and her ash blond hair fell in a cascade over her shoulders down to her slim waist. The desire to run my fingers through her blond mane was as overwhelming as it was unexpected. I was used to stroking my pony or my dog but never before had I wanted to stroke another human being. A child of my age today would have seen it all on the television a hundred times but I had never even been to the movies.

At the tea party where I first saw her I can remember edging my way across the room in order to get closer.

33

Whilst handing her a plate of strawberries I managed, quite unintentionally, to brush my free hand against her hair and experienced for the first time totally new emotions. She thanked me for the strawberries and continued talking to a fat friend. Awkwardly I stood close to her gawking at her until, self-consciously, she fidgeted with her dress and pulled it further down over her knees.

"What's your name?" I eventually blurted.

"Kitty," she replied. "What's yours?"

"Tim," I said, "I am staying at Burgage."

And so, clumsily, we started to talk and to tell each other about our lives. Kitty lived with her parents, two sisters and a brother, in a pretty Georgian house about six miles from Burgage. My immediate instinct the following day was to jump on my bicycle and pedal off to see her. Because most of the route lay along the main road between the important towns of Carlow and Kilkenny my Uncle Edward vetoed this idea immediately on the grounds of the volume of traffic on the road. As the traffic in those days consisted of about one car every five minutes I protested strongly about this decision but he was adamant; eventually a compromise was reached in the shape of the ginnet cart being substituted for the bicycle. A ginnet is a cross between a pony stallion and a donkey mare. Faster than a donkey, it is still a lot slower than a pony of the same size, and a great deal slower than an active young man on a bicycle spurred on by his first love. I readily agreed to the compromise and it took me little more than ten minutes to catch the ginnet and harness her in the donkey cart and, only forty-five minutes later, I was turning off the lane into the wrought iron gateway of Kitty's house.

At the front door I was greeted with surprise but warmth by Kitty's mother who ushered me into the drawing room where the object of my visit was seated at a grand piano practising scales. I can remember her jumping to her feet in astonishment when she saw me. But still I thought I could detect a glint of excitement in those blue eyes as, on her mother's instructions, she led me off to the large play room at the back of the house where her sisters and brothers were seated round a table playing ludo. The game had reached a tense stage and I received only a cursory greeting. After a few minutes standing awkwardly at the table I asked Kitty if she had a pony. She said she did not but her brother had one and I asked immediately if we could go and look at it.

On the way to the stables I can remember being amazed by my boldness at being where I was. If Kitty had been a boy I would have felt relaxed and natural but on that walk to the stables I realised that this was the first time in my life I had been alone with a girl. I felt tongue-tied, clumsy and out of place and fought off a desire to rush back to the security of Burgage and my brother.

To reach the stables we had to climb over a stout post and rail fence. I was first over, jumping to the ground from the top rail. Kitty, trying to copy me, caught her toe on the top rail as she jumped and landed in a heap. I quickly bent down to help her up. I grasped her hand and at that moment the battle with my uncle and all the later embarrassment and awkwardness became worthwhile.

I don't remember much of the remainder of the afternoon. But I can recall to this day the warm glow of happiness at being close to this lovely human being. Twice more during the next week I harnessed up the ginnet and drove off to see my girlfriend. We never talked about our feelings for each other but we seemed just naturally to accept that we liked to be together. At the end of the week the holidays drew to a close and I was taken off back to England and my second term at Beaudesert.

I wouldn't go so far as to say that I pined for Kitty but I missed no opportunity to talk about her and bring up her name whenever possible. Back at Beaudesert I told my friend Henry about my experiences but received the profound advice that "All girls are soppy and a waste of time and anyway they don't like aeroplanes."

In 1929 my father, who was doing well on the stock exchange, decided to go really up market on the fox hunting scene. Our Wookey Hole farmhouse was sold and replaced by a modern six-bedroom residence in the village of Great Bowden, near Market Harborough, the Mecca of English fox hunting. My brother Tel and I viewed this move with mixed feelings. The downside was that we were no longer living completely in the country. The upside was that only just outside the village were situated the solid red brick kennels which had been built thirty years before to house the famous Fernie foxhounds.

Our stable yard started filling remarkably quickly with high-class hunters and ponies. Our dachshund pack was steadily growing and now consisted of fifteen dogs and bitches, seven and a half couple in hunting parlance. The originals and a few of their favoured descendants were allowed to live in the house. The remainder were kennelled in a yard across the road from the house.

Soon after arriving in Great Bowden, Tel and I started to contact local farmers to get permission to hunt hares on their land. Being in the heart of hunting country we generally met with a sympathetic hearing and we soon found ourselves with about thirty square miles in the Welham Valley where we were free to pursue our favourite pastime.

School holidays for the following years followed a regular pattern. The first half of the summer holidays were spent at Burgage, where my relationship with Kitty grew deeper and flourished. From the start of the third week in August it was back to Market Harborough to start getting the hunters fit for the coming season and regular afternoon hunting in the Welham Valley with our dachshund pack.

Our Christmas holidays were taken up entirely with hunting. At least three days a week we spent pursuing the Fernie foxhounds. On the remaining days Tel and I would be out with our own pack of hounds hunting hares in the Welham Valley. We were invited to frequent children and teenage parties. Strangely, for such a large and rather clumsy child, I acquired a liking and a certain ability for dancing which led me into a partnership with a small and nimble girl of my own age named Susan with whom I found myself dancing regularly at many of the parties. Our efforts culminated in winning a prize as the best dancers at a big party given at Dingley Hall, the home of old Admiral Beatty who had commanded Her Majesty's Fleet at the Battle of Jutland in 1917.

The immediate result of this athletic achievement was that the admiral, who had heard of our dachshund pack, invited Tel and myself to hunt them on the following Sunday on his land. After a long and interesting chase after a hare all round his estate we were invited to tea in his large house. The admiral seemed to have taken a liking to me and over the tea table he said:

"Young fellow, I think you would do well in the Navy. I will arrange for you to go to the Royal Naval College at Dartmouth." To which I somewhat cheekily replied: "Thank you very much sir, but my father has arranged for me to go to Eton and after that I'm going to join the RAF."

It was not until I was on the way home that I realised that this was the first time that I had uttered in public my firm intentions about my future. My father, who was present at the tea table, was somewhat taken aback. But parental persuasion was to no avail and, from that moment, my sights were firmly set and I started to live with the certainty that flying was going to be my career.

Another spin-off from my success on the dance floor was that I experienced for the first time in my life the inevitable pangs of conscience about becoming involved in a relationship with two ladies at the same time. Of course they lived in different countries and were unlikely ever to meet each other but, nevertheless, I was careful to avoid any reference to the success of my dancing partner and myself. When I next met Kitty the following August, I had to administer my brother Tel a well-aimed kick when he looked like bringing it up whilst we were all sitting round a table at Burgage playing cards. Whilst at school Kitty and I had started to write to each other and it worried me a bit when one morning during my last days at Beaudesert an affectionate letter from Susan unexpectedly arrived. I asked Henry's advice as to what I should do but, as I had feared, he was totally unhelpful. After a couple of days of worrying I replied somewhat reservedly to Susan's letter saying I hoped I would see her next holidays and telling her that I was playing in the school rugger XV. Little did I realise at the time that I was getting my first experience of a situation which was to bother me often in the years ahead!

During the mid-1930s my father made the big decision to cash in his winnings on the Stock Exchange and return to his native country. The house at Market Harborough was sold and all but the closest of the dachshund pack were distributed to good homes. Whilst looking for a permanent home in Ireland, my father chose to rent a beautiful riverside house in County Kerry, Sheen Falls.

The house was situated on the point where the falls at the mouth of the River Sheen spew their waters over a rocky cascade into the head of the Kenmare Estuary. In spring you could sit in the garden and watch salmon work their way up the falls to the calm waters above.

The family move was made at the close of the hunting season in England. All but four of the hunters were put up for auction at the Leicester sale held in those days by Warner, Sheperd and Wade. It was sad to see the hunters go but, wherever we eventually settled in Ireland, we knew that only the most adaptable of them could possibly manage to jump the hairy banks and ditches they would encounter in the Irish country. They were too used to crossing the Leicestershire fences at racing speed. So, the chosen four were put out to grass for the summer on a neighbouring farmer's land to await a new home chosen for them, and ourselves, across the Irish Sea.

After looking at numerous properties in different parts of the country my father and mother eventually settled for Tullamaine Castle, near the town of Fethard in County Tipperary. It is a telling reflection on the rise in property values combined with the fall in the value of money in the 1930s that father bought this fine residence, together with 400 acres of prime farming land for only £6,000.

The old castle, bits of which are still incorporated in the present structure, had stood on the well-chosen site for many hundreds of years. Like most old houses in Ireland it had fallen down and been burnt down several times over the centuries and the present structure was of a Victorian rather than Cromwellian structure. Nevertheless, Tullamaine was a fine building and was to be our home for the next ten years and a wonderful base for my introduction to the Irish way of life.

In those far-off days the test for children passing from preparatory schools to public schools was called the Common Entrance. Full of confidence I sat for this exam when I was twelve and a half. It never occurred to me that I could fail a test which had been proclaimed by all as a walk over. A month later Mr Richardson announced that he wanted to see me in his study. With only a faint feeling of trepidation I approached his door. On entering he bade me sit down and it was only then that I realised from the look on his face, that I was in for bad news.

"Tim," he said gruffly, "I've just had your exam results and I'm afraid they're not good. You've only passed four out of seven subjects and that's not enough to get you into Eton." He must have seen the look of amazement on my face. He rose and placed a hand on my shoulder.

"Don't worry too much boy," he said kindly, "you were taking the test six months early and if you get down to work I'm sure you'll pass it next time."

Stifling tears of anger and disappointment I staggered from the room. I was shocked to the core. Up to then I had always succeeded more or less at everything which I had taken on. I simply could not bring myself to believe that I had failed at what I regarded as a simple exam. In retrospect this failure was probably the best thing that had ever happened to me. It made me realise, for the first time, that success was not just achieved by enthusiasm and brute force. I suddenly woke up to the fact that there were things in life which could only be achieved by concentrated and detailed effort. I can honestly say that those few moments in my headmaster's study changed my entire attitude towards what was necessary to get what I wanted.

I could not face up to telling my friends of my failure and avoided contact with them so far as I could for the rest of the evening. I had taken no trouble to hide my confidence of success and found it difficult to face up to the humiliation of defeat. I resolved there and then that I would never let this kind of situation occur again through my own default. For the next two terms I concentrated on my lessons with a verve spurred on by fear of a second defeat. Six months later I passed the Common Entrance with flying colours and was accepted into Eton. My first serious lesson in the dangers of over-confidence had sunk well and truly home.

CHAPTER
THREE

Eton and Crammers

I have always looked back on my four years at Eton with mixed feelings. I never felt that I was likely to fit into the school as it then was. There was a somewhat snobbish, insular and, on some basic matters, narrow-minded attitude surrounding its staff and many of its pupils. On the other hand, the extra freedom of action which Eton afforded to its inmates, especially when compared with that experienced at most preparatory schools and indeed many public schools, was an immediate joy to an independently minded thirteen year old.

About three years before my arrival at Eton another friend had entered my life. I had met John Harley whilst visiting my aunt in Shropshire. He was my own age and shared nearly all my interests. We quickly struck up a close friendship and started to visit each other regularly in the holidays. John and I arrived at Eton on the same day and naturally turned towards each other for support and companionship.

Eton was difficult for newcomers. The short jackets, black trousers and top hats we juniors wore and the same, but long-tail, coats for seniors seemed unnatural.

And, though each boy was allotted his own room on arrival, which provided a welcome privacy, it also created some loneliness. I cannot say that I experienced the same desolate feeling I had felt on arrival at Beaudesert, but I do remember being completely overawed at Eton by my strange surroundings.

I got into trouble on my first day over the custom of all boys having to go to church every day and twice on Sundays. To accommodate the many boys, around 1,100 in my day, two chapels were provided, Junior Chapel for the younger boys and School Chapel for the seniors. New boys were allocated their seats in Junior Chapel by their housemasters and were expected to be in place on time, along with everybody else.

My early experiences of crossing country when hunting had, I thought, blessed me with a good sense of direction, a fact of which I was very proud. But on that first morning at Eton my sense of direction completely deserted me. Long after everybody else was seated in their allotted places I was still blundering up and down the aisle looking for mine. The organ stopped playing in readiness for the service to begin and I could hear people starting to snigger at my predicament. I felt totally exposed to the ridicule of 400 boys and masters and near to tears.

Eventually a master came to my assistance and led me, blushing, to my place. It was a bad start. After chapel there was a short break before lessons commenced. I desperately sought out John Harley, to unload some of my discomfort on him; in the mob of boys spewing out of the chapel, John was nowhere to be found, so, disconsolate, I found my way to my classroom. My Eton education had begun.

I would be lying if I said I could remember anything that I liked about my first few weeks at Eton. I felt completely at sea. I didn't like the clothes which I was forced to wear, the food which I was made to eat, having to find my way through the town to strange classrooms; I didn't like the elder boys in my house who seemed to consider it their right and duty to make life as unpleasant as possible for new arrivals, and above all I didn't like my housemaster who seemed determined to make me feel inferior from the moment we first met.

Of course by the time I had left Beaudesert I had been pretty much a big fish in a small pond and the transition to finding myself a tiddler in a large lake was bad. John and I were in different classes for most subjects but we always tried to get together at some point of each day and we both found some solace in pouring out our troubles to each other.

We had arrived at Eton for the summer term, or "half" in Eton terminology. Two alternate forms of sport were allowed to all boys during the summer and generally speaking it was left to every boy to make up his mind which he wanted to follow. One could either become a "drybob" and play cricket or a "wetbob" and take up rowing. At Beaudesert I had been selected — through scarcity of other available talent rather than natural ability on my part — to play cricket for the school eleven. Because of this I was told by my housemaster that I must become a drybob. I was too scared to argue, even though I had no feeling or ability for cricket, which I have always regarded as a game which was either boring or frightening, depending whether you were fielding or batting. I was forced against my will to put my name down as a drybob.

Luckily it did not take long to persuade those responsible for training the house cricket team that in Vigors Minor, as I was called being a younger brother, they were dealing with material which lacked both the will and the way. It was therefore only four weeks into the half that I managed to convince the house cricket authorities that no matter how inept I might be in a boat I could not be of less service to the house wielding an oar than I would be wielding a bat. I was told to report to the house captain of rowing and try my luck on the Thames. Being strong and blessed with good balance I soon adapted to the basic skills of rowing a "rigger" by myself or sharing the effort with three others in a "four". For the first time since I had come to Eton I started to enjoy myself.

Sculling up the river by myself gave me that feeling of independence which I had sadly missed for the last four weeks. The quiet country on the river banks above Windsor made me feel more at home than the bustling streets of Eton. With my afternoons on the river to look forward to, the rough edges of school life began to wear off. I started to make some friends both in and out of the classroom and learnt to adapt myself to the everyday routine, along with my one thousand plus fellow students.

At school, lessons had to be learnt, if only after a fashion. Boats had to be rowed, either casually or at racing speed up and down the river, filthy meals had to be eaten if only to avoid starvation — or cooked for older boys each day, or at least until one became old enough to order younger boys to cook teas for oneself. Footballs had to be kicked luckily the good God had failed to bless me with any sort of an eye for a ball, moving or stationary, so football during the winter could be legally substituted by cross-country running. This to some degree alleviated the humdrum school routine; even better was the rule that allowed boys, at least once a week, to go hunting with the Eton beagles.

John Harley and I got into the habit of going for runs together two or three days a week. Apart from getting us very fit, these runs across the farmland surrounding the school gave us both a feeling of individual freedom of action which came as a big relief from the discipline of school life. Henry Maudslay had grown even skinnier and pale looking as he spent much of the time when John and I were out on our runs cooped up in his room studying the manufacture of aircraft. In order to avoid games or other forms of exercise, he would continually report sickness under false pretences. Having thus received permission to stay in his room on the grounds of a bad chest he was much more likely to be found inhaling nicotine than Friar's Balsam. John and I got quite worried about him and resolved that one way or another we would get him to accompany us on one of our runs. It took a lot of persuasion but we did eventually, one March afternoon, manage to extract

Henry from his smoke-filled room to follow us at a slow jog into the countryside.

Intentionally, for Henry's sake, we kept the pace really slow. After about half a mile we were surprised to find him still with us. John and I prided ourselves on our cross-country prowess and to find this pale, unfit, bookworm matching our pace with such consummate ease really started to bug us. As we headed back towards Eton I turned to John. "Let's go," I panted, "and show him what it's all about."

And go we did, with all the power and energy in us. To no avail. Henry coasted past us, his long easy action apparently completely unaffected by any shortage of breath. "He's a natural," sobbed John. "Natural's the word," I sighed, "he's a natural to win the Junior mile! And think of the odds we'll get with the local bookmaker." We shouted to Henry to stop. Together we all walked back towards the school. I explained my idea to Henry and told him if he would fall in with our plans we would give him a five-shilling bet for free. We also told him that he would have to go into training, which we would supervise, and that the whole thing must be kept dead secret.

Henry complied, with one proviso: "I'm not going to give up smoking," he stipulated. "Otherwise, I won't do it!" Reluctantly, we agreed to his terms. Three months later Henry won the Junior mile by nearly a lap, the darkest of dark horses. Earlier, John and I had got odds of 50 to 1 on a £1 bet with a Windsor bookmaker. He, grudgingly, paid us our £50 winnings. "That's the last time I'll take a bet from you two young scoundrels!" he growled.

Laughing, we pocketed our money. On the way back to school we risked our necks by going into a side street pub and collecting six bottles of beer for the celebration party in Henry's room.

A week later Henry, still only aged fifteen, ran over the same course in the School mile. Fighting with all his guts and courage, he threw himself across the finishing line a mere one foot in front of the nearest of his rivals, most of whom were two years older than himself.

Five years later, Flight Lieutenant Maudslay, DFC, in action against the three Ruhr dams in the "Dambusters Raid" led by Wing Commander Guy Gibson, VC, once again fought with all his guts and courage as the pilot of a Lancaster, to launch his "bouncing" mine from only 60 feet above the Eder Dam. As Henry pulled up above the parapet of the dam an explosion and a huge orange flash were seen by the other aircraft and he and his crew disappeared. No bodies were found or aircraft wreckage located. And so died my dear boyhood friend, whose love of aeroplanes was only surpassed by his fearlessness when flying them.

Soon after my sixteenth birthday it was brought home to me in no uncertain terms that unless something drastic was done about my education I had absolutely no hope of passing the exam to get into Cranwell. My father, whilst accepting quite calmly my desire to join the RAF, had made it clear for some time that he wanted me to do the thing properly and obtain a permanent commission through two years training at the Royal Air Force College. To achieve this objective I had to sit for and pass the Cranwell entrance exam, the stiffest of its kind in the country. Two cadres of just over twenty men each were accepted for Cranwell every year. Close on 200 ambitious young men like myself sat for each of these stiff tests in full knowledge that only about one tenth of them would be accepted.

In the summer of 1937 one of my schoolmates, who through his exceptional ability had achieved the exalted position of being second out of the 1,100 boys on the Eton school list, sat for the Cranwell exam and to his and everybody else's amazement, failed dismally. At this time, with little more than a year to run before I must sit for the same exam, my position on the school list was 526th.

I immediately wrote to my father telling him what had happened and suggesting that urgent consideration should be given to my leaving Eton and going to a crammer's. He replied saying that he would consider the idea and speak to me about it during half term (or "long leave" as it was called at Eton, although it only lasted for a weekend). I considered discussing the matter with my housemaster but rejected the idea. Mr Roe had always been violently opposed to my idea of joining the RAF. He had spent much time explaining to me over the years that by taking such action I was not only letting down the school and my family but, more important still, his house. He referred continually to RAF officers as "a lot of bloody mechanics!" and told me that by trying to join their ranks I was wasting all the experience of mixing with "gentlemen" which my father and he had provided. I had long since given up trying to point out to him that, in my opinion, the numerous earls and princes with whom I rubbed shoulders both in his house and the rest of the school would be unlikely to shun my company in future years just because I was flying an aircraft in the King's service. I decided not to consult Mr Roe. Instead I sought a private interview with my Classical Tutor, Fred Howe, a humane and long-suffering man who had the bad luck to be shouldered with the responsibility for my educational advancement. Old "FWH" as he was affectionately known by his students, proved most helpful and suggested that he should write to my father giving him the names of crammers he could personally recommend.

The antipathy of some sections of the Eton Society against the RAF was brought home to me vividly three years later. In mid-September 1940 the Battle of Britain was at its peak. My Spitfire Squadron, 222, was involved in the battle from the middle of August when we moved down from Kirton-in-Lindsey in Lincolnshire to Hornchurch on the eastern outskirts of London. The battling had been intense and our casualties unpleasantly high.

Somehow or other the boy who was head of the RAF society at Eton had located me and wrote to ask if I would be willing to give a lecture to the entire school. The society wanted a first-hand blow-by-blow account of the battle. Although I've always been a show-off I have never gone out of my way to lionise myself; it took some serious soul searching before I approached my squadron commander, Johnny Hill, and asked him for his permission to deliver the lecture.

"You know how shorthanded we are Tim," he said "and I can't really spare you but as long as you don't have to leave the station before five this evening you'd better go and do it. They always say that the battle of Waterloo was won on the playing fields of Eton but I can tell you as sure as hell that this battle is being fought somewhere else. Maybe you can drag in a few more players from your old school!"

I called up the boy at Eton and we arranged a date about ten days ahead. I had plenty to occupy my mind for the next ten days but whilst lying in the sunshine at dispersal between fights I started to make some notes of what I was going to say. Two days before I was to give the lecture I was called to the telephone in the Mess after dinner. I was surprised to find myself talking to the Provost at Eton who acted as a sort of second-in-command to the headmaster.

"Vigors," he said, "about this lecture of yours. I have been talking to the headmaster and we have decided that a lot of parents would disapprove of their sons being encouraged to join the RAF. Regretfully we must ask you to cancel."

I did not tell him what I thought. I just put the telephone back on the hook without even saying goodbye. I still find it difficult to come to terms with this incident.

Maybe I'm being unfair to Eton. I shall always look back on my four years there with very mixed feelings. On the one hand I have happy memories of hours spent outside the school, beagling, running, rowing and even shooting (John Harley and I illegally rented 200 acres of rough shooting from a local farmer for the last year I was there), the beautiful tree-surrounded playing fields (not that I ever played on them much), hours spent flying model airplanes with Henry, the leisurely Sunday walks with John and Henry up "The Long Walk" which stretches from Windsor Castle to the Copper Horse, discussing all the problems of teenage life and trying to unravel the mysteries of the future. Memories, too, of friends and one of the two big days in the Eton summer calendar which were, and are, the Fourth of June and the Lords cricket match against Harrow.

The Fourth of June was celebrated at Eton each year with inter-house cricket matches, picnic lunches, strawberries and cream, and a torchlight parade of boats and fireworks to end the proceedings. Many parents and Old Boys attended, bringing with them sisters and girl friends bedecked in beautiful summer dresses and frocks of every colour. The principal cricket grounds were surrounded with deck chairs and parasols beneath which these bedecked beauties relaxed, protecting their delicate complexions from the harsh rays of an English summer sun.

On my first Fourth of June my parents, due to a pressing engagement that involved a horse deal, could only attend the festivities until lunchtime. As John Harley's parents were abroad and so could not be there either, after lunch John and I wandered out onto "Sixpenny", the most famous of the cricket grounds, to see if we could, first, spot any pretty girls and, second, find out how John's house were faring in the important match being played there.

The scene was idyllic. June, for once, was behaving itself. Shaded by the green leaves of the beautiful old oak trees which surrounded two sides of the ground, and by parasols and sun umbrellas, the colourful throng of parents and guests intermingled with their offspring and friends in relaxed attitudes around the boundary.

John and I sat down in the shade of a big tree at one corner of the ground. With one eye we watched the progress of the game and with the other the parade of young ladies who strolled casually around the field with their brothers and escorts. The sound of bat on ball and an occasional "Howzat!" competed with the low buzz of conversation from the onlookers. A small biplane droned overhead. I glanced at my watch. It was five minutes to three. I lay back on the soft grass and started to doze. The biplane droned over again. I thought how much I missed Henry and his aeroplanes. Only the sound of clapping when one of the players hit a boundary or a wicket fell kept me from falling completely asleep . . .

On the other hand, there were many aspects of Eton life of which I have less than happy memories as I've already mentioned. These included the lack of any constructive relationship with my housemaster who I came to regard as a snob and a bore, the pomposity of the dress which we had to wear every day and also a similar pomposity in many of my fellow students who were wearing it. However, I did manage to compensate for the awful food by getting a job cooking breakfasts for customers in Lower Rowlands for which I was repaid with a hearty breakfast for myself.

I also found unsettling the strong undercurrents of homosexuality which ran below the surface of school life. I found these relationships unnatural but have to admit that, starved of contact with the opposite sex as we all were, I even found myself glancing around at other boys. As I grew older this became less disturbing but I did come to resent more and more the lack of freedom of movement imposed of necessity on even older boys. In hindsight, however, there is no doubt that we boys at Eton had a lot more freedom than that granted to boys at other leading public schools of the day.

In retrospect perhaps the failure of Eton to make any lasting mark on me, and my failure to make any lasting mark on Eton, was one of equal blame. Probably I am being generous to myself in my allocation of the blame. In the horse racing world we talk about horses for courses. Possibly in choosing Eton my father picked on the wrong course for a somewhat bloody-minded, wild young Irish horse!

Finally though, I must admit to being conscious of a certain secret satisfaction at being lucky enough to be part of the oldest and most famous public school in the world.

So it was that the decision was made for me to go to crammers. The institution eventually selected to undertake the formidable task of bringing me to the necessary level of competence to pass the Cranwell exam — and to be achieved within a bare six months — was situated in Camberley in Surrey. It was owned and run by a venerable gentleman by the name of Mr Tinniswood. The Cranwell exam was, basically, the same format as the exam which aspiring army officers had to pass to get into the Royal Military College at Sandhurst situated, perhaps not entirely by chance, in Camberley. However, although the papers were the same, the pass mark required to gain access to Cranwell was very much higher than that required for Sandhurst.

During my first meeting with Mr Tinniswood, he told me that he had been cramming boys to pass the army examination for over forty years. He also told me that, because of this familiarity with the contents of army papers, he was proud of his ability to forecast at least seventy-five per cent of the questions which would appear on the papers each year.

"Have you got a good memory boy?" he asked.

"I can remember poetry and the words of songs well," I replied.

"That's a good start," he said, "but there are two ways of answering exam questions. The first is to possess a sufficient pool of knowledge in your own mind to be able to construct your own answers from everything you know about the subject. The second way is to know what questions are going to be asked and to learn by heart beforehand the correct answers to these questions. Judging from what I have read of your various end of term reports which your father has sent to me, I have no doubt that if you are going to pass the Cranwell exam in six months we will have to rely largely on the second method."

"I'll learn the answers, sir. But how am I going to know what the questions will be?"

"That's my job, boy," said Mr Tinniswood. "In each subject there are normally ten questions asked. The examinee can choose any six of these to answer. I will give you the detailed written answers to ten questions on each SCB and I guarantee that at least six of these questions will appear on each of the papers which you will be required to answer."

Mr Tinniswood went on to explain that each question could be answered in about 500 words, although some questions would take more and some less. A quick calculation on my part revealed that this would require me to learn by heart about 30,000 words. A somewhat formidable task but, I reckoned, by burning the midnight oil, not impossible over a period of six months.

"OK, sir!" I exclaimed. "I'm game to try."

"You've got to do more than try boy," he said gruffly, "You've got to succeed. I've only crammed five boys for Cranwell and they have all passed with high marks. I am not tolerant of failures and you are not to spoil my record. I'll do my bit and you do yours. You're not even to think of failure." And with these stern words he dismissed me and I went off to find the digs which I had been allotted.

I was to live for the next six months as a paying guest of a widow of an Indian Army officer who owned a two up two down semi-detached in a tree-lined suburban street just off the Camberley to Aldershot road.

I attended daily classes at Mr Tinniswood's, along with the twenty other boys who were undertaking the cramming course. However, classes never consisted of more than about six boys so one received a great deal of personal attention. After classes I spent most evenings sitting in my bedroom, parrot learning answers to possible exam questions. I was absolutely determined to pass this exam and from my first day at Mr Tinniswood's I was prepared to exchange my new found night-time freedom for the long hours of work I knew was necessary if I was to achieve my objective. Occasionally I would allow myself a night off and drive to London with one of the other students who had a car and take a look at the bright lights.

But these night-time sprees were few and far between and even at weekends, when most of my companions were off enjoying themselves, I forced myself to spend hours repeating over and over again the answers to exam questions set by Mr Tinniswood. Six months later, however, these many hours reaped their reward. The exam took place over two days. As paper after paper was put in front of me I became more and more jubilant; sure enough, Mr Tinniswood's questions came up like clockwork on each of the tests I had to answer.

Four weeks after the exams I was sitting having breakfast at Tullamaine when an official-looking brown envelope was placed on the table in front of my father. Instinctively I knew what it contained. I waited with baited breath for him as he slit it open and drew out the contents. I rushed round to look over his shoulder.

"You've made it!" he exclaimed before I had time to read the contents. "You've not only made it but you've passed into Cranwell second on the list and you've got a scholarship!"

Never before, or since, have I felt such a feeling of achievement, and relief. All those long hours burning the midnight oil in the little suburban house in Camberley had paid off.

I was off to learn to fly.

CHAPTER
FOUR

Holidays, Hunts, and First Flight

Holidays away from Eton were filled with horses. By the time my brother Tel and I were fourteen and sixteen respectively we had graduated from ponies onto full-sized horses. Spoilt rotten we were, but in our defence I can say that we worked for it. We had to help to get the whole stable fit, riding the horses on the roads for up to four hours each day as the hunting season approached. We always had to ride the horses to where the hounds were meeting, this sometimes meaning a hack of twelve miles at no faster than a jog. Then, when the day was over, no matter in what direction the day's hunting had taken us, we had to ride the horses home. Very often we would arrive back in the stable yard, wet through, freezing cold, all feeling gone from our feet and hands and, even in our young and fit state, totally exhausted. Yet those short periods of tearing across the countryside after hounds, jumping everything that came into one's path, oblivious to all emotions bar the excitement of the chase, made it all worthwhile.

I remember one famous hunt with the Quorn Foxhounds. No less than 514 mounted followers were counted that day at Dalby Gate. The sight of this cavalcade, many dressed in regulation red coats, white breeches and top hats, proceeding along the lane to the first covert which hounds were to draw, was one to be remembered. A fox was soon "holloaed" away and the cavalry charge started. There then ensued one of the most extraordinary hunts which I have ever taken part in and which has been written up as such in the memoirs of the Quorn hounds.

By the time we ran the fox to ground some two hours and twenty minutes later, we had covered more than twenty miles of country and the distance run in a straight line from start to finish — the "point" as it is called in hunting parlance — was over sixteen miles.

I was mounted on a pony no bigger than the size of the average polo pony. At the end of the Quorn hunt that day, during which we certainly changed foxes at least once, only four people out of the original 514 were still with hounds. Of these four, I am proud to say, I was one.

Holidays were also filled with dogs. To my father, mother, brother and myself horses and dogs were closer than most human beings and we treated them as such. We talked to them as we talked to each other and put words into their mouths in reply. When Tel and I went back to school the dogs pined for us and to no lesser degree we pined for them.

For the last half of each summer holiday and for the whole Christmas holiday, we hunted the dachshund pack. In the Easter holidays we became involved in the point-to-point scene and when he became sixteen Tel was allowed to ride in point-to-point races. Not to be outdone, I started to hold dachshund races. I built a course in the garden using great ingenuity and comprising many obstacles in the flower beds, and even including a tunnel under the rose bed. When Mr Gates, the gardener, discovered this he nearly had a heart attack and ran shouting for my mother. After a lot of pleading on my side and indignant complaint from Mr Gates, the course was allowed to stand with some modifications one of which, of course, was the elimination of the tunnel.

Holidays were filled with music. My mother loved all forms of music as much as my father detested them. Music was therefore confined to weekdays when father was at work in London. My mother was a natural piano player but she enjoyed even more playing the piano accordion. I was lucky to inherit her natural ear and easily took to this instrument. Earlier, I had also acquired a ukelele and by the time I was fourteen had a repertoire of about fifty songs.

This small degree of musical talent I had inherited from my mother stayed with me throughout my life and hopefully has, from time to time, amused other people as much as it has myself. My piano accordion was abandoned in Singapore in January 1942, but I managed to retain the original ukelele. It has been dragged into service at such different festivities as troop concerts in India and wild pre-Derby Irish dinner parties at which it has been known to be instrumental in having guests dancing on the table before the final course was cleared!

While settling in at Tullamaine we continued to spend the summer holidays at Sheen Falls. The very beauty of the place, then and on every future visit, held me spellbound. I have never really had the patience for all-day fishing expeditions, but if I ever did enjoy the sport it was on the River Sheen. My father used to take Tel and myself out on the river immediately after an early breakfast and we spent many hours casting a fly in pursuit of the salmon we had seen jumping up the falls a few months earlier. Whilst there was satisfaction in hooking, playing and landing a big salmon with father and Tel, flogging an allotted stretch of the river not knowing where exactly the fish lurked created in me more a sense of frustration than excitement, which even the thought of a bite did not completely compensate for. My preference was to wander along the banks with a rod trying for trout. With a fly rod you could sight the fish before you cast and there was also a greater feeling of anticipation and the excitement of the chase than when pursuing larger unseen quarry.

There was grouse shooting too, with John Bell. This was a sport far removed from the tweed-clad, upper-class affair commonly pursued in Scotland from August 12th onwards.

Dear John Bell. During the 1920s at the height of the Troubles, Kenmare and the surrounding area was one of the strongholds of the Irish Republican Army, a body of men whose ideals and motivations were very much more genuinely inspired by patriotism and the desire to right old wrongs than that of their counterparts in the present-day IRA.

John had been one of the leaders of the local IRA unit during those years and his deeds of daring and cunning were legendary throughout the area. He then owned and ran a grocery store and bar in Kenmare. One evening he led me down the stairs into the basement underneath his bar. The whole area was filled with small arms. Here was an armoury of every type of light weaponry that you would not find out of place in a commando unit.

"You never know Master Tim," he said, "when we might be needing them again." To this day, I have no idea why John entrusted me with this highly confidential information. I was only about sixteen at that time and can only suppose that he recognised in me the characteristics of a born rebel, characteristics which had elevated him to his high position in the local secret army.

It was John Bell, too, who introduced me to the joys of grouse shooting. Kerry is mostly mountainous and intersected by several deep sea estuaries, each of which bites for some miles deep into the heart of the county. In each of these areas, situated on the mountains that rise steeply on both sides of the estuaries, can be found coveys of grouse. These are truly wild birds, not like those in England and Scotland that are reared for sport.

John knew of these coveys better than any other man alive, but even with his guidance it used to take my brother Tel, myself and our guide at least half a day of hard walking to discover their likely whereabouts. As soon as we were within two or three hundred yards the covey sensed our presence and took off in a flurry of squawks and wings, generally flighting out over the valley to the next mountain. We soon learnt from John that the most important thing at this moment was to keep our eyes skinned on the birds. Even as they disappeared from sight, we had to sense where they were about to land in the heather.

There was one thing which our mentor instilled in us more than any other, "Now listen boys," he would say if we were lucky enough to come within gunshot range, "don't you start firing until you see the whites of their bloody eyes, or all will be wasted." And so we would wait until at last the grouse rose up within about twenty yards of us. "Now!" John shouted, "Let 'em have it."

Six shots would ring out and never more than five grouse would fall into the heather. John would always kill two with his two shots and sometimes even three. Tel, like our father, was an excellent shot and would generally get two birds. I have never been a good shot. When grouse shooting I never got more than one bird — and often, I'm afraid to say, none! This inability of mine to shoot, even with the eight machine guns of a Spitfire at my disposal, has never left me. It was to save the lives of many a German and several Japanese.

One night after a long day in the Kerry mountains, John and I were cleaning our weapons in the gun room at Sheen Falls. My father's First World War revolver was hanging in a gun case. John picked it up and turned to me. "Now, Master Tim," he said, "if you ever have to shoot an Englishman with one of these yokes, aim at his balls and ye'll hit him in the stomach!"

One September afternoon some four years later I found myself short of petrol and ammunition 10,000 feet over Manston airfield in Kent. We had engaged some German bombers as they crossed the coast and I reckoned if I could get rearmed and refuelled quickly I could get into the air again and catch some of them on their way back to France. I quickly dived for Manston and landed there just as some Messerschmitts, which had strafed the field, were disappearing. I touched down and taxied quickly towards the nearest petrol tanker. Not a sign of life! As I jumped from my aircraft I spotted the open mouth of an air-raid shelter close by. I ran to it and down the steps. Inside in the gloom I could make out about forty figures. "Get out of here quick," I yelled. "Refuel and rearm my aircraft!"

A sergeant stepped forward, saw the pilot officer stripes on my battledress and said quickly, "Sorry sir, there's a raid on. My men are staying down here."

I took out my father's old army revolver — in action I always carried it, in a holster around my waist — and pointed it at the sergeant's nether regions.

"Sergeant," I said quietly, "I'm an Irishman and an old friend of mine in the IRA once told me that if I ever had to shoot an Englishman I should aim at his balls and I'd hit him in the stomach. If my friend was right, your guts are in real danger." I have never seen a man go up stairs faster in my life. And when he saw the insignia of the green Shamrock and crossed swords painted on the nose of my Spitfire I think he fully realised the danger that his guts had been in.

During the first year in Tullamaine, when I was about sixteen years of age, I made a new friend. His name was Rory La Terriere. He was six months older than me and lived about five miles from Tullamaine in another castle, named Kiltinan, with his mother and his sister, fifteen dogs of varying breeds and at least twenty cats. We met in the hunting field and took to each other straight away. From then on we spent much time in each other's company, hunting, shooting and generally raising hell. Rory had a bubbling personality which embodied a wonderful sense of humour and he had the ability to turn disaster into one big laugh. Although he was still only seventeen he managed to cajole his mother into letting us have the use of a rattly old car. We toured the countryside, following our sporting pursuits in the daytime and chatting up whatever girls we could find when evening came.

Happy days they were and we made the best of every minute. The last time I saw Rory was the day before I left Tullamaine to go and join my first squadron in January 1940. He shook my hand and wished me luck. I returned the sentiment. His wish came true. Mine didn't. Rory was killed four years later, on D-Day, leading his company onto the Normandy beaches.

The town of Fethard is an old walled city which dates back for many centuries. It was ravaged by Oliver Cromwell in his rampage across Ireland and, in my youth, the older inhabitants talked about it as if it had taken place yesterday. The wide main street of Fethard is well supplied with grocery stores. Behind every store in those days was a bar. In the yard behind the bar you were almost certain to find a couple of old stables housing potential racehorses.

One of the great characters of Fethard was the parish priest, Father Ryan. A red-faced, portly man, he was a regular at the meets of the Tipperary Hounds and was a staunch character to go across the country with. Although I was not of his faith he became a good friend of mine and I had many a long chat with him.

The Master of the Tipperary Hounds was the redoubtable Syvie Masters, an amazing character. Before taking on the mastership she had won over 100 point-to-point races. Even out hunting she still crossed the country as if she was riding in a race. The year I was leaving to join the RAF, I was riding along the road behind hounds talking to Father Ryan. Syvie, who was jogging along in front of us surrounded by her hounds, beckoned for us to come and join her.

"Now Tim, whatever is this I hear about you going off across there to join up with the British?"

"I just want to learn to fly Syvie," I replied, "and this way you can do it for free."

"It's over here you should be staying to make your living," said Syvie. "You know what my father always used to say about England?"

"No, what was that?"

"Ireland was Ireland when England was a pup,

And Ireland will be Ireland when England's buggered up."

"They need him, Syvie," said Father Ryan, "without a few good Irish lads like Tim, they'll never win any war!"

A few days later I was exercising a hunter in the early morning mist in a field across the road from Tullamaine, a morning I shall remember to my dying day. I heard the thunder of galloping hooves and out of the mist appeared Father Ryan urging on his mount into a gallop. What a sight; he was dressed in his priest's clothes, with his knees up to his chin like a jockey. In his left hand, he held the reins of another horse. On seeing me he pulled up and approached with an embarrassed look on his red face. "Tim," he said, "I'm training these two for the point-to-point and I haven't the time to gallop the two of 'em separately. Now, be a good lad, and don't ye be tellin' a soul or it'll get to the Bishop's ears and I'll be in mortal trouble."

Before the Christmas holidays that year my parents had moved to Tullamaine. The four English hunters were shipped over and were supplemented with three experienced Irish horses. Our first day's hunting with the Tipperary Hounds was, for Tel and myself, a complete disaster. Full of confidence we defiantly decided that we were going to ride our favourite English horses. We knew that we would be likely to be in for a fall or two but little did we know what was in store for us. The barriers which separate the fields in Tipperary, and for that matter in most of Ireland, consist of grass banks of various sizes, covered in bushes, gorse or brambles, and protected by water-filled ditches on each side. A well-trained Irish Hunter

69

will normally cross a bank by jumping onto it, sliding across the top and kicking off the far side over whatever ditch may lie beyond. Our brave Leicestershire horses knew nothing of this technique. Their natural instinct was to try to fly the whole thing.

By the end of the day Tel and I had notched up twenty-one falls between us. We had been deposited into ditches, onto banks, into brambles and, occasionally, onto the grass of the field on the far side. On one occasion I found myself lying underwater in a ditch with my horse on top of me and, had not some kind person jumped to the ground and pulled my struggling horse onto dry land, I would probably have drowned there and then. Miraculously, apart from scratches and bruises, neither Tel nor myself suffered serious injury. The only thing which was badly dented was our pride.

An old hunting character, who was to become a good friend of mine over the years, said to me at the end of the day, "God alone knows why you didn't break your bloody neck today. What you have to learn in this country, my boy, is not how to fall from your horse. You must learn the psychological moment when you choose to abandon ship."

"Thank you, sir," I replied, "I'll remember that."

And I did.

My teenage years passed quickly, full of happiness, adventure, laughter and very few tears. John Harley and Henry Maudslay both came and stayed during the summer holidays at Sheen Falls which my father continued to rent as a holiday home. They shared with me the excitement of exploring the Kenmare Estuary and the hills and the mountains which surrounded it. At school we three remained close. The companionship of John and Henry compensated to some extent for the frustration of public school life which seemed to bother me more and more the older I got.

My thoughts were constantly on aeroplanes. Before my father moved the family to Ireland my godmother, Pamela Wills, had asked me to come and stay with her for a few days. Pamela had just learnt to fly and was the proud owner of a De Havilland Hornet Moth. She knew of my interest in aeroplanes and suggested that I go flying with her each day during my visit.

In those days there was an air service between Leicester and Bristol, and Pamela had included in her invitation a free return ticket. The aircraft used on this daily service was a twin-engined eight-seater De Havilland Rapide with a cruising speed of about 120 mph. I had flown only once previously, when my father stood me a joyride at a local air show in a Tiger Moth.

This Leicester to Bristol flight was my first experience of a public air service. I was so excited I could not sleep the night before and was ready to be driven to the airfield by my mother an hour before it was necessary. Since that day I have flown literally millions of miles around the world on airlines. However, that first flight stands out in my mind even more than my first Concorde flight across the Atlantic. I can remember that what surprised me most of all was how much detail on the ground could be seen from the air. We made the journey at about 3,000 feet and I can recall being astounded that I could see white lines around a tennis court. Another aspect of flying, and one that I had not reckoned on before that day, was the effect which air turbulence would have on my stomach.

I had always been a bad sailor and had spent many miserable hours suffering on the Irish Mail Steamer as it crossed from Holyhead to Dun Laoghaire. It had not occurred to me that I well might suffer the same discomfort in the air. I was therefore horrified when after a few minutes of turbulence I began to feel queasy. Luckily we passed through the bumpy air quickly and the short period of discomfort was not sufficient to spoil my enjoyment of the flight. However it acted as a warning of things to come.

The next few days were memorable. Pamela met me at the Bristol airfield. Here she kept her own aircraft so we loaded my suitcase into her Rolls Bentley and drove straight to the hanger where the Hornet Moth was housed. With the assistance of a mechanic we pushed the aircraft out onto the tarmac and climbed in. The little cabin biplane was fitted with dual controls; as I took my seat beside her Pamela told me to be careful to keep my hands and feet away from the joystick and the rudder pedals. Given a sign from Pamela, the mechanic swung the propeller and, at the second attempt, the engine roared into life. We taxied out on to the grass field. Pamela looked over her shoulder to see that no other aircraft were in sight or landing, asked me if I was alright and strapped in, then opened the throttle. Off we sped across the airfield, running and bumping, and after some 300 yards Pamela pulled back on the stick and we were airborne.

We climbed out to the west of the field and when we had reached about 2,000 feet, levelled off and turned out over the Severn Estuary. We flew around for about five minutes and then Pamela turned to me and shouted to me to take the controls.

From my constant reading of the Biggles books and many others on aeroplanes I knew all about aircraft controls. But this was the very first time I had actually touched them. Gingerly I took the stick in my right hand and reached out with my left for the centrally situated throttle. Carefully I placed my feet on the rudder bars. I felt the nose going down and eased back on the stick. Of course, I over-corrected and the next thing I knew was that the nose was going up in the air and the right wing was dropping. I lifted it up quickly by pushing the stick to the left but immediately found myself in a shallow left-hand dive. I glanced anxiously at Pamela but she was smiling at my efforts and looking remarkably relaxed. Gradually I got the little aircraft back onto a level course and determinedly kept it there for at least two minutes.

"This is wonderful!" I shouted at Pamela, "I feel just like Biggles."

"Keep on flying," she yelled back, "I'll keep an eye out for the Fokker triplanes on our tail!"

With this encouragement I returned to the task of trying to keep us on an even keel. I was beginning to get the hang of it when Pamela shouted at me that we must head back for the airfield or we'd be late for our dinner. Reluctantly I relinquished the controls. Pamela turned the aircraft back towards the airfield and, joining the circuit on the down-wind leg, smoothly eased the Hornet into a left-hand turn and losing height all the time was soon on her final approach. I noticed that she had reduced the airspeed to about 60 mph as we crossed over the fence and the next thing I knew we were bumping over the grass as she touched down in a reasonable three-point landing.

I was ecstatic. At last I had actually flown an aircraft by myself. "Just you wait until I tell you about this Henry," I thought. Turning to Pamela as she taxied the Hornet back towards the hanger I asked, "Can we do it again tomorrow?"

"Of course we can," she replied. "Tomorrow I'll teach you to turn."

Pamela was as good as her word. For the next two days we flew for at least an hour each morning. I started to get a feel for what I was doing and by the end of the second day was completely confident of being able to control the aircraft climbing, diving and turning in the air. At the end of each flight my kind godmother allowed me to keep my hands on the controls while she landed and so, whilst I could not say that I had actually got the aircraft back on the ground by myself, I felt confident that should necessity arise, I would be able to do so without undue damage to the undercarriage.

On the fourth morning, with regret, I climbed once more into the Dragon Rapide and headed back for Leicester. The following day I returned to Eton. But something had happened to me which had made me different from my friends. I, Tim, had actually piloted an aircraft. I tried to will away the time which lay between the present and the moment I could join the RAF. My future was sealed.

Looking back on that first glorious experience of flying it is interesting to remember that when I did eventually get to Cranwell in January 1939 I was allowed to fly an aircraft solo after only the exceptionally short time of six hours and twenty minutes of dual instruction. As I landed after my first solo I thought of my dear godmother and quietly thanked her for her help in achieving my ambition.

CHAPTER
FIVE

Cranwell

The RAF College at Cranwell is situated halfway between the towns of Grantham and Lincoln, about 130 miles north of London. The country for thirty miles around the aerodrome itself is as flat as a pancake, a condition which undoubtedly influenced the Chiefs of Air Staff when, in the early 1920s, they were selecting a suitable location for the training of the elite RAF pilots of the future.

My first journey to Cranwell, in January 1939, was by train from London. On that train were twenty-three other young men who had worked their guts out in the recent exams to achieve their life's ambition. At King's Cross station I had been surprised to run into Julian Bruxner Randall, a slight acquaintance of mine from Ireland, who had coincidentally passed the Cranwell entrance examination in first position, one ahead of me. Although we didn't know each other well we naturally greeted each other warmly, laughing at the fact that us two Irish lads were in the act of joining the "enemy" forces. The Irish Air Corps in those days had only three aircraft so we would have had little chance of learning to fly with them.

At Eton it had been the fashion to wear one's hair long at the back and sides, enough to overlap the collar. My father had seen to it that I had visited the barber in Clonmel before I left for Cranwell and, as a result, my neck that morning felt remarkably bare. I was therefore somewhat taken aback when Julian turned to me and said: "Look, Tim old boy, I think you'd be smart to go and have your hair cut before you show up at Cranwell. With the length you've got it they'll certainly know you went to Eton and you may not be too popular."

"Hell!" I replied, "I just had it cut before I left home. It can't still be too long."

"Be it on your own head," responded Julian, "the barber's just down those stairs and if I was you I'd get down there quick before the train leaves and tell him to get out his shears." So down the stairs I went and sitting in an empty chair demanded a quick trim.

The next morning all the first-term cadets were paraded in civilian clothes in suits and bowler hats, which we had been told to bring with us. A large and fierce-looking warrant officer walked down the line in front of us, every now and then stopping to scrutinise his new prey. I just knew that he would make one of his stops in front of me. He halted and stared for what seemed like forever straight at me. He looked me up and down but didn't say a word and eventually moved off down the line. Then he marched slowly along behind us. Sure enough he stopped once more behind me. After a long silence he suddenly roared out, "What is your 'naime' Sir?"

"Vigors," I replied, knowing full well that for some reason this large, red-faced, parade ground bully hated me on first sight.

"Where d'yer 'gow' to school, Sir?" he demanded.

"Eton," I said, anticipating the wrath that this admission was likely to spark off in this narrow-minded savage.

"Well, Mr bloody 'Etounian' Mr 'Voigers', Sir," he bellowed at the top of his voice, for the whole of Cranwell to hear, "What do you think you are Sir, a bloody woman?! Go and 'ave yer 'air cut!" Thus my introduction to the world of Warrant Officer Digby resulted in my once more sitting in the barber's chair, for the third time in two days.

The night before, on arrival at Cranwell, I had been shown to a pleasant, although not over-large, room in the west wing of the long, low college building. I was to have this room to myself until I left Cranwell a year later. A batman, whose job it was to help initiate newcomers into the domestic routine of the college and to care for their general needs including clothing and shoes, was allocated to each ten candidates.

My batman, who was to become my trusted friend and ally in the difficult months ahead, was nicknamed "The General". At that time he was in his middle fifties. He had started his working life in domestic service in a large country house run on Victorian lines with a staff that included a butler and several footmen. During the First World War one of the sons of the house had joined the Royal Flying Corps and had persuaded The General to enlist and serve with him so that he could continue to look after his needs. In 1917 his master had been shot down in flames when the petrol tank of the Sopwith Camel he was flying was hit by a stream of bullets from a Fokker triplane, with which he was battling over the Somme battlefield. Despite The General being transferred to another officer, he mourned his old master. After all, he had looked after the young man since he was a schoolboy and, when the war ended a year later, The General returned to civilian life as soon as he could. Times, however, were hard in the Britain of the post-war years for unskilled thirty-year olds. The big houses had mostly cut down on their staff, jobs for ex-batmen were few and far between. After seven years of struggling in part-time jobs, The General had a change of luck; he was doing a one night catering job at a big reception and was recognised by the commanding officer of his old wartime squadron. His former boss was by now an Air Vice-Marshal who, on hearing of The General's difficult life over the last few years, quickly persuaded him to join, what was now, the Royal Air Force as a civilian batman. Within a year The General found himself at Cranwell, caring for the needs of cadets. Here he had stayed ever since.

The General and myself had an affinity with each other from the very start of our acquaintanceship. Maybe he saw in me something of the officer for whom he had originally worked during the First World War, or maybe it was the fact that I had been to Eton which brought out some of the latent snobbishness which is inherent in ex-butlers. Whichever it was, it was certainly my good fortune for during the next year The General looked after my every need and spoilt me rotten.

"Good morning, Sir," he would say as he woke me up each morning at 6.30 a.m., "and 'ere's yer tea Sir; it's an 'orrible mornin' Sir, rainin' cats and dogs, cold enough to freeze a brass monkey's balls off, blowin' a bloody gale, nasty mornin' for flyin' Sir but it's a great life if yer don't weaken Sir."

No matter what went wrong during the next year The General would reassure me that life was great if you didn't weaken, wise words which I soon learnt to be extremely true and a philosophy which stayed with me to the end.

On our arrival at Cranwell we were issued with uniforms, similar to those of officers, but lacking any badge of rank, and then acquainted with the programme of work and daily routine which we were expected to follow. Due to Mr Tinniswood's efforts on my behalf I had attained the highest history mark, 298 out of 300, ever to be achieved in a Cranwell exam and I was greeted by the history master as a budding historian. He took me into his study and greeted me almost as an equal. As my knowledge of history was for the most part limited to the answers to those ten historical questions which I had learnt parrot fashion, I found the somewhat highbrow historical conversation which followed my introduction to him rather heavy going. Thus, I struggled along gamely for ten minutes and then excused myself on the grounds of being late for parade. During the months ahead I studiously avoided any close relationship with the history master.

80

I'm afraid that he could never come to terms with what was to be my consistently mediocre performance in his subject, as compared to the incredibly high mark I had achieved in the exam.

On our second day at Cranwell, we were told to proceed to the aerodrome and report to our flight commanders. Now life was really starting. I had been allocated to A Flight which was commanded by Flight Lieutenant Bradford, a medium-sized, ruddy-faced gentleman into whose office I was ushered in some trepidation. He told me to sit down and relax and started to question me about my life. When I happened to mention my interest in horses he immediately interrupted. "Do you hunt?" he asked to my amazement. It had never occurred to me that anybody in the RAF would be interested in fox hunting.

"Why yes, Sir," I replied. "I have been brought up on fox hunting since before I can remember." Bradford asked about those packs of hounds I had been out with. When I told him the Mendip, the Fernies, the Quorn, the Pytchley, the Tipperary, the Limerick and the Black and Tans, he almost flipped backwards off his chair.

"I've only hunted with Warwickshire and the Blankney," he remarked with envy. "You're a lucky young devil to have hunted with all of those famous packs, Vigors."

We spent the next fifteen minutes in animated conversation about horses and hunting rather than aeroplanes. "Jorrocks", the nickname which I was soon to learn had been given to my flight commander for most of his service career, was a real enthusiast. It was however soon evident that I could probably teach him as much about the art of pursuing the fox as he could teach me about the art of flying aeroplanes.

This thought obviously crossed his mind as well for, glancing at his watch, he said quickly, "Hell! I must get on and see the rest of the new group. Anyway, Tim, I'll teach you to fly myself instead of passing you on to one of the other instructors. That way we'll have plenty of opportunity to carry on this conversation."

I rose to my feet and saluted. "Thank you, Sir," I said "that sounds great." I left his office in high spirits. I had made a new friend. Later that day, we cadets reported to the equipment store to be issued with flying overalls, helmets, goggles and flying boots. There was a mirror in the changing room in the hangar where we kept our equipment. Looking at my reflection, fully togged out in flying clothing, it occurred to me that for the first time in my life I really did look like my hero Biggles. This wasn't so very surprising as the aircraft which he flew, the Sopwith Camel, and the aircraft which I was about to fly, the Avro Tutor, were similar in many respects. They were both open cockpit biplanes, they both had radial engines and their performance was almost exactly the same.

The next morning, at 9.00 a.m., I reported to the A Flight office for my first familiarisation flight with Jorrocks Bradford. As we walked out to the dual-control Avro Tutors lined up on the grass in front of the hangar the talk was of flying and not of hunting. Strapped into our cockpits, pupil in the front and instructor behind, Jorrocks ordered the mechanic to swing the propeller. The engine fired, the mechanic pulled away the wooden chocks from in front of the wheels, and we started to taxi across the grass to the take-off position. All controls were duplicated in the cockpit in which I was sitting and I tentatively put my hands lightly on the stick and throttle.

"Keep your bloody hands off the controls until I tell you!", yelled Jorrocks through the intercom from the cockpit behind. "I'll give you plenty of warning when I want you to fly the aircraft."

Quickly I removed my hands and sat back in excitement as the throttle opened and we roared across the grass and into the air. We climbed steadily away from the field and soon the altimeter needle passed through 3,000 feet.

"First, I'm going to do some steep turns, then I'll show you a spin and then we might try some aerobatics," yelled Jorrocks. No sooner had he spoken than the left wing dropped steeply away and the little aircraft turned on its side. I felt the pressure build on my seat as the stick was pulled back and the horizon swung crazily across the nose of the aircraft. This was different altogether from the gentle turns I had performed with my godmother and I felt my mouth go dry as I clung onto the sides of the cockpit. Next thing was that the left wing quickly rose, the right wing dropped away and the horizon pivoted round in the opposite direction. My stomach felt queasy and I was relieved when the right wing rose and we were once more in level flight.

In my headphones, Jorrocks said, "Now I'm going to show you a spin. Ensure you keep your hands away from the controls."

I saw the throttle, which was situated on the left wall of the cockpit, moving backwards. The noise of the engine died away. The nose of the aircraft rose above the horizon and there was almost complete silence. Then suddenly, the nose came up and then took a sharp, vertical twisting dive to the left. Next thing the whole aircraft was corkscrewing towards the patchwork of green fields below which appeared to be gyrating in front of my eyes. I felt scared and also physically sick. Not a moment too soon for my comfort, the earth stopped spinning and the aircraft continued in a straight dive. Gradually the nose started to rise, the pressure on my seat increased and then to my relief we were once more flying straight and level. "OK, now you can try to fly her for a bit."

Gingerly, I took hold of the stick with my right hand, felt for the throttle with my left and placed my feet on the rudder pedals. Keeping the nose of the aircraft level with the horizon, as my godmother had taught me, I concentrated on keeping the wings level and, to my satisfaction, found I was maintaining a reasonably straight path.

"Excellent," said Jorrocks, "now I want you to try and turn gently to your left." I eased the stick to the left and, as I had learnt in Pamela's Hornet Moth, pulled back on the stick a little to maintain level flight. At the same time I applied a shade of top rudder.

"Hey!" came the surprised voice in my ears, "you've done this before."

"Just a little, Sir," I called back delightedly. "Can I try a turn to the right please?"

"Go ahead," said Jorrocks, "but this time try using a little bit more top rudder and concentrate on keeping the nose level with the horizon."

I was pleased to find that as soon as I had taken over the controls the feeling of air sickness which had engulfed me when Jorrocks was performing his tight turns and spin disappeared almost completely. But I was apprehensive when, a few minutes later, he called out "I've got her" and announced his intention of doing some aerobatics. My apprehension was well founded for, as we zoomed into a loop, the queasy feeling engulfed me again; then the whole weight of my body fell on my shoulder harness as we turned upside down in a slow roll. I'm bound to confess that fear of falling out of the cockpit momentarily eclipsed all other sensations. The slow roll was followed quickly by a couple of stall turns, manoeuvres which involved pulling up into a vertical climb until all speed was lost and then kicking over one way or the other into a precipitous dive. Jorrocks capped the display with two more tight loops.

By the end of the sequence my stomach was also turning somersaults and I put my hand over my mouth trying to prevent myself from being physically sick. As we flew back towards the aerodrome I started to feel a little better but, as Jorrocks sideslipped into a perfect three-point landing, I still had that nauseous feeling which I had experienced so many times when the Holyhead to Dublin Irish Mail steamer had rolled itself into Dun Laoghaire harbour after a rough night in the Irish Channel.

As we climbed down from our cockpits and pulled off our helmets, Jorrocks took a curious look at me. "Are you alright Tim?" he asked.

"Well, I'm afraid I felt a bit airsick, Sir," I admitted, "when you were doing the aerobatics." But I quickly assured him that "I'm sure I'll be OK when I get used to them."

"We'll have to see what we can do about that." Changing the subject, Jorrocks said, "From the way you were handling the aircraft before we started the aerobatics, it looks to me as though you have flown before."

I told him about the few days I had spent flying the Hornet Moth with Pamela, several years earlier. "Well, we won't take long to teach you to fly" was all he said as we approached the hangar. "Come into the office for a moment. I want to talk to you about this sickness you experienced."

I explained to him that I had always felt seasick in a boat unless I was steering it myself and I added that in the aircraft as soon as I had taken over the controls after he had completed the spin I had felt fine.

"OK," he said, "I'll try and help you through it."

Over the next vital few months Flight Lieutenant Bradford was as good as his word. I am sure that had I not been lucky enough to have had such a sympathetic teacher I would not have been able to overcome the motion sickness. Jorrocks and I soon found out that so long as I was at the controls myself my affliction was not serious. Therefore he studiously avoided any violent or aerobatic manoeuvres when he was flying the aircraft. On a very bumpy day when he was teaching me tight turns and he sensed that I had started to feel bad he straight away landed in a large field next to where some horses were grazing. We got out of the aircraft and walked over to look at the horses, talking all the time about hunting. Then we got back into our cockpits, donned our helmets, took off and continued the exercise.

Weather permitting we flew nearly every day. The rest of the time was taken up with lectures on aeronautical subjects, airmanship, meteorology, engineering and so on, plus several periods a day on history, languages, science and mathematics. We also had at least one drill parade every day during which the antipathy of Warrant Officer Digby towards old Etonians became ever more apparent.

After ten days of flight training I had logged just over six hours dual instruction. I had proved my ability to make the aeroplane do just about all normal flying manoeuvres with reasonable accuracy and had also had no difficulty in recovering from stalls and spins in both directions. After the first few attempts landing did not present me with any great problems, although I must confess to a couple of big bumps after which my instructor had to open the throttle and shout, "We are going round again."

On that tenth morning after my arrival at Cranwell I had completed a couple of good landings when I was surprised to be told by Jorrocks to taxi back towards the hangar. About halfway there he told me to stop and then proceeded to get out of the aircraft. Then, climbing on the wing beside me, he motioned for me to take off my helmet. Raising his voice above the noise of the engine he shouted, "OK, Tim, you're on your own. Just taxi back to the take-off point, do one circuit and landing and come back to me here." He gave me a pat on the shoulder, raised his right thumb and jumped back onto the grass.

There are moments in one's life which remain in one's memory so vividly that even over half a century later they are as immediate as ever they were. This was such a moment. The time was 11.20a.m. A heavy shower had passed through Cranwell an hour before and the greeny brown grass on the aerodrome still glistened with the rain which had fallen. The sky was washy bluey grey and a light wind from the west only half filled the windsock at the end of the field. I was full of emotion; anticipation battled with trepidation, deadly calm with excitement and, above all, an utter loneliness combined with a wonderful feeling of freedom.

Such a mixed bag of sensations was so overwhelming that the short flight itself was almost an anti-climax. I turned the aircraft into wind and opened up the throttle with complete confidence. Pushing forward the stick to get the tail in the air, all feelings of trepidation vanished as I eased back the stick to lift the machine off the ground. I experienced no fear as to whether or not I would be competent enough to get the aircraft back down onto the aerodrome in one piece.

As my instructor had drilled into me for the past ten days, I climbed straight ahead until I had reached 500 feet and then commenced a gentle climbing turn to the left. Now I was flying due south and had reached 1,000 feet. Glancing over my shoulder to the left to make sure my path was clear, I then continued turning to bring the aircraft onto the down-wind leg of the circuit. I felt wonderful, keyed up, but completely at ease. I watched the routine activity on the aerodrome with interest. One Avro Tutor was on a final approach to landing and another had just completed its take-off run and was climbing away to the west. I could even make out the small figure of Jorrocks Bradford standing about 100 yards in front of the hangars, watching my progress.

"I'd better put this one down really smoothly," I thought to myself, "or I'll be letting him down."

As I turned onto the cross-wind leg I throttled back and started to lose height. I was by now about half a mile to the east of the aerodrome and could see that the Tutor which I had seen earlier had now landed and was taxiing back towards the hangars. Once more, I looked over my left shoulder to make sure that my path was clear, then turned again to bring the aircraft onto my final approach leg which would bring me straight back to the middle of the aerodrome. Now, throttled right back, I could hear the sweet sound of the wind whistling through the wires which connected the top wings of the Tutor to the lower ones. I kept a good eye on my airspeed indicator to see that I kept my speed about 10 mph above the stalling speed. I held the nose of the aircraft just about on the spot where I intended to land. Then, as the boundary fence passed underneath me, I pulled back on the stick until I was flying level about five feet above the grass. Easing gently, gently back on the stick I raised the nose of the Tutor higher and higher until I could feel the wheels brushing the tops of the grass. A final pull back on the stick right between my legs and the aircraft stalled smoothly onto the ground. I am not going to boast that it was a perfect threepoint landing as I can remember that the tail skid touched the ground slightly before the wheels. But still, for a first attempt, I am proud of it to this day.

Just before the Tutor came to a complete stop, I kicked the right rudder and turned back towards where Jorrocks was waiting. I stopped beside him and he climbed onto the wing. Pulling off my helmet I shouted, "How was that, Sir?"

"OK," he replied, "with the help of the 'Man Above' we might make a pilot of you yet! Now go and do five more just the same." Full of confidence, again I taxied out to the take-off point, swung into wind and roared off. Following the same routine I flew round the circuit and straightened out for my landing. Crossing the hedge at about twenty feet I began to level off for my landing. Suddenly I felt the aircraft starting to drop out of my hands. A quick glance at the airspeed indicator gave me the reason. In my over confidence I had let the speed drop down below stalling speed and I was mushing down towards the ground. I hauled back on the stick and pushed forward the throttle. The wheels hit the earth with a bump and next thing the Tutor was staggering through the air about thirty feet from the ground. I applied full throttle and pushed the stick forwards. Of course I over-corrected and the wheels hit the ground with another resounding bang. With my heart in my mouth I opened the throttle less violently and tried to hold the aircraft steady. The wheels nearly hit the ground again and then I was climbing away, once more in reasonable control of events.

As I climbed the Tutor out over the aerodrome boundary my heart stopped thumping and I took a quick look down to the right to see if my instructor was still watching. Happily he had disappeared and I thought that with luck he had not witnessed my clumsy blunder.

Once more I flew the circuit and approached for another landing. This time, however, I kept a wary eye on the airspeed indicator and made certain to keep my speed well above the stalling level. This resulted in my flattening out over the grass going about 20 mph too fast. I drew the stick back towards me, trying to make the aircraft settle down on the ground, but the only result was to make the gap between me and terra firma wider still.

"Be patient," I told myself, "there's still lots of aerodrome left, and there's no way I am going to suffer the humiliation of having to go round again without landing this time." For another 100 yards I continued to float across the field niggling at the stick in vain to make the aircraft settle. At last, I could feel the Tutor dropping and finally, with a welcome bump, I was rumbling over the ground. Still no sign of Jorrocks outside the hangar so maybe my ham-fisted efforts had passed unseen.

As I straightened out after my next circuit I made certain to keep my speed exactly as I had been taught. Coming in over the boundary I knew for sure that this time I had got it just right and, sure enough, the Tutor greased its way onto the grass with only the rumble of the wheels to tell me that I was back on earth. Feeling a great deal happier that I had completed the routine one more time with satisfactory results, I taxied the Tutor back to the hangar. Parking at the end of the line of other aircraft I climbed down on to the ground, pulled off my helmet and, with my parachute over my shoulder, walked back towards the Flight Office. On the one hand I was experiencing a feeling of vast elation at having become a proper pilot but, on the other, I was dreading the fact that my instructor might have witnessed the mess I had made of my second two attempts at landing. Sure enough, as I drew close to the offices, a stern-faced Bradford appeared in the doorway. "Come to my office," was all he said. As I followed him down the corridor he turned on me furiously. "You silly young bugger!" he roared. "What the hell were you playing at out there? For a moment I thought you were not only going to break your bloody neck but, much more serious, write off one of my aircraft! How many times have I told you during the last ten days to watch your airspeed on final approach?

How the hell do you think we're going to win a war with disobedient, ignorant, ham-fisted young fools like you in the air force?"

"Sorry, Sir," was all I could shamefacedly mutter, "I'm afraid that after my first landing I just got a bit over confident."

"Well, let me tell you one thing," stormed the normally placid Jorrocks, "if I ever see you get over confident again, and you're lucky enough not to kill yourself as a result, I'll see to it that you're out of this place and back to your horses in Tipperary. Now get out of here!"

Both chastened and ashamed I left the office and made off for the changing room. The bubble of pride, so recently filled with satisfaction not only at going solo but also at being the first of my term to do so, was burst wide open. But looking back on that painful few minutes in the Flight Office I know that a lesson had been learnt which was to stand me in good stead during the rest of my long flying career. During that career, both in and out of action, I have had my share of near misses. Ninety per cent, particularly of those occurring out of action, have been caused by temporary fits of over confidence. If I hadn't been at the receiving end of such a fierce lecture those many years ago I would certainly have experienced more of these "incidents". Amongst them there would undoubtedly have been the incident which would have been one too many.

Life at Cranwell proceeded apace. I lagged behind my mates in most of the educational subjects. Science is a subject which has always been way beyond my grasp. Likewise, mathematics has continually caused me frustration and trouble. Engineering lectures left me cold. The very thought of a small cog in a piece of machinery, on which I was dependent to keep me in the air, revolving at 20,000 revolutions a minute, was a piece of knowledge that my brain quickly rejected. History was a subject at which I felt obliged to work hard, if only to make some effort to justify my reputation as a budding historian. All forms of team ball games were anathema to me and I would go to most lengths to avoid them. I much preferred, when time was available at the weekends, to go riding with Jorrocks on two horses borrowed from a neighbouring farmer. I like to think that in return for what he was teaching me about flying, I was able to give him some help with the finer arts of horsemanship.

Cranwell, whilst similar in many ways to the life that I had led at Eton, provided more freedom of movement. Cadets were allowed to have cars of their own and, as an eighteenth birthday present, my father gave me a secondhand Ford 8 which quickly became my pride and joy. Some evenings, along with a few of my friends who also had cars, we would arrange cross-country rally races between one public house and another — some 20 miles apart.

The only rules were that you could take whatever route you liked along the country lanes and the last man home paid for the drinks. There were a number of minor prangs during these races and a couple of major accidents which resulted in cars being written off and drivers hospitalised. I was proud to say that my car, "EGO" — named after her registration letters, I prefer to think, rather than the character of her owner — never suffered so much as a scratch during these events. Moreover, I never once had to pay for the drinks and managed to reach the winning pub first on several occasions. Of course, the Cranwell authorities were tipped off by the local constabulary about what was afoot and before long these races were forbidden on pain of having one's car confiscated.

I had been at Cranwell for about two months when, for the first time, the dangers involved in flying were brought home to me. After initial flying training, cadets were moved up from the simple Avro Tutors onto the more sophisticated and faster Hawker Harts or, if they were selected for twin-engined aircraft training, onto Airspeed Oxfords.

One sunny morning two of the senior cadets who were involved in a practice dogfight in their Harts, misjudged their distances, collided and crashed in flames. Entangled in the wreckage of their own aeroplanes neither managed to get free to make use of their parachutes. If they weren't already dead both were killed instantly as their aircraft, still locked together, hit the ground. By chance I had been talking to both of them half an hour earlier as we strolled down to the hangars. It therefore came as a real shock to me when I heard of the accident. Somehow, up until then, I had regarded flying as a marvellous game. Death in the air belonged only in Biggles books. The real dangers of what we were doing had never occurred to me.

Two days later we attended the funerals. The two coffins were lowered into their graves to the sound of the Last Post and we witnessed the grief of the bereaved parents standing around the graveside. Only then, for the first time, did it occur to me that it could easily be me in one of those coffins. Looking back now over all these years, I believe that it was at that moment that I left schooldays behind and became a man.

The clouds of war now darkened the summer skies. A sense of urgency entered our training at Cranwell. Flying training especially was gradually stepped up at the expense of other subjects. The expression "when we're at war" was substituted for "if the war starts".

"Thanks be to God yer don't 'ave to go to war with a rifle, Mr Voigers, Sir," remarked Warrant Officer Digby one morning on parade, "the bloody Germans would have a walk over!"

"Afraid yer going to 'ave to beat the bastards again!" said The General.

"No hunting for us next season," said Jorrocks.

"Gentlemen," said the Air Officer Commanding, Cranwell, "the time has come when all our efforts have to be doubled."

About this time I had to choose between flying Hawker Harts or the twin-engined Airspeed Oxfords. For some reason I plonked for Oxfords. "I think you're better suited mentally to be a fighter pilot," Jorrocks advised me.

"I know, Sir," I replied, "but somehow I just want to see if I can fly a twin."

"OK, but don't come running back to me in a month's time saying you want to get back onto singles."

At first I enjoyed the sensation of flying the twin. A low-winged monoplane with two radial engines, the Oxford was a much greater challenge to fly than the little biplanes I had by now grown used to. Instructor and pupil sat side-by-side in the Oxford and could converse relatively easily without the use of headphones. For a time I got a big kick out of rumbling around the surrounding countryside imagining I was an airline pilot and feeling greatly superior to those of my companions who had opted, or been recommended by their instructors, for the single-engined Hawker Harts. But gradually I started to miss the excitement of aerobatics which were forbidden in Oxfords and to realise that my instructor had been right in his assessment regarding my temperament. However, the die had been cast, and it was too late to do anything about it.

Although the pressure of work was being stepped up we were still allowed a certain amount of time for play. My fellow cadets and I took full advantage of this. During one weekend off in London I managed to contact my former girlfriend Kitty, who was staying with an aunt in London. With several friends we spent the evening dancing wildly in a nightclub off Regent Street. Kitty and I left at about 3.00 a.m. and returned to my car. Daringly, I suggested to her that she should come back for a final drink at my hotel.

Nothing untoward happened between us but it all went wrong when we reached the hotel. Collecting the key at the desk we got into the lift and ascended to the tenth floor. Just as I was opening the door to my room there was a shout from the corridor behind me. A large night porter was emerging from the second lift. "What you doin' takin' that young girl to your room?" he yelled. "You only booked a single and anyway she's far too young for those kind of tricks."

Kitty cried all the way back to her aunt's house. When I stopped the car she jumped out and left without so much as a "Goodnight". I drove back to the hotel feeling embarrassed, ashamed, angry and frustrated. Looking back on this rather sordid affair it is hard to imagine how it could have come about. At least it is a reflection on the moral standards of night porters of the pre-war era. The sad sequel was the letter Kitty sent me four days later telling me that she never wanted to see me again. And she got her wish; we have never met since.

The short summer leave was soon over and by the end of August we cadets were back at Cranwell, where a sense of urgency entered into every part of our lives. More and more time was spent in the air instead of in the classroom. I was getting on well with the Oxford and enjoyed trying to hit targets laid out on the bombing range, using practice bombs which were carried in the racks below the aircraft's wings. But I watched with envy as my friends who had opted for single engines took off in their Hawker Harts for practice dogfights.

Within a couple of days we heard of Hitler's invasion of Poland and the realisation hit us that we were on the verge of war. On September 3rd, at 10.30 a.m. we were told to assemble in our ante room to listen to an important announcement to be made on the radio by Mr Chamberlain, the British Prime Minister. We all knew what it was he was going to say. An air of intense excitement pervaded the room. At 11.00 a.m. his stern voice came over the speakers. He announced that he had issued an ultimatum to the German leader but no reply had been received. Britain was therefore now at war with Germany.

There were about fifty cadets gathered in that ante room and, as one man, we jumped to our feet cheering with excitement. There was not one amongst us who would not have been bitterly disappointed had the declaration of war not been made. I wonder today whether our cheers would have been as enthusiastic had we known that within five years all but a handful of us would be dead.

The first difference war made to our lives was that we were immediately issued with gas masks. These we were told to carry with us at all times, except when we were in the air. The second difference was that at night a blackout was to be rigorously imposed, necessitating black blinds being installed on all windows and black masking tape placed on about seven-eighths of the surface of car headlights. The former made it harder to wake up in the morning if, like me, you automatically awoke at first light, and the latter finally eliminated any cross-country racing between pubs after dark.

Our term consisting of twenty-three cadets was now amalgamated with the term of twenty-four cadets who had been ahead of us. We were all told that we would be completing our training within the next three months. Working hours were to be increased and even more attention given to flying and its related subjects.

I pleaded with Jorrocks to get me transferred from Oxfords to Harts. "It's no bloody good Tim," he said, "I told you not to go for the Oxford and that I wouldn't be able to do anything about it if you changed your mind."

"Right enough, Sir," I agreed, "but then I didn't know war was going to be declared."

"Too bloody bad! Now get cracking and go and fly your bomber." It seemed that my fate was sealed.

The next months at Cranwell passed quickly. Up till now flying had been a lovely game. Now, every moment spent in the air was deadly serious. Each new exercise bore the stamp of cold reality; in the days ahead what we learnt now might mean the difference between life and death. No more trips to London were allowed as all leave was cancelled and weekends were spent either in the air or swotting up for final exams which were due to be taken in early November.

The most important of the exam tests which had to be passed were, of course, the flying tests. These included written exams related to airmanship. The reward for passing was the right to have the coveted RAF wings sewn onto one's uniform jacket above the left-hand breast pocket. Only two of my term failed the flying tests and they, poor devils, had to work for another two months before sitting for the tests again. For myself a great surge of pride and excitement ran through me when I heard my name called out as a successful candidate.

The other exams in maths, history and science were of little importance compared with the flying tests but they too had to be passed if one's progress was not to be retarded. It was science which really worried me. Realising that there was no way that I was going to achieve the necessary pass mark in this subject, I decided that I must resort to more devious means. The gentleman who, for nearly one year, had shouldered the task of instilling into my unreceptive brain some scientific knowledge, was a kind, scholarly man who had never yet lost his temper at my hopeless efforts. One evening I approached him in the Mess and asked him if he would care to come and have a pint with me at a local pub. He looked at me with surprise but nevertheless agreed.

"Look, Sir," I said, "as you are only too well aware, I have no chance of passing the science exam the day after tomorrow."

"So far, I agree one hundred per cent with what you say," he remarked dryly.

"Well Sir," I continued, "Flight Lieutenant Bradford, my flight commander, tells me that my flying ability is above average. I believe I can pass all the other exams without any trouble. But if I fail to pass the science exam I will fail to pass out of Cranwell this term. That means joining a squadron three months later than I should."

My teacher said nothing. I staggered on. "Do you think, Sir, my lack of scientific knowledge is going to make any serious difference to my ability to shoot down Germans? I know I'm a pretty good pilot and believe I can make a fair contribution to the war when the fighting really starts. We all know that the RAF is short of pilots. Do you think that they should be made even shorter at this critical time by my inability to understand physics?"

He listened calmly to my impassioned appeal. "Let's have a think about this," he said. He remained ominously silent for a long time. Placing his now empty tankard on the table he eventually turned to me. "You weren't born an Irishman for nothing. You've certainly got the blarney! Nevertheless, there is something in what you say. I have never been asked to do anything like this before and what we have said must remain secret. But, OK, I'll do it for you. You do your best and I'll give you the pass mark. But I repeat, never tell a soul or you'll cost me my job. And good luck to you." He was true to his word and I scraped through the exam with the requisite pass mark.

Only a few days remained before our final passing out parade. I made one last appeal to Jorrocks to recommend me for fighters, cornering him in his office.

"How would you feel, Sir, if I asked you to go hunting on a cart horse?"

"Uncomfortable and scared," he replied.

"Well, that's just how I feel having to face up to the prospect of fighting the war in a bomber," I said. "Please do me one last favour and put me up for fighters."

He relented. "OK, I'll recommend you for twin-engined fighters. There are a couple of Bristol Beaufighter squadrons knocking around and I have heard that there are one or two Blenheim squadrons being converted to a twin-engined fighter role. Now that is as good a compromise as I can manage. Now get the hell out of here. I'm busy."

I was jubilant. "Thank you, Sir. One day I'll mount you on the best horse in Ireland." Out on the tarmac the first person I ran into was my pal Bob Holland. He had come to Cranwell at the same time as me and had quickly shown himself to be a fantastic performer on the piano. Possessed of a natural talent he played jazz to a professional standard. My amateurish efforts on the piano accordion and the ukulele had drawn us together from the word go and we had shared some noisy evenings.

I told Bob my news. "Good for you. Now, I'll tell you something really exciting. Fats Waller and the Mills Brothers are playing in Nottingham from tomorrow and I have four seats in the front row for their first show. You'll come of course."

And so it was that the following night, which was actually the last night before the passing out parade, off we went to Nottingham. After a short overture the show began with a chorus of pretty girls. Our appetites wetted, the lights dimmed and the spotlight shone on the grand piano in the centre of the stage with its small stool opposite the centre of the keyboard. An enormous black man came on stage, grinning, and placed one cheek of his large backside on the stool and looked round over his shoulder.

The magic started. After four or five songs the audience were clapping so much Fats rose to his feet and lumbered to the front of the stage, waving his big hands in acknowledgement. Looking down at us cadets sitting in the front row in our RAF uniforms he hollered above the din, "Good to see you fellows! Come and see me after the show!"

Next were the four brothers, singing a succession of favourite songs and miming saxophones and clarinets as they sang. More applause and more dancing girls and more of Fats. As the show ended Fats Waller stood in the centre of the Mills Brothers and once more lent forward to us and once more shouted, "Don't you guys forget to come and see me!"

As we made our way to the street, Bob said, "I believe Fats meant it. Let's give it a try." We entered the stage door and at that moment a big figure appeared on the landing above and we could hardly believe it when we saw it was Fats himself. He beckoned us to come on up.

We followed him into a large room which seemed to be filled with people, all with glasses in their hands and all talking nineteen to the dozen. The Mills Brothers were all there, and the dancing girls. Also there was the theatre manager with his pretty blonde daughter, who Bob was dating, and who had done us proud in providing the front row tickets.

Near the centre of the room stood an upright piano. After some quick introductions we were given drinks and mingled with the crowd. Somebody shouted for Fats to give us a song but he said that he had been working all night and wasn't there somebody else who could play the piano? "My friend Bob can hold his own," I shouted, "come on Bob, get to work!"

Bob was reluctant to leave his girlfriend or perform but after some encouragement from Fats he sat down and launched into his version of "Basin Street Blues". Everybody stopped talking and started to crowd around the piano. One of the Mills Brothers started singing. "Hey, that fella can hit those keys!" roared Fats. "Let's have more."

And so began a most memorable two hours. Soon we had Fats at the piano with the Mills Brothers accompanying him. Then Bob was persuaded to draw up a chair beside Fats and they launched into a succession of remarkable duets. Fats soon had a large plate of sausages and mash and a pint tankard of beer on top of the piano in front of him. The whole room was dancing and singing. There had been magic in the theatre but this was something else.

I glanced at my watch. It was after 2.30 a.m. We were due on parade at 9.30 a.m. and we had a long dark drive ahead of us. Reluctantly I tapped Bob on the shoulder and pointed at my watch. He nodded assent and, accompanied by Fats and the Mills Brothers and the rest of us singing, he launched once more into "Basin Street Blues". Amidst wild applause he rose from the piano and we started to say our goodbyes. As Bob shook Fats by the hand the big man looked him straight in the eye and said: "When you're all through with those aeroplanes, boy, you just let old Fats know and we'll make some music together. We sure could turn an odd buck."

The theatre manager had pressed some bottles of beer on us before we left in case we got thirsty on the way home. By the time we had driven ten miles Bob and I had only got through one bottle but our companions in the other car drove up beside us signalling that they had run out of beer and could do with another bottle. I let them go on ahead and then carefully pulled alongside them in formation. Bob opened the window and passed the bottle to the driver of the other car. Just as he took the bottle from Bob it slipped from his fingers. In doing so he turned the steering wheel of his car and hit the side of mine. I pulled away but he swerved to his left and disappeared over a steep embankment.

"Goddam clumsy fool!" shouted Bob. "He's broken the beer!" I remarked to Bob that maybe we should find out if the other driver had broken his neck.

We found the car upside down in a ploughed field. The occupants appeared unhurt and, covered in mud, clambered back up onto the road. It was nearly 5.00 a.m. by the time we turned in through the gates of Cranwell.

The General woke me. "It's 'arf past six sir and it's raining cats and bloody dogs. Warrant Officer Digby wants to see you personally at 'arf past seven after you've 'ad your breakfast, Sir."

Peering bleary eyed at the grey rain splashing against the window, I sat up and held my head. "Now 'ere's yer tea," said The General. "Yer uniform is all pressed and 'ung out on the chair, Sir. And yer'd better get up quick and not be late this morning, Sir, 'cos you've got the passing out parade at 'arf past nine."

I don't know how I got through that morning. I snatched some coffee and a slice of toast in the dining room and made my way to the office of my tormentor. Ever since that first bowler-hatted parade, nearly a year ago now, a running battle had existed between Warrant Officer Digby and myself. It was not just the fact that I had been schooled at Eton. Many of my other fellow cadets had been to similar schools. It was probably more to do with an underlying trait in my character which automatically makes me react against authority of any kind.

I entered Mr Digby's office, expecting the usual tirade of insult and abuse. I was taken by surprise, however. He rose to his feet and asked me to sit down opposite him. I awaited developments. "Now, Mr Voigers, Sir" he began. "You and I 'ave been 'avin a rare old battle this past year. Yer going to leave 'ere as an officer tomorrow and I don't want you leaving with a bad taste in your mouth about me. I don't want yer to feel that I hold you any malice. I've had ter lick you into shape a bit because when you arrived here yer was just like a rag doll with two left feet. You're a bit of a rebel and I admires yer for your independence. I just want to shake your hand and wish yer luck wheresoever you goes." He held out his big hand. I jumped to my feet and clasped his hand. We stood for a moment looking at each other straight in the eye.

"Thank you Mr Digby. You have been a great help to me and I can only apologise for the trouble I've caused you. I appreciate every word you have said."

As I turned to leave the office he had one final dig. "One last thing Mr Voigers. On this 'ere passing out parade would yer make a big effort not to drop yer rifle!"

"I can assure you Mr Digby, that with the hangover I've got I'll be lucky to get through the parade without dropping myself! But I promise I'll do my very best."

The parade assembled at the east end of the college, ready to line up in squadrons. Thank goodness it had stopped raining and even a little wintry sunlight was working through the clouds. The parade ground was now surrounded by parents and relations of cadets, teaching staff and various local dignitaries. We were marched onto the main space in front of the college and were put through our paces, then stood at attention for inspection by the Air Marshal of Training Command. We presented arms whilst the sword of honour was presented to the most virtuous of my contemporaries.

Under the command of Warrant Officer Digby we were marched off the main parade ground back to where we had assembled. He stood us at ease and then advanced to where I was standing in the front row. With a large grin on his face he yelled at the top of his raucous voice, "Congratulations, Mr Voigors, Sir. Yer didn't drop yer bloody rifle!"

When the parade was dismissed I returned to my room, collected my suitcase and said a fond and grateful farewell to The General. I loaded my belongings into my car and bade goodbyes to my friends who were doing the same. Then, on some instinct, I got into my car and drove down to the hangar.

Jorrocks was at his desk. I saluted and stood to attention in front of him. "I've just come to say goodbye, Sir."

"Relax Tim," he said, "I've some good news for you about your posting. You've been changed from Bomber Command and are now to go to the Fighter Operational Training Unit at Aston Down for training on twin-engined fighters. Report there after Christmas."

I could not resist a yell of joy. I shook his hand. "You've been a real friend, Sir. Just wait 'till I can get you on those good hunters in Tipperary!"

"Don't you worry, Tim," he laughed. "I'll be there." I bade him goodbye with more thanks, saluted and left his office. Poor Jorrocks never did ride my good horses across Tipperary. A month after our last meeting he got himself transferred to Fighter Command and four months after that he met his end in the skies over Norway.

Thinking about it reminds me, too, that as I left the hangar for the last time I bumped into Bob Holland. We talked about his piano playing with Fats Waller and maybe having a drink later on in Grantham. Bob was to play his last tune three years later, in a tented camp near Calcutta. The next day he met his death at the hands of a Japanese Zero pilot in the skies over Burma.

And so ended my days at Cranwell. It was now December 23rd 1939.

CHAPTER
SIX

Tipperary and Aston Down

After leaving Cranwell I packed my belongings into my car and set off for London. I left the car in a garage near King's Cross and then made a slight diversion to wish some friends a happy Christmas. In the evening I boarded the night mail train for Holyhead. This train had nostalgic memories for me. I had travelled on it often as a schoolboy returning home for the holidays. Now the holiday was only going to be of four days' duration and after that came fighters and the war!

The train pulled up alongside the mail boat in Holyhead harbour at the usual ungodly hour of 2.45 a.m. I ran up the gangway of the boat and proceeded straight to the purser's office to get myself a cabin. I have always found the effects of sea sickness less if I am horizontal rather than vertical.

The next morning I packed my uniform into my suitcase and donned an old tweed jacket before we docked. Ireland was a neutral country and if I had appeared in my RAF uniform I would have been immediately arrested and interned.

In Dublin I set out for the Shelbourne Hotel in one of the "jaunting cars" (or sidecars as they were often known) that were pulled up on the hill leading from the quayside to the main road. The jaunting car is an open, horse-drawn conveyance with two big wheels over which the driver and three passengers sit back to back, facing outwards, two one way and two the other. When it rained a mackintosh sheet was provided on each side of the vehicle and drawn over the occupants' legs.

The three miles to the Shelbourne took only 20 minutes along roads almost devoid of motor traffic of any kind. Strict petrol rationing was already in force in Ireland and horsedrawn vehicles of all kinds abounded on the street, interspersed only occasionally with the odd bus, a few taxis and some official cars.

Drawing up outside the hotel, I was greeted by Matty, the hall porter. "Good mornin' to you Mr Tim!" he said and shook my hand. "Is it on leave you are, Sir?" Taking my suitcase from me, he asked, "Did you run into any of those old Germans?" Matty had been a friend of mine almost as long as I could remember. My family had always used the Shelbourne as their Dublin base and, on countless occasions, I had breakfasted there after arriving on the mail steamer.

"No, Matty. I've only been training yet but I think I'll be joining a Spitfire squadron soon."

"Spitfire," said Matty, "and what would that be?"

"The best and most modern fighter aircraft in the world, Matty!" I replied.

"Sounds to me more like a woman than a bloody airyplane!" said Matty. "Spitfire," he said again, "haven't I been knowin' a few like that myself!"

After a hearty breakfast I said goodbye to Matty. "Good luck now Mister Tim," he said. "You be careful in those new fangled airyplanes and don't be gettin' shot by any of those old Germans."

I took the train to Thurles. Watching the fields of Kildare flash by outside the window it crossed my mind that it might be a very long time before I made this familiar journey again. My father met me at Thurles station. We climbed into the trap behind his good grey mare, Biddy, and set off along the lanes and over the hills to Tullamaine.

We drew up on the wide gravel sweep in front of the house and my mother and two brothers rushed out to greet me. My white lurcher was jumping all over me covering me with licks, my mother was hugging me and my two brothers were shaking me by the hand. I felt like the original hero home from the wars. Tel was only just out of bed from a severe attack of pneumonia complicated by pleurisy which had come close to killing him and which was to delay his joining the RAF for a further six months. Patrick, six years my junior, was on holiday from his Dublin school.

I had to tell them, jointly and individually, of my life since war was declared. My mother seemed to greet with mixed emotions my news about being posted to a squadron equipped with Spitfires. She was only now waking up to the fact that her second son was likely, in the very near future, to have his neck on the line.

The next morning my father and I set off for a race meeting at Mallow. We drove to Clonmel behind Biddy and then caught the train to Limerick Junction, where we changed for Mallow. We were on the racetrack by 1.00p.m., enjoying a sandwich and a drink, where we watched father's horse run a good second in a two-mile hurdle race.

After the fifth race that day a friend of my father's, Andrew Knowles, invited us to come back for a drink at his house. On our way back to the house he said to my father, "I'd like to show you my two young jumpers on the way back. They are with a new young trainer who is having a bit of success with very few horses. Do you mind? We'll take a taxi, it's only a couple of miles out of the way."

We arrived outside a farm yard. It was starting to get dark as we got out of the taxi and walked over to a row of loose-boxes near to the hay barn. A small, neat figure appeared out of the gloom and walked towards us.

"You want to look at the horses I'm sure, Mr Knowles."

"Yes," said Andrew, "I'd like to show them to Major Vigors."

Turning to my father he said, "Ashmead, I'd like to introduce you to Vincent O'Brien. Vincent, this is Major Vigors, and his son, Tim, who is in the air force." We looked at the two Knowles horses and then at the other three or four which comprised the trainer's string. They were all good sorts and looked in the best of health. We stopped and chatted with O'Brien for a short time and it was dark by the time we got back in the taxi.

On the way back to Clonmel that evening we were sitting chatting to a couple of trainers on the train. They had both run horses at Mallow that day.

"Did you ever hear of a new young trainer named Vincent O'Brien?" my father asked.

"I did so," replied one of the trainers, "he's had a couple of winners lately and they say he's a bright young lad." Little did any of us realise that the young trainer we had just met would, years later, create more records with his jumpers than had any other trainer before him and be acknowledged as the greatest trainer of horses in the flat-racing world.

The next day was Christmas Day and we had a family Christmas, eating and drinking and relaxing. When we were walking the dogs, my mother asked, "Are you allowed to keep a dog now that you're an officer?"

"Yes, we are," I said, "as long as you look after it well and don't take it into the public rooms of the Officers' Mess."

"Well then," said mother, "take Snipe back to England to keep you company. Don't you think that's a good idea Ashmead?"

My father agreed and so it was decided. Two mornings later, as I stood on the steps saying goodbye to my mother and brothers, Snipe was sitting in the trap behind the faithful Biddy waiting for me. We set off down the drive and I turned and looked back at the house, thinking of these last happy Christmas days.

Aston Down lay on a flat plain in the Cotswolds, about four miles west of Minchinhampton in Gloucestershire.

I joined the other new arrivals at the station headquarters on January 18th and was told to report to Flight Lieutenant Montagu, who commanded B Flight. When my turn came, I walked into the office and saluted.

"Sit down Vigors," said my new flight commander. "And in future don't salute me. As a pilot officer you only have to salute squadron leaders and above."

"Sorry, Sir. I'm so used to being a flight cadet I forgot that I'm now a pilot officer."

"OK. By the way I know your name. Our families have crossed paths somewhere but I can't remember where."

"I'm from Tipperary," I said, "but have lived in Leicestershire and Somerset." We couldn't track it down but we had established a link of some sort which was going to prove important to me.

Montagu told me that Cranwell had given me a good report on my flying ability. "They say that you have been flying Twins but want to get back onto single-engined fighters. Is that correct?"

"Yes, Sir," I said, "that's one hundred per cent correct. But I will settle for twin-engined fighters if there's no hope of getting onto singles."

"Well," said Montagu, "let's see how you fare. Meet me outside in half an hour and I'll give you a run round in a Blenheim."

The aircraft strength at Aston Down comprised a fairly varied collection: some half a dozen twin-engined Bristol Blenheims, the same number of single-engined Gloster Gladiators and a couple of two-seat, low-winged single-engined Harvards. The Gladiator, although a biplane, was at that time the hottest and most popular of the RAF fighters although it was soon to be outshone by the Hurricane and the Spitfire. For now though I had set my sights on the Gladiator.

Prior to meeting Montagu, I visited the stores and got myself equipped with a parachute and flying helmet. We walked out to a Blenheim, climbed on to the wing and into the cockpit. The layout was in the same configuration as the Oxford and had dual controls. I sat in the left hand, or first pilot's seat. "I'll give you a quick demo circuit and landing," said Montagu, "and then I want you to take over and we'll see what you make of it."

In the air I could see that, apart from the fact that there was more power in the Blenheim's engines and the whole thing was a bit faster, it was all very like flying in the Oxford. We went round the circuit quite quickly and landed.

Now it was my turn. "You reckon you can manage that?" asked Montagu.

"It's very like the Oxford," I said. "I'd like to try." Without any difficulty I taxied back to the end of the airfield. Turning into wind I eased forward the throttles and, juggling a little with the rudder, held the Blenheim on a straight course across the grass. On the controls I recognised the moment when we had sufficient speed

117

to lift off and I edged back the control column until we were climbing comfortably away.

I didn't attempt to turn onto the down-wind leg until the altimeter showed we had an altitude of 1,000 feet and then, without any worry, I dropped the port wing and made a gentle turn so that we were flying parallel to our take-off path.

The controls were crisper than the Airspeed Oxford I was used to. Otherwise I felt perfectly at home. Being careful to keep the speed well above the stalling level I started another 180 degree turn to bring us back onto our approach for landing, dropping off height as I turned. Straightening up about a quarter of a mile from the airfield I gently drew back on the throttles as we crossed about ten feet over the boundary fence. Then, easing back on the stick, I slid the big aircraft onto the grass with not much more than a rumble of wheels.

"Couldn't do it better myself," said Montagu. "OK, now taxi back and take off again and we'll go up and fly around for a little while and I'll show you how she stalls."

We took off again, climbed up and topped out at around 2,000 feet and my instructor told me to try out some tight turns, both flying straight and level and climbing. After this he made me practise some stalls with the engines off and also cut back at half power. Again, I found it all straightforward and simple.

"OK, let's go home and we'll have a talk," said Montagu. I turned back for the field and once more managed to get the Blenheim back onto the grass with hardly a shudder. In the office Montagu told me that he had paid very careful attention to my flying and that in his opinion Cranwell's assessment of my flying ability was correct. "You handle an aircraft much more like a potential fighter pilot than a bomber boy. So, I'll give you a run around in a Harvard after lunch and if you can handle that as well as you did the Blenheim I'll put you onto Gladiators."

My heart rose in my mouth. "Thanks a million," I gulped, "that would be super!" An hour and a half later I was strapped into the front seat of a Harvard with Flight Lieutenant Montagu in the cockpit behind. "OK," he said in my headphones, "I'll do a quick circuit and then you can have a go."

The Harvard was a low-wing monoplane with a round radial engine which was inclined to block the forward view when on the ground. We had to zig-zag on the way down to the take-off position in order to make sure we could see no other aircraft in our path. Then Montagu turned the Harvard and we roared off the ground in a much more spritely fashion than we had in the Blenheim, round the circuit and back over the fence for a smooth landing.

"OK, you've got her," said Montagu. "Be careful to swing your nose right and left when you're taxiing and let's see you do a circuit." I felt completely at home and thrilled to the power and lightness of the controls the moment I opened the throttle. Turning onto the final approach for my landing I sideslipped off a bit of extra height and rolled the aircraft smoothly onto the grass.

"Well done, Tim. Now we'll take off again and do a couple of spins." As we taxied back to the take-off point

Montagu continued, "There's one thing you've got to remember about the Harvard. It's not the easiest aircraft to get out of a spin. If you let the spin get too flat you may not recover it. Remember, as soon as you get into a spin push the stick right forward and keep it there until you've straightened out and started to recover."

I took account of his words as I climbed to 3,000 feet, stalled, kicked on the rudder and got into a spin. I remembered to keep the nose pointing at the ground until I had stopped the gyrations by applying opposite rudder and was in a straight dive. After a couple more spins my instructor told me to return to the airfield, where I had no difficulty in putting the Harvard down. Back in the office Montagu handed me a book. "These are the handling notes for the Gladiator. Spend the rest of the afternoon reading them and spend half an hour sitting in the cockpit of one of the Gladiators. You can find one under maintenance in the hangar. If the weather's good tomorrow morning we'll get you off in one."

Hardly believing my good luck I thanked him profusely and left the office. As instructed, I spent the rest of that afternoon studying the notes, most of the time sitting in the cockpit of a Gladiator. I immediately felt at home. It was just like a big, powerful, Avro Tutor on which I had learnt to fly. The next day I reported to the Flight Office on a dark, wintry morning. The grey cloud base formed a ceiling at about 2,000 feet.

"Good morning," said Montagu, "did you familiarise yourself with the Gladiator?"

"I certainly did," I replied, "I spent three hours at it."

"Right," he said "I've just got to do one bit of duty in a Harvard and as soon as I land we'll get you off; that is, if the weather doesn't get worse."

He walked away towards the line of Harvards where he met his pupil and climbed into the back cockpit. I stood on the tarmac and watched them take off. The aircraft climbed away and turned back over the airfield under the cloud base at about 1,500 feet. Immediately over the centre of the field the aircraft slowed and the nose rose slowly into the air. Next thing the nose dropped and the Harvard flicked into a spin. "Bit low," I thought to myself, "but he knows what he's doing."

The spinning Harvard reached about 500 feet. It was only then that I realised the nose of the aircraft was unusually high. It was literally in a flat spin. "My God," I yelled to a mechanic who was standing beside me. "He's not going to pull out."

Helpless, we looked on in horror as the aircraft spun down. When it was about 100 feet above the ground, we were near enough to see Montagu and his pupil sitting in the cockpits. There was a large explosion and a sheet of flame followed by a cloud of black smoke. As we ran towards the crash, we were overtaken by the fire engine tearing across the grass. The heat was far too great to get anywhere near the wreck. All we could do was stand and watch as the foam from the fire engine slowly brought the flames under control. Gradually the smoke cleared. The Harvard was nose down in the ground. By some Herculean effort Montagu must have got the aircraft into a possible recovery position just before impact. The front cockpit was concertinaed into the engine. In the rear cockpit, plain for all to see, sat the charred hulk of what had been Montagu.

As I walked sorrowfully away, the thought occurred to me that it might so easily have been me in the cockpit. I was in a state of some shock when I got back to the crew room in the hangar. This was the first time in my life I had seen somebody killed within minutes of talking to them. In a more selfish vein I worried that my own fate hung in the balance. If Montagu had not talked to his second in command about his decision to let me train on Gladiators there was now very little chance that I would receive the same understanding treatment from anybody else.

About a dozen pilots gathered in the crew room, roughly one half of them pilot officers and the remainder sergeant pilots. The flying officer who had been Montagu's No. 2 entered the room and we all stopped talking.

"This has been a nasty experience for all of us. We have lost a fine officer and, to those of us who knew him, a good friend. His pupil was unknown to most of us as he only got here yesterday but we can only be sorry for his family and friends. But the war must go on." He paused and then continued. "As soon as the wreckage has been cleared off the airfield we will carry on flying, as planned. Just all of you remember not to practise spinning any aircraft when you are too low." He then read out those names of pilots he wanted to see in his office. My name was included. On my way there, I passed the airfield and saw that, alongside the

122

fire engine, a long low-loader had pulled up beside the crash followed by a mobile crane. I wondered, morbidly, whether they would be able to remove the bodies before they hoisted the remains of the Harvard onto the truck or whether they would just load the whole thing, lock stock and barrel.

When my turn came to enter the office I did so with some trepidation. The flying officer stood behind the desk looking through some notes. This was my first meeting with him.

"What's your name?" he asked.

I told him and quickly added that I had spent yesterday with Montagu flying Blenheims and Harvards. "Alright, Vigors, relax. Our late friend told me all about you last night. He recommended that you should be trained on Gladiators." I heaved a big sigh of relief.

"The weather's a bit lousy for a first solo this morning but the Met people say it's going to clear up this afternoon. You just spend the morning reading through those notes again. If the cloud base has gone up we'll get you off this afternoon."

I did as I was told. The weather was improving all the time and by early afternoon a watery sun was filtering through the clouds, the base of which had lifted to about 4,000 feet. The flying officer led me over to one of the Gladiators lined up on the grass. He told me to get in but to keep my helmet off for the moment. Then he climbed on to the wing, leant into the cockpit and gave me a thorough briefing on the Gladiator drill. "Remember one thing," he said, "this engine is one hell of a lot more powerful than anything you've flown before so look out for the effect of torque on take-off. And be prepared to use full right rudder to hold her straight until you get her tail in the air." With this he slapped me on the shoulder and jumped down from the wing. I got the engine started and taxied to the down-wind end of the field. Final cockpit checks made, I opened the throttle and I was off. I immediately learnt about the torque and made ready to counteract it. Before I knew where I was the aircraft was off the ground and climbing. I pulled back the stick to take up the recommended best rate of climb, at about 105 mph. It was like going up in a fast lift. I just couldn't believe it. "Hey!" I shouted in excitement. "This is something else! This really is flying!"

At long last I was in a proper aircraft and I whooped with joy as I swung into a tight climbing turn watching the earth fall away below my port wing tips. Throttling back, I levelled the aircraft out at about 4,000 feet and then flew around for a while, putting the Gladiator through gentle trials including a power-off stall which I found to be straightforward but quite sudden. Then I turned back towards the field and sideslipped in happily for my landing. Over-confident as usual I tried to ease the aircraft onto the ground whilst I still had too much flying speed and, as a result, bounced a couple of times before settling down on the grass. I was mad at myself and quickly took off for another circuit. This time I got it right and my Gladiator touched down lightly and rumbled to a halt. I kicked the rudder, opened the throttle again and started taxiing towards the hangar. After about 100 yards I found myself passing close to the circle of black grass and earth where the Harvard had so recently spun into the ground. Shamefacedly I thought of Montagu who had so recently died there and without whose help I would not now be sitting in this glorious aircraft. My joy became tempered with sorrow and I taxied soberly back to the hangars.

The following three weeks at Aston Down were filled with flying, interspersed every day with lectures on fighter tactics and gunnery. Aerobatics, cross-country navigation, formation flying, and practice gunnery filled the days. The weather, although cold, was kind to us and there was hardly a day when we were not able to get into the air and continue our training. For me everything went pretty smoothly, apart from the gunnery practice. Although I felt in total control of the aircraft and seemed able to get it into the right position for shooting at the right time, for some reason I continually missed the target drogue being towed by its aircraft. The problem in shooting straight that had dogged me since my early years, and when grouse shooting with John Bell in Ireland, was again catching up with me.

The Gladiator was a wonderful aircraft to fly. Its power and manoeuvrability was unsurpassed by that of any aircraft I have flown since, including the Spitfire. Once you had the hang of it, you could line the Gladiator up for take-off, stand on the brakes whilst opening the throttle to bring the tail off the ground, and then release the brakes. The aircraft would accelerate for some 200 yards before gaining flying

125

speed. Holding the wheels just off the ground, you could roar across the field to the far boundary, gaining speed all the time until, crossing the far fence, you would ease back on the stick until you were in a vertical climb. As the speed fell off you would pull the stick back further in the first half of a loop which would bring the aircraft into a position on its back flying in the direction from which you had started. Holding inverted flight for a minute you could then pull back on the stick again which would manoeuvre you into the second half of the loop, soon to bring the aircraft into a vertical dive towards the ground. Allowing speed to build up once more you would pull out of the dive and, kicking the rudder right and left to drop off excess speed, glide over the fence to land in exactly the position from which you had taken off a couple of minutes before. This completed what was a vertical circuit, a manoeuvre not recommended for the inexperienced.

Aston Down was only a few miles from Beaudesert Park, my first school, and most days I would pass over the fine old building standing in its beautiful grounds on the slopes above the village of Nailsworth. Looking down on the playing field where I had met Henry that first Sunday at school, and where he had allowed me to retrieve his Warnford Monoplane, I thought to myself, "That is where this all began." And wondered, too, "Where is it all going to end?"

We were due to complete our training at Aston Down in a month so that we could join our squadrons as quickly as possible. The heat was on and we spent many hours each day in the air. I enjoyed the formation flying and the dogfighting sessions in which we pitted ourselves against each other and also against our instructors. But still the air-firing gunnery sessions continued to frustrate me. For some reason I didn't seem able to achieve with my guns the degree of accuracy enjoyed by my fellow trainees. I was reminded of the hours I had spent walking across the Tipperary bogs shooting at snipe and duck with my friend Rory La Terriere and my annoyance when, at the end of every day, he had got twice as many birds in his game bag as I had in mine. I was worried that the standard of air gunnery which I was achieving might prejudice my chances of getting into Fighter Command.

When I was called into the station commander's office, I thought my fears were justified, especially as it was the day before we were due to finish our course at Aston.

I stood before his desk. "Vigors," he said, "your training here is completed and you have been posted to 222 Squadron at Duxford."

"What aircraft have they got, Sir?" I queried eagerly.

"Blenheims," he replied. My heart sank; the Blenheim was usually thought of as a bomber rather than a fighter. He must have seen my face drop. "Don't worry," he reassured me, "remember that 222 is a fighter squadron. Their commanding officer is 'Tubby' Mermagen and he's a friend of mine. He tells me that 222 is going to be re-equipped with Spitfires shortly." I saluted, left his office and rushed back to the crew room to tell my friends of my good luck.

CHAPTER
SEVEN

Duxford

On February 24th, after a spot of leave, Snipe and I collected the car at King's Cross and we set off for Cambridgeshire.

Passing through Bishop's Stortford at about 40 mph, I was waved down by a police car. "You're in a bleedin' 'urry, young man. Don't you realise you're in a 30 mph limit?"

Snipe, sensing an enemy, started to growl and I quickly told him to shut up. "Sorry, officer. I'm in a hurry to get to Duxford to join my squadron."

"Well, your squadron will just 'ave to wait 'till I get's your particulars. All of you young air force officers is just the bloody same, drivin' round like a bunch of bloody loonies like the end of the world was comin'. 'Arf of you lot is more dangerous to the English public than the bleedin' 'Uns themselves!" I showed him my driving licence.

"Actually, I'm over here flying aircraft to help you people out of your troubles. I'm a bit on the late side for reporting to my squadron and I would be really obliged if you'd let me off with a caution this time. I promise to be more careful in the future."

He did let me off. I thanked him and set off once more for Duxford. Half an hour later I turned into the gravel drive outside the Officers' Mess. Snipe got out of the car at the very same moment as one of the most beautiful girls I had ever seen in my entire life emerged from a door to the side of the main entrance. "Oh! what a beautiful dog," she cried as Snipe walked towards her.

"Oh! what a beautiful girl," I exclaimed. I was unable to take my eyes off this dark-haired vision. I introduced both myself and Snipe. "We have both just arrived from Ireland."

"I'm Jill Addison. My brother-in-law is stationed here and I'm visiting him with my sister."

"I hope we can meet up again," I said awkwardly. "I'm sure Snipe would like that as well," I added, laughing. Snipe did his bit by nuzzling Jill's hand.

"That would be nice," she said, "but I must fly now as I'm late for lunch." With that she patted Snipe on the head and hurried off to a small car parked in the drive.

And that was the start of a close friendship which was to do much to help keep me sane during the traumatic events of the next year.

I put Snipe back in the car and entered the Mess. There was a WAAF clerk behind a typewriter who told me that in view of current overcrowding in 222 Squadron I would have to share a room with a Pilot Officer Edridge, who had arrived the day before. I just hoped that my new room mate liked dogs. I fetched my suitcase and Snipe from the car and located the room. I gave Snipe a drink of water, put his rug on the end of my bed and told him to get on the bed and go to sleep.

It was coming up to lunch so I went off to find the dining room.

There were about twenty officers standing round the ante room, mostly from the other RAF squadrons that shared Duxford. I did not know any of them so I ordered a pint of beer and tentatively mingled with the crowd. The steward pointed out Edridge, a fair-haired officer standing by the fireplace. "Are you, by any chance, Edridge?" I asked him.

"That's me," he said, "what can I do for you?"

I explained about sharing his room. We shook hands. He was a slimly built man of about my own age, with smiling eyes and a sensitive face. "I hope you don't mind dogs," I said. "I've brought mine from Ireland."

"What sort is he?" Edridge asked. I explained that Snipe was a lurcher. We had another drink.

"Have you had lunch yet?" he asked. During lunch he told me that he too had been posted to 222 Squadron. But, unlike me, Edridge had joined the RAF the year before on a short-service commission and had come from another officer training unit where he had been flying Blenheims. His first name was Hilary. He lived in Bath and liked any form of music, but especially classical. Although our upbringing had been totally different, we hit it off with remarkable ease and had soon established a good feeling between us.

We went back to our room, so that Hilary could meet Snipe. They immediately made great friends with each other. Then I drove down to the hangars and reported to the squadron adjutant. He told me that the squadron commander would decide later which flight I was to join and that meanwhile I should go along to the crew room and meet up with my fellow pilots.

I found Hilary chatting away with a couple of other pilot officers. I gathered from them that the word was the squadron was definitely going to be re-equipped with Spitfires within the next few weeks. Meanwhile we were to take delivery of a Harvard to start conversion training back onto single-engined aircraft for those of us who had been flying Blenheims.

While we were talking, a broad-shouldered, dark-haired, determined looking flight lieutenant much older than any of us entered the door at the far end of the room. "Marvellous how he can get along without 'em," remarked one of my companions.

"Without what?" I queried. The man in question looked to me to have just about everything he needed.

"Without his legs of course."

This was my first sight of Flight Lieutenant Bader. My informant said that Bader had lost both his legs when he crashed a Bristol Bulldog, doing a slow roll straight off the ground some ten years before. He was out of the service for a long time but managed to get back in just before war was declared. "He's a character, I can tell you. He's in charge of B Flight."

Bader strode across the room towards us, moving with only the slightest of stiffness apparent. "Are you Vigors?" he said, his piercing blue eyes looking straight into mine.

"That's me," I replied, holding his gaze.

"You've been put in my flight. Come on over to my office. I want to talk to you." I followed him out of the door. We walked down the side of the hangar at a brisk pace and I just couldn't believe that the man striding out beside me had no legs. He must have guessed what I was thinking for as we turned into his office Bader said, "Yes, it is a bloody nuisance having no legs." He lowered himself into his chair, motioning me to sit also. "But it has its compensations. One of these days a Hun may shoot me through the legs and then who will be laughing?" He opened a file on his desk. "Now, this report on you from Cranwell and from Aston Down", he said. "Your Cranwell flight commander has given you an excellent flying report and I gather from Aston Down that you took to the Gladiator like a duck to water. What a hell of an aircraft that is," he smiled. "Pity we can't fight the war in it."

"Anyway," he continued, "although you're the latest arrival in the squadron it seems that, apart from myself, you are about the only pilot who has had recent intensive experience on single-engined aircraft. We have heard today that our first Spitfires will be ready for collection from the factory within the next few days. A Harvard is arriving here tomorrow for us to get people used to flying behind one engine again. We don't want to start breaking Spitfires. They're hard to come by at the moment. Meanwhile I'll check you out on the Harvard as soon as it arrives, just to make sure of you myself and then you can get on with collecting Spitfires."

"That sounds pretty good to me," I replied, delighted with this unexpected responsibility. He opened a drawer and handed me a booklet. "Here are the Spitfire handling notes. You can sit up and burn the midnight oil tonight, because by tomorrow morning I want you word perfect."

I took the notes and got up to leave the office. "What's your first name?" Bader asked.

"Tim" I said.

"I don't like unnecessary formality and you and I have got a lot of work to do during the next few weeks. So, call me Douglas. Oh! And there's one last thing. Reading through your reports I did notice that 'tends to be over-confident' appears at least twice. Don't get me wrong, I like people with plenty of confidence in their own ability. But too much confidence can break necks and aircraft. I don't give a damn about your neck, but if you break one of our new Spitfires through trying to be too bloody clever, you'll rue the day you ever left the Tipperary bogs."

I left the office, collected Snipe from the car and took him for a walk along the airfield. Entering the crew room once more I introduced him to those of my fellow pilots who were still sitting around. A short time later the commanding officer of 222 Squadron, "Tubby" Mermagen, came into the room with Douglas Bader. Neither Hilary nor myself had met the CO since we had arrived but now Bader introduced us.

Tubby ordered all those pilots present to sit down. He said that an experienced Spitfire pilot was to spend the next couple of days with us and would give a series of lectures on the aircraft. Our first Spitfire was scheduled to be ferried from the factory in three days' time. Meanwhile, as from tomorrow, a series of training flights would commence on the Harvard, which the squadron should soon be receiving. After the journey from Ireland I was ready for bed early that night. I took Snipe for a final walk and then he curled up on the end of my bed as I fell asleep.

Early the next morning one of the Supermarine factory pilots arrived in a light aircraft. He was to be our instructor over the next two days. "It has many great virtues, and a few tricky habits," he advised us that first morning. Without delay, lectures were scheduled. Assisted by diagrams and photographs he was able quickly to get us familiar with the aircraft. After each lecture he was bombarded by questions, all of which he answered patiently.

Meanwhile, the newly-arrived Harvard was being put to good use and, apart from refuelling breaks, was never on the ground. Douglas grabbed it for 20 minutes on the first day and gave me a short check out which apparently satisfied him. "That was OK," he said as he slid down off the wing onto the grass, "but remember when you fly the Spit that the controls are going to be a hell of a lot lighter than they are on this old tub."

One morning in March the throaty roar of a Rolls-Royce Merlin engine brought us all running out onto the tarmac. A whoop of admiration and joy rose from a number of throats as a Spitfire swooped down over the hangars and pulled up into a steep climbing turn. I can remember to this day the glow of excitement which ran through me as I watched this superbly graceful aircraft climbing away into the sky before turning to glide in over the fence, to a perfect three-point landing. The only other aircraft which has ever given me the same thrill to watch is the magnificent Concorde. Although many years apart I have always felt that the two are sisters under the skin.

For most of us pilots, the camouflaged "Spit" that taxied along the Duxford tarmac that morning was our first close-up look. This was the aircraft that, during the coming year, was going to be for the fortunate a passport to life and, for those who were less fortunate, a way of death.

The Spitfire taxied to a halt in front of us, the pilot shut off the engine and the propeller kicked to a stop. It was much smaller than I had imagined. Its enormously long nose dwarfed the cockpit itself and I worried that I might be too big to get into it. The small wheels on the retractable undercarriage were set very close together, giving rise to justified fears of swinging and ground loops. The wings were so thin that it was difficult to see how eight machine guns were fitted into them.

The pilot climbed out of the cockpit and jumped from the wing to the ground beside us.

"OK," he said, "she's all yours."

At this moment we were joined by Tubby Mermagen and his two flight commanders. He was carrying his helmet and parachute pack and wore his leather fur-lined jacket. Tubby had already done a conversion course on Spitfires. "How much fuel has she got left in the tanks?" he asked the pilot.

"About 45 minutes flying at cruising speed, Sir."

"Alright," said Tubby, "I'm going to have a quick go round in her." He climbed on the wing, slid down into the cockpit, signalled an airman to connect the starter battery and was soon taxiing out to the down-wind boundary. Tubby put on a nice flying display for our benefit and included some aerobatics before making a smooth landing.

"I'm next," said Douglas as the Spitfire taxied back to us. A tanker was sent for and the aircraft was refuelled. Douglas climbed into the cockpit and had some final words with Tubby and then taxied away for his take-off. As the Spitfire left the ground I could see that the nose bobbled up and down a little. "Remember that," I said to myself, "I'll bet she's delicate fore and aft once you're off the ground."

Douglas flew for about 15 minutes and couldn't resist making a low pass over our heads before joining the circuit for his landing. "Did I say yesterday that it was a pity that we couldn't fight the war in Gladiators?" he remarked to me as he climbed out of the Spitfire and rejoined us. "Well, I take it back. I just want to fly this baby when I first meet the Huns!" He chatted to Tubby Mermagen for a short time and came back to where I was standing.

"Alright, Tim, you're next. Run back to the crew room and get your flying jacket, helmet and parachute. The squadron leader wants to give you some final words of advice before you take off." I could not believe my ears. I was filled with a mixture of excitement and apprehension.

136

"OK, Douglas." I tried to remain calm. "I'll only be a minute." Snipe ran back with me to the crew room where I collected my equipment and then ran back at the double to the Spitfire. "Lucky bugger," said Hilary, and then added, "Good luck."

"Hang on to Snipe," I called out to him. I joined the squadron leader, who was waiting for me beside the aircraft.

"Hello, Vigors," Tubby said. "I'm afraid I've been so damn busy these last few days there just hasn't been time to talk to either you or Edridge. Anyway we have had good reports on your flying and Douglas is quite happy about the way you flew the Harvard. We need pilots to start collecting our Spitfires soon so you'd better get going and learn quick."

I climbed up onto the wing and, grasping the sides of the cockpit with both hands, slid myself down into the seat. It was a tight fit; there was about half an inch to spare on each side of my shoulders.

Tubby ran over the main points which, after constant study of the Spitfire handling notes, were already pretty familiar to me by now. "Just take off, fly around for five minutes and then come back and land," he said. "If you're happy with everything do another couple of circuits. Just remember three things. First, if you don't put the propeller in fine pitch before you take off you won't get off the ground and you'll end up in the far fence. Second, mind the torque on take-off; but as you've flown Gladiators you should be used to that. Third, remember how sensitive the fore and aft control is the moment you're airborne. OK, good luck!" And

137

with a pat on my shoulder he jumped down off the wing. I was on my own.

In moments of extreme tension in life one is inclined either to panic or to go deadly calm. I have done both in my time. Luckily this was one of the occasions when my mind went crystal clear and I felt nothing but confidence in my ability.

Taxiing out I immediately noticed, as I had been warned, that the forward view was blocked entirely by the long nose sloping upwards in front of me. Gently kicking the rudder right and left I zig-zagged down the field to get a clear view of what lay in my path. At the end of the field I turned into wind, did the final cockpit checks and made doubly sure that the propeller was in fine pitch, gently opened the throttle and started to accelerate across the grass. The torque was expected and didn't worry me. Quite quickly by holding the stick forwards I was able to get the tail off the ground which immediately gave me a clear view in front. About two-thirds of the way to the far fence I gingerly eased back on the stick and lifted the Spitfire firmly off the ground.

"All's well so far," I said to myself, "now to get that damned gear up." The undercarriage of the Spitfire Mark I had to be manually operated by means of a hand pump protruding from the side of the cockpit, next to the pilot's left foot. It needed about a dozen pumping motions to retract the wheels completely into their housing in the wings. As I reached down for this pump I inadvertently pushed the stick forwards a little and was amazed by the immediate drop of the nose towards the ground. "They weren't exaggerating about the fore and aft sensibility," I said to myself.

Gently, I tried to pull the pump upwards and downwards without moving the stick backwards and forwards. Despite my best efforts, I knew that the spectators on the ground would see that telltale bobble. It was only later that summer when I realised that, until the Spitfire Mark II was produced, you could always judge the experience of a Spitfire pilot by looking for the bobble after take-off.

With the gear up I quickly levelled off at about 1,000 feet and headed in an easterly direction towards Newmarket. I was amazed by the smooth power created by the big Merlin engine and by the delightful sensitivity of all the controls.

"This Spitfire is a real thoroughbred," I thought to myself. And at that moment, coincidentally, Newmarket Heath and its two racecourses came into view. I knew it well having attended races there with my father and it was where, in the years which lay ahead, I was to experience so many moments of excitement, triumph and disaster in connection with the breeding, buying, selling and racing of thoroughbred horses.

I turned back towards Duxford and rejoined the circuit where I talked myself down, the handling notes fresh in my memory. Reduce speed, lower undercarriage on the downwind leg, turn cross-wind, flaps down, propeller in fine pitch, turn into wind, too high so throttle back more, cross the fence at about twenty feet, throttle right back, glance at the airspeed, hold off gently, back gently, so gently, with the stick, a little shudder through the wings denoting the aircraft was down to stalling speed, stick right back, a little bump and then rumble, rumble, rumble as the Spit rolls across the grass.

I taxied back to the down-wind boundary and then took off again for a couple more circuits and landings, each time eliminating "the after take-off bobble" a little more but still a long way from controlling it completely.

After my third landing I taxied back triumphantly towards where Douglas and Hilary were talking. Snipe, who had been lying peacefully beside Hilary now jumped to his feet when I was still about 100 yards away and started running towards my aircraft. Turning alongside me he trotted about five yards from my wing tip. This habit became automatic with him whenever I was flying. Later on, when the airfield was alive with Spitfires he could still tell one from the other.

And he never made a mistake.

Douglas joined me. "Well done, Tim. That was A1 but we've both got to get rid of that bobble after take-off."

The next day I did two hours flying on the Spitfire and Douglas did the same. The other pilots flew a Miles Master, an incline-engined, low-winged trainer with tandem cockpits. It was in constant use as a supplement to the Harvard. The following morning when I reported to Douglas he said, "Starting now, you and I have a lot of work to do. There are about twenty Spitfires waiting to be collected in Wiltshire. Tubby is too busy to help us and, at the moment, it's just you and me who are qualified to fly them. An Avro Anson has been allocated to us with a pilot for the next week to ferry us down there and we have got to make full use of it. Be ready with your flying kit and parachute in half an hour."

During the next few days I not only got to know the route to Wiltshire, and back, like the palm of my hand but I also learnt a lot about the Spitfire. On top of this a link grew between Douglas and myself which gradually turned into a close friendship. I began to understand his remarkable character; he was often direct to his superiors to the point of rudeness and appeared not to have a grain of fear in his mind or body. Although he demanded a lot from his friends, he gave more than he received.

During that first week, although twice grounded by weather, we managed to collect nearly all the Spitfires that were ready for us. After a few days, most of our 222 Squadron pilots had been let loose on the Spitfire. The two other squadrons on the station were also both being re-equipped so during all daylight hours Duxford turned into a very busy airfield.

Towards the end of the week Douglas invited me to have dinner the following evening. "I think you met my sister-in-law, Jill, the day you arrived here. Well she and my wife, Thelma, are coming to spend the weekend at the Red Lion at Wittlesford and we hope you will join us."

"Thank you very much Douglas, I'd really enjoy that. Would you mind if I bring Snipe along as well?"

"Of course not," said Douglas, "I'm not sure if it's your dog or you who Jill wants to see again."

The next evening I donned my best uniform, got my batman to give my shoes an extra polish, brushed Snipe's long white coat until it shone, got into EGO and drove the short distance to the Red Lion. This lovely old coaching inn dated back to the 18th century and, being so close to the airfield, it had become almost an extension to the Duxford Officers' Mess.

As I entered the bar I was surrounded by many familiar faces. Douglas came in and asked me to join him in the residents' sitting room. I walked through with Snipe and there, sitting on a large sofa, was the vision I had first met outside the Mess on my arrival. Douglas introduced me to his wife Thelma, a charming, vivacious woman who was to become a close friend during the coming year. Jill said good evening to Snipe. We ordered drinks and I sat down beside her. I had thought a great deal about her and as we chatted away it was obvious that there were strong feelings between us. When we went in for dinner, I made the right noises to the head waiter about Snipe's good behaviour and he was granted permission to sit on the floor alongside myself and Jill.

It was a pleasant evening with plenty of laughter and a relaxing contrast to the hectic work of the previous week. Thelma and Jill made me feel very welcome. Later, I asked Jill to have dinner with me at a restaurant in Cambridge the following night, and she agreed. At about 10.30p.m. Douglas said we would have to break up the party. "The war doesn't stop on Sundays and Tim and I have got to go flying Spitfires in the morning. Up to bed with you all now!"

The next morning was cold but pleasant, with some frost on the grass and a hint of sunshine above the broken cloud, the base of which was at about 3,000 feet. Douglas announced that he was going to start practising formation flying. Each Duxford squadron was divided into two flights, A and B. For operational purposes each flight was divided into sections of three aircraft each, making a total of twelve aircraft in the air together when the squadron flew at full strength. Douglas had decided that, for the moment, Hilary and myself would fly in his section as part of B Flight. "We will take off individually, but get off the ground as soon as you can after me. I'll wait for you at 2,000 feet and five miles west of the field. Join up in formation as soon as you can. You'll be my No.1, Time so you fly on my right. Hilary will be No.2 and will be on my left. All understood? OK, let's get cracking."

As instructed Hilary and I waited for Douglas to get airborne before we took off behind him. We could see him ahead of us and he slowed to allow us to catch up as planned. I gradually eased my Spitfire in towards him and Hilary was doing the same on his left. When I was about twenty feet away from him, with my wing tip slightly behind his, I straightened out and held my position. Hilary did the same. Douglas looked over his shoulder first at me and then at Hilary. Then his voice came over loud and clear. "What the bloody hell do you boys think you're doing, dancing the old fashioned waltz? Come on, get in really snug like you would if you were smooching with your girlfriend, cheek to cheek."

Hilary and I began to edge in closer until our wing tips were no more than five feet from our leader. "OK that's better," Douglas said. "I'll expect both of you to be a lot closer than that in a couple of days. Now I'm going to start a gentle turn to the left."

Desperately trying to hold our positions we followed him round the turn. As the practice went on the turns became steeper and steeper until after half-an-hour Douglas was doing practically vertical turns with one of us positioned on our side immediately above him and the other in the same position below. "Now we're getting on. That's more like it." He levelled off until we were flying in a straight path again. "Now I want you with your wing tips inside mine," he said, "and I mean really inside."

Again, Hilary and I edged in until the tips of our wings were only about ten feet from the side of Bader's aircraft and the arc of our propellers was dangerously close to his own wing tips.

"That's more like it," called Douglas. "Now you can break off. Go and climb above the clouds and throw the aircraft around a bit and then go back to base."

I pulled away to the right in a steep climbing turn, and held my climb through the broken clouds to reach about 6,000 feet. Easing back on the stick before I had reached the fluffy tops of the clouds I climbed vertically until I felt the speed dropping off to stalling point. Then I kicked hard on the left-hand rudder and the Spit flipped over into a stall turn and was diving back down into the clouds. I did a couple of loops and a "roll off the top" of the third and then cut the motor and

144

glided back through the clouds where I was pleased to see that my instinct had been right and that Duxford lay straight ahead of me. Joining the circuit on the down-wind leg I lowered the undercarriage and then, turning left all the time, sideslipped the last 100 feet losing height quickly until I whistled over the fence for the smoothest landing I had yet achieved in a Spitfire.

That evening I picked up Jill from the Lady's Room in the Officers' Mess. She was having a drink with Thelma and some friends. We talked a little, bade polite goodbyes, then went to collect Snipe. We drove to Cambridge, delighted to be on our own, and found a pleasant restaurant overlooking the river. We ordered dinner and talked through the meal about our childhoods, our parents and our schools. There was something indefinable growing between us which made us completely at ease in each other's company. Jill told me about the battle Douglas had waged to get back into the RAF before war started. He had finally issued a challenge to one of his former colleagues, by then a wing commander in Fighter Command, to the effect that if they would give him a fighter to fly he would prove his ability. He promised that unless he could perform all manoeuvres as well as any pilot in the whole of Fighter Command he would stop badgering them. Eventually they had taken him out to an airfield, put him in a dual-controlled trainer and let him have a go. There followed a display of the most immaculately performed aerobatics which anybody had witnessed for a long time. Douglas had won his case and was reinstated in the RAF with the rank of flight lieutenant, the rank he had held when he crashed in the Bristol Bulldog in 1931.

Jill and I talked of many things that evening. With Snipe alongside us, we walked along the river bank. It was a cold night but the stars shone brightly, reflecting in the black waters of the river. I took Jill's hand and we walked on in silence. Turning back onto the road we returned to the car and drove back to the Red Lion. I got out and helped Jill from the car. I wished her goodnight and she thanked me for dinner. Now the end of the evening had come and we were loathe to part. The ghastly ending of my relationship with Kitty was on my mind, so I was determined not to prejudice the glorious warm feeling which was growing between Jill and I. After a quick kiss on the cheek and a squeeze of the hand, I led her to the hotel and watched as she went inside.

The next four or five weeks passed quickly. Whilst the Germans had made no move as yet on the Continent and had hardly shown their presence in the skies over England, there was a general feeling afoot that, come the spring, the war, which so far had only been a charade, was going to start in earnest.

We spent many hours a day in our Spitfires, practising formation flying, aerobatics, air combat, interceptions and air-to-air gunnery over the Wash. As ever, this shooting business continued to give me problems.

I wrote to Jill and she agreed that, if ever I could get a night off to spend in London, she would meet me there. Hilary and Snipe and I spent many evenings wandering in EGO round the neighbouring pubs, drinking beer, playing darts and chatting up the locals. Everywhere there was an uneasy atmosphere, the lull before the storm.

Douglas kept us doing formation take-offs and landings and, although he did not insist on such close proximity as before, there was still uncomfortably little space for straying from a straight path after we had touched down. These manoeuvres were soon extended to six aircraft at a time and eventually to the whole squadron which left a very small margin for error on the airfield, which was only 1,000 yards square.

Douglas told me that he was going to fly down to Farnborough to spend a night at Thelma's parents' home near Camberley. He asked me if I would like to come along. Two days later we took off in our Spitfires and flew to Farnborough, where we landed in close formation, just to impress the locals! Thelma and Jill were there to meet us and we drove back to their house in high spirits. Both Thelma and Jill had asked their own parents to join us and we could not have had a friendlier or more hospitable welcome.

I was delighted to see Jill again and her parents suggested that I should take her out to dinner, to which I happily agreed.

We spent a pleasant evening together and everybody else had gone to bed by the time we returned. We sat talking until after 3.00 a.m. When we said goodnight, I kissed Jill and she responded warmly. We stood together for a moment and then with a final kiss went off to our separate rooms.

The next morning the girls drove Douglas and myself back to Farnborough and we flew back to Duxford. I had left Snipe with Hilary for the night and they were there to meet us on the tarmac as we landed.

"Have you heard the news?" Hilary shouted as we got out of our cockpits.

"No," replied Douglas. "What's kicking?"

"The Huns have invaded the Low Countries! It's just been announced on the radio."

"Thank God we're at war at last!" shouted Douglas and, whilst I was still greeting Snipe he was off, literally running on his tin legs back to his office.

During the day the news filtered in. The German panzer divisions, paying no regard to Belgium's neutrality, had swept across the borders of that country. Completely bypassing the so-called impregnable Maginot Line, of which the French had been so proud, the German armoured columns were advancing fast towards the positions held by the French and British armies.

At Duxford, all squadrons were placed on immediate readiness. Rumour had it that we might be called upon to go to France to reinforce the Hurricane squadrons already there. We were ordered to pack essentials in kit bags which would follow us on ground transport to France as soon as possible. I made arrangements with my batman to look after Snipe and told him that in the meantime I would try to make arrangements to get Snipe back to Tullamaine.

During the next week, as German tanks were sweeping over Belgium and into the heart of northern

France, overcoming all opposition using their new Blitzkrieg tactic, a battle was being fought in Whitehall which was to have an even greater immediate effect on the lives of us Spitfire pilots.

Winston Churchill, vowing complete unity with France, was determined that the Spitfire squadrons in England would go to the aid of the outnumbered French-based Hurricanes. "Stuffy" Dowding, Commander-in-Chief, Fighter Command, thought otherwise. Dowding realised that no matter how many Spitfires were sent to France, and we only had a very limited number of them anyway, they would not be sufficient to stem the tide of the German armies. He reasoned that when Hitler held all mainland Europe in his grasp, the day would come, in the not too far distant future, when he would launch his mighty air strength and his armies against mainland Britain. When that happened there would be only one hope. And that hope was the Supermarine Spitfire, undoubtedly the finest and most effective fighter aircraft of that time. The Hurricane, although a first-class aircraft, was inferior to the Spitfire in a number of ways and, argued Dowding, we would be unlikely to get many back from France in any case. However, Churchill stood firm. Dowding, a quiet and dour man with none of Churchill's verbal flair, but all and more of his guts, would not budge. As came to light later, Dowding actually told Churchill that if one Spitfire squadron was ordered to France he would resign his commission. Churchill wavered and England was saved.

News of this confrontation between two great men came back to us in dribs and drabs. Tubby Mermagen had a friend who was personal assistant to a member of the Air Staff. Douglas had several old colleagues in high places. All of us, to a man, having no understanding of the strategic implications that were at stake, were rooting for Churchill against our own C-in-C. All we wanted to do was to get into the fight as soon as possible, and put our wonderful aircraft and our own skills to the test against the Huns.

After one week of immediate readiness, the atmosphere became a little less electric. Word had filtered through that there was no question of the Spitfire squadrons being sent to France. We felt frustrated and waited impatiently for something to happen. The news from the war front was worse every day. Both the British and French armies were being driven back down through northern France and were also retreating towards the Channel coast. Out-gunned, out-flanked and out-manoeuvred, even their most determined rearguard actions could not stem the advance of the German tanks.

The Hurricane squadrons in France were having a really tough time. With no early warning system to help them, apart from visual sightings, they were continually caught on the ground, resulting in their aircraft being strafed before they could get airborne. When they did get into a fight they were always hopelessly out-numbered and suffered casualties. The high-wing Lysander aircraft, most of which were used as a reconnaissance aircraft, were sitting ducks against the

German fighters and the Blenheims could achieve very little in their bomber or fighter role.

Stories came back to us daily, of heroism and disaster and all we could do was to sit on our hands and wait. Of course training intensified even more. Now that we knew it could only be a matter of weeks before we ourselves were involved in life and death combat, each hour we spent in perfecting our skills had an added significance.

Days turned into a week and the weeks turned into a month and, although there was only bad news from across the Channel, there was still no sign of German aircraft over England, nor of us going into combat.

I managed to get 48 hours leave at the end of April and arranged for Jill to come and meet me in London. She had a friend she could stay with and I checked into a hotel, but not the Regent Palace! We met and spent a relaxed and fun weekend together. Each night we ended up at the 400 Club which was the Annabels of its day and of which I had become a member. Snipe accompanied us everywhere apart from the 400 where, despite all our persuasion, he was banned. Each night I dropped Jill back at her friend's house in the early hours of the morning before returning to my hotel. By this time we accepted that we were in love but, although we never discussed it, we were both determined to keep it just a friendship and not get hopelessly or physically involved. We both knew that it was virtually certain that soon I would be in action, and this added a certain poignancy to our time together.

151

I arrived back at Duxford in time to hear the rumour that the British Army was to evacuate France. If this was the case we were certain to be involved in covering the evacuation. Again we were ordered to pack a kit bag and warned we might have to move at short notice. But it was another two weeks before the call came.

We were in the Mess, on the point of going to bed, when Tubby came in and said that he wanted to see all 222 Squadron pilots immediately. We assembled in the dining room, knowing that something serious was afoot. You could have heard a pin drop.

"Right, boys!" he smiled. "This is it." A murmur of excitement ran round the room. "The following pilots will assemble at dispersal point at 5.00 a.m. tomorrow morning." He read out the names of 11 pilots which, not including himself, made up the fighting strength of 222 Squadron. Both Hilary and I were on the list. We glanced at each other with mutual satisfaction. "Those pilots whose names I have called will all make sure that kit bags with essential clothing, etc., are packed as they won't be sleeping here tomorrow night. We will take off at first light for the beaches of Dunkirk from where the British Army is being evacuated. I will brief you all in more detail when I see you tomorrow. All those pilots whose names I have not called will report to the squadron adjutant at 8.00 a.m. when they will be given further orders as to their deployment. Goodnight gentlemen and sleep well."

Excited conversation filled the room. I singled out "Dave" Davies, a friend of mine whose name had not been on the list. I asked him if he would agree to drive my car, kitbag, and Snipe to wherever the squadron was going to be in future. He very kindly agreed. I tried to console him about not being on the list. I told him, "This old war is going to go on for a long time." I was wrong. Dave Davies died six months later in a dogfight over Kent.

In the morning, I said goodbye to Snipe and told him that I would see him that evening. "Hell!" I thought suddenly. "I hope I'm telling him the truth."

CHAPTER
EIGHT

Dunkirk

For some time now all our aircraft had been kept in open, bomb-proof, bays. They were sited around the airfield and gave some protection against an enemy bombing raid. The aircraft belonging to each squadron and flight were grouped together and these areas were known as dispersal points.

When Hilary and I arrived at dispersal that morning it was all action. Ground troops were everywhere, getting aircraft ready for departure. The scene was lit by dim arc lights giving just enough light to allow people to see what they were doing. These arc lights were only for use in an emergency.

Tubby called all the pilots together. "In half an hour we should have sufficient light to get airborne. We will take off in flights, each section using a different side of the field to avoid us getting too close together in the bad light. Douglas, I will fly on a heading of 130 degrees and will stay throttled back until you catch up with me. We will then take up a loose line astern in battle formation and climb to 10,000 feet. It will take us about 50 minutes to reach Dunkirk. Before we get there, Douglas, I want your two rear section aircraft to take up weaving positions above us. We will patrol the beaches at this height and you are all to stay in formation unless I order you otherwise. Alright, get yourselves ready. I'll be giving the order to scramble in about 20 minutes. One final thing. If we get split up you are to return to Hornchurch."

As I walked towards my aircraft my mouth was dry. For the first time in my life I understood the meaning of the "taste of fear". I suddenly realised that at long last the moment had arrived. We were going into action. Within an hour I could be battling for my life being shot at with real bullets by a man whose sole intent was to kill me. Up till now it had been something of a game; like a Biggles book, where the heroes always survived and it was generally only the baddies who got the chop. Now it was real war. I was dead scared and knew I had somehow to control this fear and not show it to my fellow pilots.

Hilary came over and we chatted a bit, both of us trying to appear nonchalant. A few minutes later Douglas levered his way down the steps of the dispersal hut.

"We're off," he shouted almost running to his aircraft. Hilary and I ran to ours and climbed into the cockpits. Engines started to roar and in a couple of minutes the squadron was on the move.

We took off as planned and closed up on the leading flight led by the squadron commander. After climbing to 10,000 feet in semi-darkness we saw the sun edge up over the horizon in front of us. Soon we crossed the coast near Ipswich. The sky was virtually clear of clouds and visibility, even in the early morning haze, was about twenty miles. Long before we reached Dunkirk we could see a pall of black smoke in the sky ahead of us. The sea below us was dotted with craft of every variety, from small motor boats to large steamers and warships, all plying their way either to or from the Dunkirk beaches. This was the armada of craft making its way to the relief of the British Army, to save as many troops as possible from the predicament into which they had been forced. These great mountains of smoke above and the stream of boats below became part of the scenery with which we were to live for the next ten days.

As we approached the coast line this first time we could see that much of the smoke came from oil tanks which had been bombed by the enemy and set ablaze.

"Green 2 to Red leader," sounded in my headphones, "Bandits at six o'clock below us!"

This warning came from one of the two rear section Spitfires that Tubby had positioned to fly above us, weaving from side to side as our watchdogs. It meant that enemy aircraft had been spotted flying below and in front of us. We had practised these spottings and warnings many times during our training but this was the first time we had heard it for real. Words of this kind were to become part of our everyday life over the months which lay ahead. "Tally ho!" replied Tubby. He had spotted the bandits. "Douglas, you and your boys stay on top to protect us. A Flight follow me."

The leading six aircraft peeled away and Douglas led our B Flight in a broad circle above them.

"Tally ho!" shouted Douglas suddenly. "There are more bandits above us, at three o'clock. I'm climbing up to meet them. Follow me."

Looking down I could see streams of tracer where Tubby was engaging the enemy, some 3,000 feet below. Then I quickly swivelled round to address what appeared to be a formation of Messerschmitt 109s, crossing our path 5,000 feet above. They had either not seen us or didn't intend to attack for the moment. There were twelve of them and by now were getting away from us. Douglas was bringing B Flight from underneath and behind them. When we were less than 1,000 below, one of the Messerschmitts must have spotted us for they started a steep right-hand turn. We swung after them getting closer all the time.

"Green section will go for the leaders and you boys at the back go for the last six," called Douglas. The enemy were now diving and trying to turn to face us. With sticks hard back we were trying to cut inside their turn. Suddenly I saw a line of white tracers flying past my port wing tip and at the same time heard a yell in my headphones. "Look out! More bandits behind us!"

A quick glance over my shoulder revealed an enemy 109 unpleasantly close to my tail, and still spewing tracers. My first reaction was extreme fear which temporarily froze my ability to think. This was quickly replaced by my overwhelming desire for self-preservation. From experience in practice dogfighting, I knew that if I tried to climb out of trouble the Hun would have a good chance of pulling up inside my arc and of keeping his sights on me. The opposite action gave me a better chance.

I pushed violently forward and sideways on the stick which flung my Spitfire into a sudden and violent dive. My whole weight came unpleasantly hard against my shoulder harness. But thankfully the tracer disappeared. I pulled into a steep turn looking desperately over my shoulder to try to assess the situation. The enemy fighters had apparently passed clean over my head as I could see a wild circling mass of Spitfires and 109s interlaced with many white lines of tracer.

My manoeuvre had lost me a lot of height, a bad tactic in a dogfight. Loss of height generally put one at a disadvantage. On this occasion it had probably saved me but nonetheless I immediately started into a steep climbing turn so as to get above the rest of the fighting aircraft. I was now continually glancing over my shoulder, checking to see that I was not likely to be attacked again from behind.

I began a dive towards the action.

Below, a 109 was chasing a Spitfire in a tight circle and I manoeuvred in behind him. Trying hard to get him in my sights, I pulled back on the stick. My hand closed on the spade grip at the top of the control column. The firing button was positioned in the middle of the column and now I pressed it with my right thumb to fire my first shot in action. The Spitfire shuddered and tracers arced out of the machine guns in my wings. I could see the tracer passing harmlessly below the Messerschmitt. Keeping my finger on the firing button I hauled back even further on the stick trying to drag the nose of my own aircraft above him. Gradually the tracer came closer to his tail but, just as I thought I had him, he realised his danger and flicked over on his left side and dived. I stopped firing and tried to follow him down in a vertical dive. I got my sights near him again but his quick manoeuvre had lost me ground and I was now about 300 yards behind him. I opened fire again in the hope that I might catch him with a lucky bullet and I thought I saw a piece of his tail fall off as we dived towards the sea. At this moment a tracer once more came whipping past me from behind. I heaved back on the stick and blacked myself out as I wrenched the aircraft into a climb. Quickly regaining my senses I saw my attacker dive by me and I tugged my Spit into a steep turn to try to get around onto his tail. I lost sight of him whilst in my turn and started to look around me. To my amazement I couldn't see another aircraft in the sky.

Only moments before, the whole sky had been filled with circling and diving aircraft. I was to learn later that this transition from a mass of milling aircraft to an empty sky was a common occurrence. The sky is a big place and when aircraft are travelling at speeds of up to 350 mph they can very quickly put a lot of distance between each other. My altimeter indicated that I was now down to 3,000 feet. I could see the coast line but during the fight I had moved away from the town of Dunkirk and the landscape looked to be empty. I searched for black smoke from the burning oil tanks and was surprised to see it billowing into the sky at least fifteen miles to the south.

Evidently, I had covered a lot of ground in the last few minutes. I started to climb in the direction of Dunkirk. Then, suddenly, I thought better of it; at normal cruising speed the Spitfire carried enough fuel to stay in the air for over two hours. By throttling back at high altitude this could be stretched, in extremis, to three hours. Equally, with the throttle wide open at low altitudes flight duration could be reduced to little more than one hour. My instruments showed that I had been in the air for one hour and fifteen minutes.

Hornchurch, the airfield situated on the eastern outskirts of London, to which we had been told to return, was a lot closer to Dunkirk than Duxford. But it would still take at least 30 minutes flying to get back there. I realised, too, that in the last ten minutes I had been using extreme ranges of throttle movement, which was well known to eat up petrol.

Still searching for any other aircraft, I set a course which would hopefully bring me back to the mouth of the Thames. Hornchurch was on the north bank of the river. To conserve fuel I throttled back and, still keeping a wary eye for enemy aircraft, started to relax. The events of the last few minutes flicked across my mind.

First, I thought with relief, I was still alive. My Spitfire also appeared to be completely unscathed. Second, apart from possibly knocking a bit off the tail of a Messerschmitt 109, I had done nothing to harm the enemy apart from causing them a little distraction. But on the plus side, I had managed to help at least one of my colleagues out of trouble by firing on his attacker. "Not a great start to the fighting career of Tim Vigors,"

I thought, "but at least the balance sheet is fairly square so far."

I was worried, however, about how deadly scared I had been when I first saw those enemy bullets streaming past my wing tip. I had never known fear like that before in my life and knew that I was likely to experience it many times again in the near future. Flying home that morning I just hoped fervently that I would be able to keep my fear under control.

Flying much lower than on my outward journey, I could more clearly see the armada of vessels below me on their way to, and returning from, Dunkirk. The variety was immense: naval frigates, pleasure steamers, trawlers, fishing boats, Broads cruisers, even sailing yachts, all wallowing along in the Channel swell. I even saw several ordinary open rowing boats powered by outboard motors. One thing they all had in common if they were heading for England — their decks were crammed with khaki-clad soldiers rescued from the beaches. It was indeed a remarkable, if also a very sad, spectacle.

Most of the boats below me were heading for the vicinity of Dover, the closest landfall, and I soon left them behind on my left. Soon I saw the mouth of the Thames beginning to open in front of me and I altered course a little offshore to pass by Southend and then down into the Hornchurch area. As I approached, I saw several other Spitfires converging on the airfield and started to wonder how many of my squadron had made it home safe.

I circled above the airfield to get the lie of the land and then joined the circuit and landed. Another Spitfire turned off to the left in front of me so I followed it to a dispersal point. As I taxied to a halt, I recognised Douglas heaving himself out of the cockpit. I jumped down and walked over to his aircraft. Douglas said,

"Glad to see you made it Tim. How did you do?"

"Not great," I replied, "but I think I damaged one. To tell you the truth, I was too damn busy most of the time looking after myself."

"So was I," said Douglas, "but I definitely got one. I saw the bugger go down in flames."

"Well done yourself," I laughed and shook his hand. "Did you see any of the rest of the boys?"

"Well, I saw one Spitfire landing in the sea just off the beaches," he said. "Hilary's OK too and so is Tubby. Both of them actually landed just before me."

"Have we come to the right dispersal point?" I queried.

"Yes," said Douglas, "I radioed the tower and they sent me over here."

We walked to the hut where several pilots were standing talking. I saw Hilary and straight away went to him.

"Glad to see you're in one piece," I exclaimed. "How did you do?"

"Never ever been more scared in my whole bloody life," he laughed. "And I'm afraid I didn't make any sort of a dent in the German Reich."

"That makes two of us," I replied, "I was shit scared from the word go. I think I knocked a bit off a 109's tail

162

but not enough to stop him." While we were talking another Spitfire taxied up to dispersal. We could see bullet holes in the tail unit and hurried over to greet Sergeant Pilot Baxter.

"What happened to you?" I asked, looking in awe at the ragged holes stretching in one line from the middle of the fuselage back across the tail fin and rudder.

"Some bastard got on my tail and I couldn't shake him off. Those bloody Huns know how to fly alright. I guess I'm lucky to be alive." Baxter took off his helmet. His usually rather florid complexion was now two shades lighter.

And so, one by one, our friends came back. Eleven Spitfires were drawn up around the dispersal hut by the end of the morning. The intelligence officer had arrived and, in turn, we gave him our first combat reports. The only pilot who was missing was another sergeant pilot from A Flight and we assumed that he was the pilot of the Spitfire which Douglas had seen landing in the sea. Later we learned that he had been rescued by one of the many boats picking up troops from the beach.

Our final tally of enemy aircraft amounted to two confirmed kills and three definitely damaged, not counting my own which I didn't consider serious enough to claim. Thus, the squadron had both drawn, and spilled, first blood.

There was nothing much we could do for the rest of that day (May 28th) as our ground support party were still on the road from Duxford. Our aircraft were refuelled by Hornchurch personnel but, despite Tubby's efforts to borrow some armourers from the other squadrons based there, nothing could be done about getting our Spitfires rearmed until our own people arrived.

We were driven to the Mess in a station truck and were allocated rooms. After lunch we walked down to our dispersal point again to await the arrival of our ground convoy. First to arrive on the scene were Dave and Snipe in my car. As soon as the car stopped Snipe jumped out of the open car window and smothered me with licks. The main convoy arrived soon after and went straight to work. The armourers got down to loading up our guns and the mechanics started checking everything on the aircraft. Sergeant Baxter's aircraft was taxied over to the maintenance hangar for repair and Tubby waited impatiently for the moment he could report the squadron once more operational.

Our move from Duxford to Hornchurch had brought us under the jurisdiction of 11 Group, Fighter Command, which controlled the whole of the south-east corner of England, from which air cover for the Dunkirk operation was being organised and from which 90 per cent of the action in the Battle of Britain was to be fought three months later.

At Duxford we had been under the command of 12 Group, who controlled Cambridge, Suffolk and Norfolk. This redeployment did not affect the lives of us lowly pilot officers in any way but for Tubby and Douglas it meant quite a major change as 12 Group was commanded at that time by Air Vice-Marshal Leigh Mallory who was a great personal friend of theirs. They were not so well acquainted with Air Vice-Marshal Park, Commander of 11 Group.

The armourers and mechanics finished their work at about 5.00p.m. When Tubby told Group, he was advised that we were not needed again that night and that we could stand down. Hilary, Dave, Snipe and myself investigated the local hostelry that evening but were all in bed by 10.00p.m. in anticipation of an early start next day.

By 5.35a.m. we were on our way back to cover the Dunkirk beaches. There was no sign of enemy air activity and we were back at Hornchurch for breakfast. At 11.00a.m., bound for the beaches again, we soon made contact, intercepting a squadron of Heinkel bombers. As we attacked them, their Messerschmitt fighter escort became involved.

"Get those bastard Heinkels first," yelled Douglas. "We'll look after the 109s later." We dived down on the Heinkels as they ran in on their bombing run towards the beaches. Douglas opened up on the leading aircraft and it burst into flames. I got my sights on one but my tracer passed harmlessly underneath him and I hauled back on the stick to bring them up into his fuselage. As this was happening, tracer was passing me and I realised I had a 109 on my tail. I took a chance and pulled up, sharp right, and blacked out as the G-force took effect. I came round to find the 109 still on my tail and still firing but having to climb to engage me. I kept turning as hard as I could and looking back was happy to see that my turn was taking me inside him. Now we were on opposite sides of the circle in a classic dogfight.

I again pulled back on the stick, on the verge of blacking out once more. Gradually I was gaining on the 109 but as I readied to shoot he flicked onto his back and dived for the sea. I followed him down and opened fire, my bullets ripping his starboard wing and then suddenly the 109 became a ball of flame.

"Got you, you bastard." I was exultant as I watched the Messerschmitt go down. At that moment there was a tug on my right wing and to my horror I saw holes appearing in the wing tip. The jubilation of a minute before changed to fear. A 109 shot underneath me and I climbed away, turning desperately. Suddenly, once more, the sky was empty with not another aircraft to be seen. I looked anxiously at my wing tip. There were several holes across it, about two feet from the wing tip. However, the Spitfire was flying normally. The tension eased and I gingerly turned for home.

Keeping a wary eye open for any more trouble, I started to think about the events of the past five minutes. There was no doubt that I should have got the Heinkel. That was just damned bad shooting, a failing to which I had grown used. On the other hand, I was more than happy to have made my first "kill" and was experiencing that same satisfaction that I had known in Ireland when out pigeon shooting on a summer's evening.

I was aware that I had killed a fellow human being and was surprised not to feel remorse. Of course, Hitler's atrocities had been well publicised and we had got into the way of identifying all Germans with their leader. In hindsight this could not have always been right. But the way I saw it then was, "Poor son of a bitch. He was probably a nice guy and we would probably have got on well had we met. But he was on the wrong side. He shouldn't have signed up with that bastard Hitler!" The fact was, and remains to this day, Germany was wrong in every way allowing itself to be bamboozled by one of the most evil monsters the world has ever seen. Thus, the consequences when Germans met their fate was just their bad luck. And so, philosophising about the wrongs and rights of the world, I eased my Spitfire round the Hornchurch circuit and smoothed her onto the grass.

I was still about 50 yards from dispersal when Snipe came running. My mechanics were soon there too, having already noticed the line of holes in my wing tip.

"Are you OK, Sir?" one of them asked.

"Sure!" I replied. "Let's have a look at the damage." On inspection, there appeared to be no major structural problems and the damage there was looked to be quite easy to repair. The aircraft went into the hangar and I went to dispersal to make my combat report to the intelligence officer. Apart from telling him about my score I also reported having seen Douglas shoot down one of the Heinkels. Douglas himself landed shortly and came over to say that he thought he had got another Heinkel as well, but had had to take violent evasive action from an attacking 109 before he could confirm that his second victim actually crashed.

The following days took up a regular pattern. Every morning we seemed to be on the dawn patrol and often we only had time for breakfast before we were in the air again. If we didn't do a second sortie in the morning we were sent over Dunkirk in the afternoon or evening. Sometimes we did all three. On most patrols we ran into enemy aircraft of one kind or another. We had some losses but were satisfied that our scoreboard was ticking over almost three to one in our favour. A couple of our pilots were killed and one landed behind the German lines, which were now practically on the beach, and was taken prisoner. Another arrived back at Hornchurch covered in blood with a bullet through his shoulder. Although the two pilots who were killed were both good acquaintances of mine, they were nothing like as close to me as Hilary, Douglas or Dave and at the end of each day I was always glad that all we four were unscathed.

Each morning on waking, the question in my mind was would I sleep in that bed ever again, Somehow we all learned to live with this threat to our existence. For myself, I was blessed with a sublime confidence; always, it would be the other guy who "bought it".

The stream of boats ploughing between Dunkirk and Dover never varied in size. Gradually, the entire surviving British Expeditionary Force was brought to safety.

Our last dawn patrol was on June 4th. A couple of quick scraps and we were heading home for our breakfast. Then once again we were ordered to go and for the last time found ourselves heading for Dunkirk. By now the town and its surroundings were a Dante's Inferno, all the remaining oil stores, fuel supplies and equipment which had not burnt already were now set on fire by the departing troops. Vast clouds of flame and smoke billowed into the air. The Germans had reached the coast on both sides of the town and, as in the past few days, tracer and puffs of anti-aircraft fire greeted our arrival.

We saw Junkers 77 aircraft attacking shipping lanes. Once we engaged we were, as usual, set upon by Messerschmitt 109s. I got into an individual fight with one of them and was delighted to send him scurrying for home with white smoke trailing from his engine. My further plans for his fate were interrupted by my catching sight of a Spitfire being fired on by a 109, unpleasantly close to his tail. I interfered and soon was following the 109 in a dive towards the ground. I fired on him but, as so often, missed and found myself, by now about 1,000 feet from the ground, engulfed in a hail of bullets fired by enemy ground troops. I considered discretion the better part of valour and headed for home at sea level, landing first at Tangmere. I passed close to the stream of boats and waved wildly at their occupants and received many a wave in return.

Half an hour later I was back at Hornchurch. At dispersal, Hilary ran over and slapped me on the shoulder. "Thanks a million, pal!" he cried, "You probably saved my life. I couldn't shake that bastard off, and I was more than happy that you interfered. Come on up to the Mess. I want to buy you a large drink."

Later, Tubby Mermagen came into the Mess. "It's all over, fellows." He told us that the last British troops had been taken off the beaches and we would not be patrolling Dunkirk again. "You can have the rest of the day off."

Hilary and I went back to my room. "What shall we do with ourselves?" he said.

"Do you want a big laugh, Hilary?" I asked him, glancing at the morning paper.

"Sure do," he replied.

I showed him the paper. "See the date? It's the Fourth of June. Let's go to Eton."

And so we did, six years after my first visit to the day and hour, June 4th 1940. Now I lay dozing on that same piece of grass. The same sound of clapping awoke me. I glanced at my watch. It was 2.55p.m. I looked around. All was as it had been, six years earlier. The same sun shone down and June was, once more, bursting out all over. The same crowd of Eton boys with their parents, sisters, friends, and girl friends bedecked in their same colourful summer dresses, relaxing or strolling around the same green cricket field. The sound of ball on bat and an occasional "Howzat!", the same low buzz of conversation.

All the very same, except that instead of John Harley, lying beside me on the soft grass was my friend of six months, Hilary Edridge. And now we were wearing the uniform of the Royal Air Force and the coveted wings, for which we had worked so hard, and stripes of our pilot officer rank. Moreover, we knew that the peaceful scene which we surveyed would soon be rudely shattered. For Hilary and me lying by that cricket field, the change had already come. Hilary summed it up.

"It's just bloody crazy," he said, "but I suppose this is what we are fighting for."

The contrast in emotions which I experienced that June day will live with me all my life. For my friend Hilary it was different. He died four months later in a blazing Spitfire 20,000 feet over Kent.

CHAPTER
NINE

June and July 1940

On our way back from Eton we stopped at a pub in the East End. There was an atmosphere of subdued shock. Up till now the British people, always phlegmatic about major crises, had pretty much turned a blind eye to the disaster which was facing their country. Unlike us few pilots, with our grandstand view of the evacuation, and those who had actually taken part, the public did not really know what had being going on. There existed a degree of escapism which refused to accept the fact that the British Army, as a fighting force, had been virtually annihilated. Now the official announcement that the last British troops had left France had been published, a realisation was growing that nothing stood between Britain and the armies of Hitler than the thin strip of the English Channel.

An unspoken truth was becoming accepted. For the first time since 1066, England was in imminent danger of being invaded by her enemies.

We happened to be the only people in the bar in uniform and the other patrons cast glances at us as if we had arrived from the moon. "You boys are going to have to go some to look after us now," said the portly lady behind the bar. "I just hope there's enough of you."

"Madam," Hilary said, "it's the quality that counts, not the quantity! Now look at this fine Irishman standing here beside me. Only three hours ago I was sitting over there with a Hun on my tail doing his best to kill me and, thank God, along comes my friend here. The Hun sees the murderous look in these wild Irish eyes and dives so fast for home that he nearly pulls the wings off his aeroplane."

Embarrassed, I kicked out at him under the stool. But his remarks had been heard. People crowded round us. An old grey-haired man sitting beside us asked, "You boys really there this mornin' fightin' those bloody Jerries?"

"Yes, but that's what they pay us for," I replied. A flood of questions were directed at us.

"Give 'em a free drink Mabel!" cried our neighbour.

"No thanks," I said. "I'm sorry, but we are late for an appointment and we must get going." Resisting all requests to stay, we fled. I was angry. "What the bloody hell were you shooting that line for?" I demanded of Hilary.

"I'm sorry, Tim," he replied "but to tell you the honest truth I'm really grateful for what you did this morning. Without your help, I might well be dead now. I just wanted to tell somebody about it."

Driving through London we saw little traffic. Petrol rationing had, by this time, really started to bite. It had not affected us pilots too badly as, quite illegally, we used to top up the tanks of our cars from the petrol bowsers used for refuelling aircraft. As long as this was done reasonably discreetly the authorities kindly turned a blind eye. What effect 100 octane fuel was having on the pistons and cylinders of my Ford 8 remained to be seen. So far EGO was still going like a bomb. In fact the diet seemed to suit her.

The next day I found a telephone box and called Jill. She was free and agreed to have dinner with Hilary and I. She sounded pleased to hear that I was still in the land of the living. We drove over to Bagshot to pick her up and spent the evening laughing and joking about the events of the past week. Jill seemed somewhat surprised by the rather callous way in which Hilary and I referred to casualties. We had already started to learn the hard lesson that the only way to cope with the constant loss of close companions was to laugh rather than cry.

After dinner we dropped off Jill and drove back to Hornchurch. It was after midnight by the time we walked into the Mess. There was a note for us on the board saying dispersal was not until 9.00a.m. the next day. We heaved a sigh of relief and retired to our rooms for a welcome sleep.

Although the immediate flap was over, 222 Squadron was not going back to Duxford. Our new base was to be in Lincolnshire, at Kirton-in-Lindsey, and we were to leave that day. As my Spitfire was still unserviceable, due to the damage inflicted the day before, I was given permission to drive to Kirton, stopping at Duxford to collect my belongings.

I set off on the long haul to Lincolnshire, passing through Bishop's Stortford with particular circumspection, and drove through the gates of RAF Kirton-in-Lindsey later that same day. Hilary had got me a room next door to his and, having unloaded my kit and some baggage that I had collected for him from Duxford, we made a tour of inspection.

Kirton was pretty much what we had been used to and the squadron settled down into what was a comfortable way of life after the traumatic events of the past two weeks. It was obvious that it would not be long before the Germans made a major assault on the British mainland but, for the first few weeks after Dunkirk, there was a complete lull in the battle and very few German aircraft were seen.

Those which did venture out were mostly night raiders, some of which were causing concern over Midland towns such as Birmingham and as far north as Manchester. Shortly after our arrival at Kirton, I was dispatched with a section of Spitfires to act as night protectors over Manchester. With Hilary and one other pilot our three-aircraft section flew to Ringway Airport where we were to be based indefinitely. In fact, we were only there for about ten days and during that time no enemy aircraft were tracked by the radar in the area.

This was a rather boring period. Situated in the centre of the row of hangars which bordered the north side of Ringway was a high control tower and, for want of anything better to do, I suggested to Hilary that it might be amusing to take some pictures from the top of this tower. My idea was to have the photographer take a

175

picture from above a Spitfire, if only to provide a change from countless other photographs of Spits which were taken from every angle, but invariably from below. There was a photography unit on the airfield and, enlisting their help, we made the necessary plans. Our first attempts were simple and easy to complete.

We put the photographer up in the tower about thirty feet above the ground and I flew my aircraft at some 200 mph close to the base of the tower and about ten feet above the ground. The result was an excellent picture of a downward view of a Spitfire. Then we got more ambitious. "If we can do it with one aircraft," said Hilary, "why can't we do it with two?"

"You mean two of us, flying in formation?" I said.

"No," said Hilary. "I mean the two of us flying in opposite directions and crossing under the tower!"

"Well, it's going to take some pretty accurate timing. But let's give it go." Luckily for us, the only other air activity at Ringway at that time was the training of parachute troops. Aircraft took off, dropped the students, and then landed about twenty times a day. We knew that we would need a lot of practice to perfect our little stunt so we fitted our own training around the parachute school's schedule.

To avoid causing too much irritation to people working in the vicinity of the hangars, we decided to do our training on the other side of the airfield where there were no buildings. We placed a packing case on the grass and then Hilary and I took off and flew away in opposite directions. We climbed to 500 feet and, at prearranged points the same distance from the airfield,

176

we turned 180 degrees and dived on a collision course towards the packing case.

Crossing the airfield boundary, I would pull out of my dive and, keeping as close to the ground as I dared, fly straight at the box. Allowing for the arc of the big propeller this would mean that the bottom of my fuselage was about eight feet above the grass. Hilary, now flying straight at me, would maintain a height of about twenty feet and would flash over my head. We closed at a speed of roughly 400 mph which, by itself, was easy; the trick was to time it so that both of us would pass above the box at the same moment.

The first few times we got it hopelessly wrong but by the end of our second session we were regularly crossing within ten yards of the target and had even, so our friends on the ground told us, got it bang on right a couple of times. Soon, we were getting it right more often than wrong.

We positioned the photographer in the tower for the "shoot". The word had spread and most of the station turned out to watch. The first couple of times we misjudged it and Hilary passed over my head well before I reached the base of the tower. But the next time we were spot on. As I whistled past the base of the tower, Hilary streaked over my head right below the photographer and we both let out a yell of glee. We decided on one more pass for luck, and this time crossed right under the tower.

We waited impatiently for the film to be developed. To our delight, the best of the three photographs showed the nose of Hilary's aircraft exactly above the

177

tail of mine. The rest of my Spitfire was practically hidden by Hilary's, apart from the wings which emerged from behind the wings of his aircraft.

We were soon to leave Ringway but not before I learnt that something about parachuting which was to save my life over Penang some months later. And I did keep the Ringway photographs. I don't know whether any other pictures of Spitfires in this position were ever taken. I have certainly never seen any like it. I kept the photographs but they were lost along with the rest of my gear when I had to get out of Singapore in a hurry eighteen months later.

We found life back at Kirton very much the same as when we had left. There was a temporary lull in hostilities and the Luftwaffe had not yet started to make its presence felt over England in day time. However, an increasing number of German bombers were venturing over the country at night. As yet there was no sign of any mass raids but every night the enemy would cross the coast in ones and twos, apparently feeling out the defences more than being intent on causing any major damage. It was therefore decided that night flying practice was to be stepped up and the squadron was to keep one aircraft section at readiness every night.

Until one got the hang of it the Spitfire Mark I was not the easiest animal in the world to fly at night. On each side of the nose were six exhaust outlets and, on the early Spitfires, no kind of muffler was fitted to the exhaust to hide the exhaust gases from the pilot. Of course, in the day time this did not matter as the exhaust fumes were practically invisible. But at night these same gases appeared as bright flames which were of sufficient intensity to cut out all forward vision. In addition, fore and aft sensibility in the Spitfires made the first moments off the ground a tricky affair, even if the pilot could see ahead. With the blinding effect of the exhaust gases, no visual horizon of any kind could be seen in front of the nose so that the pilot had no indication as to whether the aircraft was climbing or diving. Forward pressure on the stick at this moment could plummet the aircraft into the ground. It was therefore inadvisable to start pumping up the undercarriage before the altimeter was registering 200 feet or more. The drag of the undercarriage affected the climbing ability of the aircraft at low speeds so, during the first few seconds at take-off, the pilot could be in a "catch 22" situation.

By midsummer, 222 Squadron Spitfires had exhaust mufflers and constant speed propellers fitted. These provided a better climbing performance off the ground, but in those early days, initial night flying training on a Spit was still a bit hairy.

Pilots on night readiness always slept down at dispersal. There was a lot of rivalry between different sections concerning who could get all three aircraft off the ground in the shortest space of time from the sounding of the alarm bell. Characteristically, Douglas was determined to prove that his section was the fastest. This led to many hours of rehearsal.

Our three camp beds were placed close to the door of the dispersal hut. Douglas's Spitfire was positioned slap bang outside the door with Hilary's and mine near by. In order to sleep better Douglas liked to remove his false legs before retiring. Lowering himself onto his bed he would hand his right leg to me and I would place it at the foot of my bed. Hilary's responsibility was the left leg. Wherever we were, Snipe liked to sleep on my bed and somehow or another he managed to squeeze himself beside me on the narrow mattress.

On the sound of the alarm bell my first responsibility was to seize Douglas's leg and place it onto the stump of his thigh which he would be sticking over the end of the bed. Hilary would be helping him with his left leg. At the same time his fitter and rigger, the two mechanics who were responsible for the maintenance of the engine and airframe of his aircraft, would have rushed through the door. Seizing him under the arms they would carry him bodily out of the door and down the steps onto the grass. Lifted by them onto the rear edge of the wing he would grab the sides of the cockpit and lever himself into his seat. Hilary and I would run to our Spitfires and hit the starting buttons as our bottoms touched the parachutes, already positioned on the metal seats. The three engines would splutter and roar into life and, with Douglas taxiing fast in front, we would head for the big floodlight which marked the end of the take-off area. Opening the throttles we would roar off the ground in loose formation about twenty yards apart.

Spurred on by Douglas's unswerving determination, we managed to reduce the interval between the sound of the alarm bell and all three Spitfires being off the ground to two minutes and fifty seconds, at least thirty seconds better than the time achieved by any other section.

Day flying activity during those early summer months was mostly taken up with mock dogfights and formation practice. From time to time, operating from an advance base on the north-east coast of England, we carried out convoy patrol duties, guarding merchant ships passing up and down the coast from enemy air attack.

One morning, Douglas, Hilary and myself were on convoy patrol when we spotted a couple of German torpedo bombers diving out of the clouds towards the leading merchant ship below. With guns blazing we dived straight at the Germans. One of them disappeared in a flash of flame and the other pulled up and ran for the clouds. I was close behind him trying to pull my sights up through his fuselage when bullets smashed into my own aircraft. A large star appeared on my bulletproof windscreen and I could see even larger holes in the engine cowling. Evidently, the rear gunner in the German aircraft was a better shot than I was; it was just as well for me that seconds later he disappeared into the cloud.

I levelled out and surveyed the damage as best I could. Automatically, I turned back for the coast which lay out of sight and told Douglas that I had been hit and was heading for home. Shortly afterwards he and Hilary appeared beside me. I was relieved to find that, despite the pounding it had taken, my engine was still functioning reasonably normally.

The most vulnerable parts of the Merlin engine in a battle were the system of cooling pipes which intertwined the various parts of the big cylinder block. If a bullet fractured one of these pipes a white cloud of vaporising glycol would spurt from under the cowling, warning the pilot that the engine was about to overheat and seize up. My engine was running very rough but I was happy to see no signs of escaping glycol. I was still some twenty-five miles off the coast.

With Douglas and Hilary beside me I limped back towards land and heaved a big sigh of relief as I crossed the coast about ten minutes later. As everything was running fairly normally I decided to head back for Kirton rather than land at one of the coastal airfields where, although much closer, maintenance facilities were minimal. It was a beautiful clear morning and soon Kirton came into sight. I glided down and, with the engine bursting into unnatural splutters, landed without incident and taxied back to dispersal.

Snipe and my ground crew were there to meet me. Also there was my fitter, who was responsible for the maintenance of the engine. He stood gazing with awe at the jagged holes in the engine cowling. "Looks like a bleedin' sieve!" was his immediate reaction. "You're bloody lucky to get home with that load of lead in your motor," he added.

We took off the cowlings and inspected the damage which was considerable. Looking at the mangled pieces of metal it was difficult to understand how the faithful Merlin had kept running after such punishment. My fitter, by this time, was standing on a ladder with his head in the engine. "Look at this," he cried, "you must have gone to church last Sunday, Sir."

I climbed on to another set of steps to have a look for myself. When I saw the cause for the fitter's excitement I agreed that the good Lord had been on my side. One of the glycol pipes which ran along the top of the cylinder block had been furrowed by a bullet for threequarters of its length. One fraction of a millimetre more and the skin of the pipe must have been broken. I quickly stopped myself imagining what might have been . . . "Come on Snipe!" I muttered. "Let's go and get a drink."

Not long after this incident I was taking off in loose formation with Douglas. About halfway across the field I realised that there was something wrong with his aircraft. Instead of lifting off at the expected moment his wheels were still trundling across the grass. I lifted off normally and, looking over my shoulder, watched in horror as I saw his Spitfire plough into the fence at the end of the field and stand on its nose. I hauled round in a steep turn, still only about fifty feet off the ground and completed the fastest circuit and landing which I had ever achieved. As I pulled up at the end of my landing run the ambulance and fire engine were just drawing up by Douglas's upturned aircraft. I leapt out of my cockpit and ran across to give a hand. Douglas was sitting in his cockpit swearing. Climbing on the wing I could see that the engine had been squashed back by the impact and was pinning his legs, preventing him from moving. Mercifully there was no sign of fire.

183

"I'll have to take my bloody legs off!" Douglas fumed. "Tim, be a good fellow and fetch my spare pair from my room whilst these fellows are getting me out."

When I returned, Tubby Mermagen, Hilary and several other pilots were gathered round the wreckage. The ambulance men had lifted Douglas out, minus his legs, and he was sitting fuming on the grass. "It's no damned good making excuses for myself Tubby. I left the prop in coarse pitch. How many young pilots have I sworn I would kill if they were ever so bloody careless as to do that. Now you'd better kill me!"

"You're damned lucky not to have killed yourself," Tubby remarked drily, "but let it be a lesson to us all." At this moment one of the fire crew came over to us holding out the remains of Douglas's legs which he had managed to extract from the wreckage. Both legs were bent and broken halfway down the shin bone.

"Now all you boys can see that there are, after all, some advantages in having tin legs," said Douglas. This was the only time that I ever knew Douglas to be careless with anything apart from his own skin for which, when he got into action, he never appeared to have any regard whatsoever.

Not long after this incident I nearly caused a fatal accident myself. Tubby had received an invitation to a cocktail party from a friend who commanded 19 Squadron at Duxford. He and Douglas were unable to go, so the commander of A Flight, "Matty" Mathieson, and myself were asked to represent the squadron.

Matty and I duly took off about 5.30p.m. on the following Saturday. We flew our Spitfires in formation down to Duxford and spent a pleasant evening with many of our old friends, swapping stories of our different experiences since we had last met before Dunkirk. At about 7.30p.m. I suggested to Matty that it was time we headed for home. We had been drinking pretty hard and I didn't want either of us to go over the top.

"Let's have one for the road," said Matty, "and then we'll get on our way." The one extended to two and, as is so often the way, to three. It was nearly 8.30p.m. by the time we managed to get moving and neither of us were feeling any pain by the time we clambered into our Spitfires.

"You lead, Matty," I called over the R/T. And off we went. About halfway home a silly idea occurred to me. Matty was wandering round a bit and I thought I'd give him a shock. The moment I saw him looking the other way I flipped my Spitfire onto its back and continued in close formation in this position. As Matty turned his head back towards me, I saw the look of horror appear on his face. In his slightly befuddled state his immediate reaction was that it was his aircraft which was upside down and not mine. He took immediate action to correct the situation. Somehow, in performing this manoeuvre, he pushed his nose in the air and closed his throttle. A moment later he flicked over in a stall and was diving, inverted towards the ground. The horror of what I had done suddenly hit me. "Pull out," I yelled. "For God's sake Matty pull out."

His reactions were terrifyingly slow. I was diving beside him and could see the grass fields rushing up towards us. Gradually it seemed to sink into his head what was happening and he started to haul back on the stick. I was, by this time, flying level once more about 300 feet above the ground. With a deep sigh of relief I saw his aircraft level out just above the trees and start climbing towards me.

Dusk was starting to creep in when we landed back at Kirton. Tubby Mermagen and Douglas were waiting at dispersal when we taxied in. "I told you two to be back by 8.00 p.m." said Tubby sternly. "And both of you have had too much to drink!" he added.

Matty and I acted repentant. Snipe was standing beside me with my fingers in his mouth, a habit he had developed when he sensed there was trouble afoot.

"You can both be on night flying duty for the next week, and neither of you are to go off the station during that time." Tubby strode off. The following week passed slowly. We had a couple of night scrambles in search of German bombers which had been picked up on radar but which we failed to intercept. Otherwise, boring days and nights passed without visits to the local pubs to break the monotony.

On July 24th we had completed our week of punishment and to celebrate I asked a pretty member of the WAAF, who worked in the control room, to come and have dinner with me in Lincoln. I did admit to a slight feeling of guilt as I helped my new companion for the evening into the car's passenger seat. It was the first time since I had met Jill, six months before, that I had taken out another girl. Snipe got into the back and acted a bit offhand towards my passenger.

After a good dinner in Lincoln we moved on to the saloon bar of the King's Head, the most popular bar for RAF pilots in the area. Meeting up with some bomber pilots from Helmswell, who I had run into before, we got seriously stuck into the beer and by the time the landlord was calling time all of us were in a fairly advanced state of inebriation.

One quality with which the good Lord has blessed me is the sense to stop drinking the moment I feel that I am losing control of my ability to walk straight or drive a car. When Snipe, the WAAF and myself settled ourselves in EGO that night I realised that for once the Man had let me down. With great care and concentration I managed to drive back to Kirton. I bade my pretty companion a warm but quick goodnight outside the WAAF's quarters and then parked EGO as close to my room as possible. Giving Snipe a moment to relieve himself on the grass, I wended my way to my room and, donning a pair of bright red pyjamas, I gratefully slid into bed.

The moment my head touched the pillow I knew the worst had occurred. I was suffering from bedspin, the curse which overtakes those who have heavily over-indulged. I lay there for about five minutes before turning off the light, hoping that the feeling of nausea would pass. No such luck. I had just turned on the light again when the Tannoy, which was sited in every part of the Mess, blared into life.

"One pilot of 222 Squadron to report immediately to dispersal!" The command came over loud and clear and even infiltrated my befuddled brain. I staggered off the bed, slid into my green silk dressing gown, donned my flying boots and weaved my way back to the car. Snipe followed, looking somewhat bemused. Even with maximum concentration on the drive to dispersal my path was alarmingly erratic. "My God," I thought to myself, "I've never been as drunk as this before."

At dispersal a rigger came running towards me carrying my parachute. "You're to get off the ground quick," he shouted, "they say that a lot of Huns have crossed the coast."

I hesitated for only a moment. I couldn't admit I was drunk, particularly after the rocket Matty and I had received only a week earlier. But, in this state, God knows if I could get a Spitfire off the ground in daylight, let alone at night. I started to run towards my aircraft, trying not to wobble. The rigger followed, carrying the parachute. I scrambled onto the wing of the Spitfire, took the parachute from the rigger, strapped it on and clambered into the cockpit.

My rigger handed me my helmet. I pulled it over my head, connected the oxygen, and turned it on full blast. Somewhere, I had learnt that the best cure for a hangover was a strong dose of oxygen. I hoped fervently that it would have the same effect on bedspin. I switched on the R/T. The voice of the controller came over the headphones. "Scramble immediately, and call up for a vector when you're airborne."

I pressed the starter button and the engine roared into life. Resignedly, I raised my right hand and waved it right and left in the acknowledged signal to the ground crew to pull away the chocks from in front of the wheels. Uncertainly, I started to taxi towards the light that marked the take-off point. My head spun and I felt a wave of nausea. I realised that, in my present state, there was no hope of a visual take-off. To make matters worse, rain started to splatter across the windscreen.

I reached the light marking the take-off point, aimed the Spitfire down the line of flares which marked the runway, stuck my head in the cockpit, said a short prayer, and opened the throttle.

Only a few minutes before I had been lying in bed trying to regain my sense of equilibrium. Now I was sitting in the cockpit of a most delicate fighter aircraft, roaring up into the black night. I stared fixedly at the illuminated airspeed indicator, artificial horizon, and altimeter. Remarkably, the old rule of "Look at the light!" seemed to be working.

The controller was trying to call me over the R/T but I switched him off. "One thing at a bloody time," I thought. Miraculously, the altimeter showed 300 feet and climbing rapidly. Somehow, I had got the aircraft off the ground and stable. I resolved there and then to do nothing else but climb the Spitfire to 20,000 feet before I took my eyes from the instruments. And that is what I did.

As the altimeter passed 20,000 feet, I chanced looking around me. To my relief I found myself in a clear moonlit sky, with a white blanket of cloud at least 10,000 feet below me. I heaved a big sigh of relief. And I felt the horrible clinging effects of the alcohol I had consumed gradually slipping away from me. I decided it was time to get in touch with base.

It took me several moments to realise that the radio was dead. I switched to another channel. Same result. I tried the emergency frequency. Not a sound. I sat back and took stock of my situation. Without instructions from the ground there was no hope of me intercepting an enemy aircraft. My most important task was to get the aircraft and myself back onto the ground in one piece. I knew that I had taken off in an easterly direction and had done my best to keep a straight course during my climb. I had been in the air for roughly fifteen minutes and, climbing at 120mph, I must therefore be about thirty miles east of the airfield. But I knew the cloud base was under 1,000 feet and it was raining. It was going to be the devil of a job to find anywhere to land, let alone get back to my own base.

I reckoned the best thing I could do was to let down once more at about the same speed as I had maintained during my climb. I must keep a westerly course and hope that when I broke cloud I might be near Kirton. Small hope but a beggar couldn't be a chooser. As I started my 180 degree turn my eye was suddenly caught by the silhouette of another aircraft crossing the almost full moon. I turned quickly towards it. I suddenly realised that my luck had not entirely deserted me. The aircraft had two engines and was obviously one of our bombers returning from a raid on Germany. All I had to do was to close in near enough to follow him down through the cloud back to his home base.

190

I was about 300 feet below and behind the other aircraft and closing fast on it, when I saw tracer bullets streaming towards me from its tail. I took evasive action and dived beneath him. As I looked up, from about fifty feet below, the silhouette of a Heinkel III with the famous Maltese cross on the underside of the wings presented itself to me.

Throttling back to get behind him again, I pulled up my nose to bring my eight machine guns to bear on the underside of his tail. As I opened fire, the rear gunner managed to get me in his sights again and tracer spurted at me. I could see my bullets tearing into his fuselage and suddenly black smoke started streaming from his port engine. I felt my own aircraft shuddering as bullets struck my tail and I dived away to get clear. Over my shoulder, I saw the Heinkel diving towards the clouds and I turned to follow him. Smoke was now pouring from his engine and I managed to get in one more burst before he disappeared into the cloud. "That's one Hun who as sure as Hell won't be going home," I shouted with delight.

It was only then that it occurred to me that I was back to where I had started. Unless I was damned lucky, here might be one Irishman who might not be going home either. I considered my plight one more time. During the course of my brief encounter with the Heinkel I had probably travelled twenty miles from where I was when I first spotted him. There was absolutely no hope now of retracing my steps to Kirton. The best I could do was to let down through the cloud and hope, when I broke through the lower base, that I might see some runway from which RAF bombers were either taking off or landing. I knew that, heading east, I was letting down over the flat country of Lincolnshire and decided that I could safely come down in the cloud to 1,000 feet without any danger of running into an unseen hill. I was glad that my aircraft was flying normally and reckoned that any damage which had been inflicted was superficial.

At 1,500 feet, despite my scanty clothing I started to sweat. I was still in thick cloud as I descended. The altimeter was indicating 1,000 feet and still there was no sign of breaking out of the cloud. I decided to give it another 200 feet or so and, if I still could not see anything, climb up to 3,000 feet and bail out.

At 900 feet I was still in the cloud and losing height fast. The moment of decision had arrived. "Give it another 200 feet," I said aloud to myself. With the altimeter showing 700 feet, I suddenly broke through the base cloud. Unbelievably, right in front of my nose, the dim lights of a flare path shone through the rain. "The devil looks after his own one more time," I remember thinking when I saw those lights. I flew straight over the lights on a westerly course, made a tight turn, throttled back and eased over the airfield boundary and touched down at the start of the flare path in a three-point landing of which even Douglas would have been proud. Completing my landing run, I swung the Spit towards the lights of a hut which I could see on the edge of the airfield.

A figure detached itself from the crowd of people standing around the doorway of the hut and climbed onto my wing as I shut down my engine. I pulled off my helmet and instantly recognised "Tommy" Thomas. When I was at Cranwell he had been an instructor in Jorrocks Bradford's flight and I had often flown with him.

Everyone had a good laugh, at my expense, when it was discovered that I was wearing a green silk dressing gown over red pyjamas. And more laughter when I had to admit that I didn't have a clue where I had landed.

"It's Barkston, Tim," said Tommy. "You must remember where you used to practise forced landings with me not so very long ago."

Slowly the penny dropped. Barkston was a grass field about eight miles south of Cranwell which had been used as an auxiliary airfield for a number of training purposes. "You are a lucky fellow young Tim," said Tommy, as we entered the hut under the curious stares of the other pilots and ground crew. "We had stopped night flying training because the cloud was getting so low. We were just about to switch off the flare path when we heard your engine."

In his small office Tommy produced two bottles of beer. He removed the caps and handed one to me and insisted on me telling the whole story. I had just finished the beer and the story when the flight sergeant in charge of maintenance came in to report to Tommy and demanded I tell it all again. We went out and inspected the damage to my tailplane, which turned out to be superficial. The Spitfire was passed as airworthy.

Tommy had a twinkle in his eye when he mentioned that he had never managed to get his hands on a

Spitfire. He followed this up with, "Do you mind if I fly your Spit back to Cranwell? You will need some sleep, so come back with us now."

"Help yourself, Tommy. And I'll fly one of your Hawker Harts. I've never flown one of those either."

As dawn broke we fuelled up my Spitfire and I gave him a rundown on the cockpit drill and the aircraft's flying characteristics. Then he did the same for me on the Hart. Ten minutes later we were both airborne on the five-minute flight back to Cranwell. Tommy found me a room and I fell asleep as I climbed gratefully into the bed.

About four hours later I awoke to the sound of a familiar voice. "'Ere's yer tea, Sir" said The General. "It's a lovely morning for flyin' Sir, and where's yer uniform?" Once again, I had to tell the whole story.

"Yer bleedin' lucky to be alive is all I've got ter say!" he exclaimed. "I'd better get yer some breakfast in yer room 'ere. Yer wouldn't 'arf look a sight in the dining room dressed like that!"

Good as his word The General brought me a large breakfast. And he managed to borrow a razor for me and also an overcoat so that, when I walked down to the hangars half an hour later, most of my strange garb was covered up and only a small splash of red pyjama showed between my overcoat and the top of my flying boots. But, as luck would have it, Cranwell's station commander happened to be passing. He stopped me and angrily demanded an explanation. When I told him what had happened he insisted on taking me back to his office and hearing the whole story and then driving me down himself to my Spitfire.

I thanked him, said goodbye to Tommy and was soon airborne on the short flight back to Kirton. It was only then that I suddenly realised that I had completely forgotten to inform my squadron what had happened to me. Obviously, they must have given me up for lost. Approaching the airfield, in a fit of wild joy at being alive, I dived almost vertically on our dispersal hut. I meant to pull out about ten feet above the ground but as I heaved back on the stick I had left it too late. The nose came up but the aircraft was still sinking and the tail wheel just brushed the ground, and then I was climbing away.

Douglas was mad at me for not letting him know I was safe. Tubby was mad at me for nearly writing off both my aircraft and myself in what he was pleased to call "a blatant piece of showing off". Snipe was just mad to see me.

Word had come through of the Heinkel. It had crashed in the River Humber and was assumed to have been shot down by me, flying the only fighter in the area at the time. Eventually, everybody calmed down and I got into my car with Snipe to return to my room for a bath and change before resuming duties.

CHAPTER
TEN

August to December 1940

Historians generally demarcate the start and finish of the Battle of Britain as August 1st to October 31st 1940. Many words have been written about it. Today it often appears in histories as an individual incident, like the battles of Waterloo or Trafalgar, a meeting of enemy forces confined to a certain place and time. In fact this was not the case.

After the evacuation of the British Army from France and Belgium there was a lull in hostilities whilst both sides took stock of their relative situations.

The Luftwaffe had fared well during the past months against the air forces the British and French had deployed against them. But they had not yet met the hard core of the well-organized RAF Fighter Command Spitfire squadrons. As well as being a long way from their home bases, the Luftwaffe were somewhat over-confident of their ability to win command of the skies over England.

The outlook for Britain was more bleak but less complicated. The British Army, a large proportion of which had been committed in France, had in parts been virtually wiped out. Although thousands of troops had survived and been brought back to England, virtually all their fighting equipment and most of their weapons had been lost.

The British Navy was still in command of the seas. Whether they could stay in command in the confined space of the English Channel, whilst under heavy bombardment from the Luftwaffe and whilst they tried to sink fleets of enemy invasion barges, was a question yet to be answered.

The Royal Air Force was, still, mostly in one piece. Due to the incredible foresight of Air Marshal Dowding all the Spitfire squadrons were untouched. Radar, a virtually secret weapon at that stage of the war, had not yet started to play its vital part. And Bomber Command was fast building its strength and flexing its muscles.

Not unnaturally, Hitler was full of confidence from his recent overwhelming victories. But now he hesitated, probably the greatest mistake he made in his evil life. Had he struck immediately, whilst Britain was still reeling under the frightful moral impact of the defeat in France and the evacuation from Dunkirk, he might well have installed his forces successfully across the Channel.

The fighting men who took part in the battle are thought of as the pilots of Fighter Command and, more especially, those pilots situated in the area of 11 Group which covered the whole of the south-east of the country.

To my mind, the Battle of Britain started the day the last soldier in the British Army was evacuated from the

French shore during the first week of June 1940. The end of the battle, in my opinion, did not come until Hitler's invasion barges were finally scattered and sunk during the last six weeks of that fateful year.

We fighter pilots may have been the spearhead which was used to thrust at and repulse the enemy. But the troops who fought the battle were the people of Britain themselves, who stood up to the strain not only of the day and night time bombing of their homes and work places but also to the continual threat of invasion which hung over the country during those long, tense months. And we must also remember the bomber boys, who suffered heavy losses in attacking the invasion barges waiting in their French harbours, the ships of the navy patrolling the English Channel, the army gunners manning anti-aircraft guns all over the country, and the RAF personnel operating the vital radar stations which were to come under continual aerial attack, and without whom the defence of the country would have been in no way possible. All these, men and women and children, made up that one army which threw back Hitler's one and only chance of bringing Britain to its knees.

For the pilots of 222 Squadron, stationed at Kirton-in-Lindsey, those summer months of 1940 passed quickly. Continual convoy patrol work from our advance base on the east coast, occasional night sorties interspersed with the training of new pilots in the art of aerial warfare, took up most of our time. On an occasional weekend off, Douglas and I would slip off in the two-seater Miles Master trainer to spend the night at Bagshot and enjoy precious time with Thelma and Jill.

Soon, Douglas was promoted and posted to take command of a Canadian squadron. He asked Hilary and myself if we would like to go with him. We all discussed it at length but we declined his offer and decided to stay put with our own 222 Squadron. "That mad bugger will get us all killed quick when the proper war starts!" laughed Hilary. Fond as I had grown of Douglas over the past six months, I completely agreed with these wise sentiments.

During the latter part of July formations of German bombers launched daily attacks on targets along the south coast. These attacks stepped up and in Lincolnshire we felt left out of the action. Tubby Mermagen was also promoted and posted and was replaced by Johnny Hill, a quiet and pleasant leader with whom I became close friends over the months ahead.

By the end of the first week in August the Battle of Britain was in full swing and it became obvious that Hitler had launched his major drive to gain command of the skies over the Channel. It was not until after the middle of August that the welcome word came through that the squadron was to proceed once more to Hornchurch.

We landed at Hornchurch the following morning, just as Spitfires from the other two squadrons based there were coming back in ones and twos after intercepting a German raid. We were directed to our dispersal point on the south-east corner of the grass

199

field and after being allocated lockers in the dispersal hut for our flying gear, were driven to the Mess for lunch. Pilots from the other two squadrons, several of whom I knew, were crowding round the bar discussing, with an understandable degree of animation, their morning encounter with the enemy. We were back in the war.

Hilary and I saw a friend of ours who had been in the morning battle and got him to join us for a pint. "What's it like?" asked Hilary.

"Well," our friend said, "it's difficult to put in words. But I can tell you one thing. The whole bloody sky seems to be full of Germans!" We were to learn all too quickly that our friend could not have summed up the situation more accurately.

After lunch we were returned to dispersal and the station commander, Wing Commander "Boy" Bouchier, arrived to give us a briefing. "Here's the situation," he began, "the Huns are now launching two or three raids a day on our sector. Average size of the raids is 40 to 50 bombers escorted by 60 or 70 fighters. Our radar is detecting them as they form up over the French coast so, generally speaking, we have reasonable warning of their arrival. If it is just one raid we try to get a wing or more to tackle them but if another raid starts, and squadrons from other stations are on the ground refuelling, we sometimes have to split up the station wing into two or three parts to deal with the various enemy formations. The main thing is to get as much height as you can as quickly as possible. The bombers are flying at anything from 10,000 to 20,000 feet but the enemy fighters protecting them are stepped up to over 25,000 feet. No need to tell you boys how important it is to try to start above them."

"What types of enemy aircraft are we mostly dealing with, Sir?" asked Johnny Hill.

"The bombers are all Heinkels or Dorniers and practically all the fighters are Messerschmitt 109s. But we are also starting to see quite a few twin-engine Messerschmitt 110s. Their main targets at the moment seem to be our radar stations and airfields. They haven't hit us at Hornchurch yet but no doubt our turn will come."

The wing commander had hardly finished speaking when the telephone in the corner of the hut started ringing. Johnny picked it up and listened intently for a moment. Then with an excited expression lighting up his face he turned to the station commander. "Sorry, Sir. That was an order to scramble. Come on boys let's get going."

Seizing our flying gear we ran out to our aircraft which had already been refuelled by the advance crews who had been sent down by road from Lincolnshire the previous day. Soon we were taxiing out in rough formation to the end of the field where the other squadrons were also arriving. We took off in threes as instructions from the controller were crackling in our headphones. It appeared that a raid of 100 plus bandits had been detected in the Calais area and were approaching Dover. Their estimated height was 15,000 to 20,000 feet.

201

The three squadrons in our wing gradually arranged themselves into a loose formation. The two rearmost aircraft in each squadron took up a position above and behind and weaved backwards and forwards keeping a constant guard on our tail.

Passing through 10,000 feet Johnny gave the command to switch on oxygen. Despite the fact that it was a warm summer's day it soon started to get cold. We were all dressed in fur-lined leather jackets and wore flying boots and fleece-lined gloves but by 20,000 feet extremities were starting to hurt. "Your bandits are now about fifteen miles to the south-east," the controllers advised over the radio. "Look out, because some of them are still above you."

"Tally ho!" yelled one of the weavers behind us. "Hundreds of bandits at three o'clock!" I looked to my right and there they were. The sky was full of what looked like black specks, stretching from way above us to thousands of feet below us.

"OK, I've got 'em," called the wing leader, "we'll keep on climbing and then swing in over their tails."

It was obvious that we weren't going to get above them all before they had passed us. I could now distinguish the twin engines of the bombers below us and the sharp noses of the masses of 109s protecting them from above. "Bandits attacking from above nine o'clock!" came a yell in the headphones. The next moment the sky was full of tracer and about 12 Messerschmitt 109s dived straight through our formation from our left quarter.

"Turn starboard and attack the main formation!" yelled the wing leader. "Take the fighters first if you can and then go for the bombers." Clawing for height our squadron swung towards the enemy. I could see two Spitfires dropping away from our formation, one enveloped in white steam and another with black smoke pouring from its engine casing.

And then we were amongst them. I saw a 109 flash across in front of my nose and pressed the firing button wildly. Tracer bullets from my eight machine guns streamed past his tail. "Damn!" I muttered. "Should've got that one." There was no time to reflect before I was diving onto the bombers. Their rear gunners were putting up a hail of fire. I got a Heinkel firmly in my sights, pulled back on the stick to bring my guns to bear on the cockpit, and pressed the button. This time there was no mistake. The Heinkel literally exploded in front of my eyes. But tracers were tearing past my cockpit from behind and, glancing round, I could see a 109 diving on me only about fifty feet from my tail. I pushed forward on the stick and the whole weight of my body hit the shoulder straps as the negative G force took over. I was diving vertically for the ground far beneath me but I had evidently evaded my attacker. I eased back on the stick to pull out of my dive and, looking continually backwards in both directions, started climbing back to where I reckoned the action was taking place. Not an aircraft of any kind was in sight.

I searched around. All I could see were puffs of anti-aircraft smoke about ten miles to the north. I started climbing towards it as it was in the direction of home anyway. When I reached 15,000 feet I saw a formation of 109s about 3,000 feet above me heading home to France. They were too far away for me to do anything.

Looking around again I could see that three Hurricanes were flying in the same direction as myself. Most of the Hurricane squadrons had been sent to France early on in the war. Many aircraft were shot down and their pilots lost whilst battling gamely with, but hopelessly outnumbered by, the Luftwaffe. Nearly all these squadrons had now been reformed and equipped with the Hawker Hurricane, the performance of which could not quite match that of the Spitfire. Nonetheless, the Hurricane was due to play a prominent part in the battles over England which lay ahead.

Still no sign of the German bombers. My fuel gauge showed that I had already used nearly threequarters of my tank. I put my nose down and saw the Thames Estuary appearing on my starboard side. I headed back for Hornchurch.

About half the squadron had already landed. We waited anxiously whilst the rest of the aircraft returned in ones and twos. We were lucky and lost no one in that first fight. The two Spitfires which I had seen go down belonged to the other squadrons in the wing. On the plus side we reckoned that, including my own Heinkel, we had scored one other confirmed victory and two probables.

About an hour after we had all landed we were released from readiness and returned to the Mess to be allocated rooms. That evening Hilary, Dave Davies and myself, who were all in the same flight, set off on a quick reccy round the local pubs before turning in. Snipe came too and enjoyed the attention from the inhabitants, some of whom recognised him from our Dunkirk days. He was to become a well-known character round the nearby pubs during the next ten weeks.

We were aroused for dawn readiness at 4.30 a.m. and were ordered off the ground before 6.00 a.m. This time the squadron was unaccompanied by the rest of the wing and given the job of intercepting a smallish raid which had been developing in the mouth of the Thames Estuary. We were told to climb to 25,000 feet as quickly as we could in order to get above the attackers. Apart from the cold there are other discomforts which are caused by flying above a certain height in an aircraft which is unpressurised. The least important of these is the feeling that one's stomach is blowing up like a balloon, caused by the increasingly rarified nature of the air the higher one climbs. This is, of course, an illusion but it is a disconcerting and uncomfortable feeling. These before-breakfast climbs were always more unpleasant than those performed later in the day, as an empty stomach is more affected by this phenomenon than a full one.

The second, and much more serious, discomfort is "the bends", a pain similar to that experienced by deep-sea divers who are hoisted back to the surface too quickly. This complaint is caused by oxygen bubbles forming in the blood and the result is intense pain in the joints. Sometimes it attacks just the elbow joints and sometimes the knee or shoulder joints, sometimes all three at once. There is no cure, apart from getting down to a lower level as quickly as possible and we found it advisable not to do even that too quickly.

These unpleasant sensations, combined with the extreme cold, which got worse and worse the higher the aircraft climbed, made early morning patrols a far from pleasant experience. Hangovers, from which many of us suffered at 6.00 a.m., did little to improve matters.

On that first morning we had reached 27,000 feet before we caught sight of the enemy. Even the 109s escorting their flock of bombers were flying below us and we dived in for a perfect attack, each singling out our own targets. The 109 pilot who I had made my particular quarry saw me before I opened fire and quickly threw his aircraft into a tight turn. I followed him round trying to bring my sights to bear. For a moment, I thought I had him and hit the firing button only to see my tracers pass well below his tail. Glancing quickly over my shoulder I could see one of his companions unpleasantly close behind me. I heaved back on the stick, both in an effort to bring my bullets closer to the aircraft in front, and also to evade the fire of the one behind. For a moment I blacked out, the centrifugal force sending blood rushing down from my head and temporarily blinding me. I eased the stick forward a shade, but as my sight returned the target was nowhere to be seen.

Not so my friend behind me. A stream of tracer was flashing by my starboard wing tip and I hurriedly whipped my Spitfire into a left-hand diving turn and then pulled hard back to try to get above him. I saw him go fast and away below and at the same moment a Dornier 17 appeared in front of me, about 200 yards away. As I prepared to fire the Dornier exploded and a Spitfire, with guns still blazing followed him down. I just saw the registration letters of Hilary's aircraft on the side of the fuselage and yelled with delight.

Once more the sky was empty. I flew around for a little while but there was no more sign of friend or foe. Back at Hornchurch I told the intelligence officer about Hilary's Dornier. "I didn't hit a thing, but Edridge got one right in front of my eyes."

Just then Hilary joined us. I clapped him on the back. "You were really quick on the draw this morning, Hilary. You blew that bloody Dornier up just as I was going to press the button."

"Oh! So it was you, Tim. I did feel a bit guilty poaching that one."

We got into EGO and drove up to the Mess for a good breakfast of fried eggs and bacon. The other pilots from our squadron arrived at the table in dribs and drabs. Once more the squadron seemed to have been comparatively lucky. One of the sergeant pilots from A Flight had been seen to bail out and had already telephoned the squadron to say that he was OK. My friend Dave had his wing tip hit by a cannon shell but he had managed to get his aircraft back in one piece. It seemed that we had downed three or four of the enemy.

After breakfast we returned to dispersal and resumed our state of readiness.

We waited for the next call.

And so we slipped into a routine which was to be our daily life for the next ten weeks. There were busy days and quiet days. Some days we would be scrambled as many as four times, some days only once, although the latter was rare. We had good days and bad days. More often than not we managed to cause more damage to the enemy that we received ourselves. But there were days when the reverse occurred also. On one really bad day the squadron had nine aircraft either destroyed or damaged with only four confirmed victories to our credit. Death and wounds amongst our companions became commonplace and were taken with an exaggerated lightness which we found was the only possible way to bear the losses and remain sane.

Tiredness started to creep over the survivors and, in some cases, a resignation to the fact that soon one's day would come. For myself I would just not let a fatalistic attitude take hold. I was absolutely determined to survive.

This single-minded attitude to survival, adopted by most pilots at that time, but which succeeded in the case of so few, was to be helped in my own case by two factors. First, by that stage of the war I was a very well trained and capable pilot. So far as flying the aeroplane was concerned, I was probably a natural for the profession I had chosen. If I had been as good a shot as I was a pilot I would certainly have shot down at least three times the number of German aircraft with which I was accredited, which was only a paltry eight.

Second, and a much more important factor in my make up than my flying ability, was the fact that I am an Irishman. As such, I considered myself a mercenary. True, I had spent a lot of my youth in England and had been to school there but, from a very early age, I had identified myself with Ireland. I had joined the RAF principally as a means to an end. I was determined to learn to fly and the RAF was the cheapest and most effective way of doing so. Whilst I believed from everything I had heard that Hitler was a monster and that the Germans were the "baddies", I was not possessed of that wild uncaring patriotism which caused so many young British men and women at that time unselfishly to lay down their lives for their country. To put it bluntly, whenever I found my life in extreme danger — which was then about half a dozen times a day — my immediate reaction was to place priority on the safety of my own skin rather than that of killing the enemy. I like to think that if any of my friends were in danger I was prepared to take big risks in order to help them. But invariably I looked after number one.

Had the Battle of Britain been fought over the green fields and purple mountains of Tipperary in all probability I would have been fired with the same wild protective feeling for my country which was responsible for the deaths of so many of my brave friends and, almost certainly, I would not be alive today to write these words. (When I was writing this book, my darling young wife, Diana, whose father lost a leg fighting as a

209

commando and who would have laid down his life for the royal corgis let alone for the Monarch herself, frowned as she read the last paragraph. "What's wrong?" I asked her. "Don't you like the last bit I've written?" She looked at me and said, "No. I'm just a little disappointed that you were not brave enough to get killed like all your friends!" Such is the logic of beautiful ladies.)

About two weeks after we had arrived at Hornchurch, Hilary failed to return from a morning fight over the south coast. None of us had seen him get into trouble and I waited anxiously for news. Deaths had become everyday occurrences by now but, as I paced up and down outside the dispersal hut with Snipe, I found it difficult to treat the possibility that my good friend had been killed with that same studied lightness which, like everybody else, I had learnt to affect in these circumstances.

"Please God let him be alright," I said to Snipe, who seemed to sense my worry and was walking along beside me with his head down. Living lives of such contrast, between extreme danger and normal daily comforts, it was natural to crave the close companionship of another human being. With them, one could share one's hopes and fears. Hilary and I had grown very close over the past few months and now, confronted for the first time by the stark reality that he might have been killed, I suddenly realised how much I relied on his sympathy and humour. Luckily, my anxiety on this occasion was short lived.

"He's OK Tim!" yelled Johnny Hill from the doorway of the dispersal hut. "Biggin Hill have just called to say that he bailed out and landed nearly on their airfield. He's got a bit burnt, but they say not too bad."

Johnny gave me permission to take a few hours off the next day. As it turned out, the following day did not prove a good one for hospital visiting. Soon after 6.00 a.m. we were scrambled to try and intercept a raid which was approaching the coast near Dover. There was cumulonimbus cloud building up over the coast, the tops reaching over 20,000 feet. At the crucial moment when we should have been getting into visual range of the bandits, one of these huge clouds got in our way and by the time we had flown around it the raid had passed north of us. We flew fast in pursuit but never managed to make contact with the enemy. Frustrated, we returned empty-handed to Hornchurch. We were sent off for our breakfast and were told to be at readiness again by 10.00 a.m.

We had just returned to dispersal when we were ordered off the ground again in a hurry. A large formation of German bombers, escorted by a fighter force which had crossed the coast earlier, had been heading north-east but had suddenly swung due north and was approaching Hornchurch. All squadrons were told to get off in a hurry but most of us were still taxiing out to the end of the field when the bombers came into sight, flying straight in our direction and only just south of the Thames. As we opened our throttles to

211

get off the ground, regardless of any sort of formation, the bombs started to fall.

As my Spitfire got airborne and started to claw for height, the ground on my right erupted in earth, smoke and flames and completely engulfed three Spitfires which were just taking off. I saw one break into three parts and another slither into a ploughed field beyond the boundary. As I climbed away I looked over my shoulder and saw the whole airfield being torn apart by bombs. I could see the bombers above me turning for home immediately after they had disgorged their loads and, together with several other aircraft from my own and the other squadrons in the wing, I now climbed to attack them from below. Of course, in full knowledge that we would be at the mercy of the escorting fighters, this was asking for trouble. But the insult of having our own home bombed had, I suppose, got our adrenaline going and we climbed into the attack regardless of the consequences.

Just as we were opening fire the sky around us suddenly became full of flying tracer and the 109s were amongst us. I dived sharply to the left and then pulled up again under the belly of one of the bombers. I managed to get in a quick burst which made him reel out of formation and then had to dive away again to escape the attention of another wave of 109s. I saw a Heinkel falling from the sky with smoke pouring from both engines and a Spitfire explode in a ball of flame. A 109 dived by me with a stream of white smoke erupting from his engine and then once more I had a Heinkel in my sights. I let him have a long burst of fire and, as I

212

passed underneath him, I could see the rear gunner slumped over his gun. Another 109 flashed across my nose and I hauled my Spitfire around onto his tail. A quick burst, which I could see just passing underneath him, and then he had flipped onto his back and was diving for the ground. I followed him down in a vertical dive but he was travelling faster than me. As he pulled out of his dive I let him have one last burst which would have been lucky to have caused him any damage. Then I started to climb again hoping to come up once more with the bombers.

About 10,000 feet above me I could see some specks heading south. I started to climb in pursuit. No other aircraft were in sight and, approaching the Channel coast, I realised I was on a wild goose chase and turned back for Hornchurch. Landing would be tricky I thought and this was confirmed on the R/T. The controller advised that a clear path amongst the craters had already been marked out and that it was possible to land providing great care was taken. Approaching the field I could see that a sort of runway had been staked out with yellow flags and I lined up, cautiously, for my landing. Taxiing back to dispersal was a real problem as there had not been time for the ground personnel to mark out individual craters and, given the Spitfire's appalling forward vision, great caution had to be exercised to avoid ending up in a hole.

There was a lot of destruction and a pall of smoke still hung over the whole station. The wrecks of several Spitfires which had been hit, either in their dispersal bays or taxiing out, were scattered around. A hangar had been struck and there was a jagged hole in its roof. For the most part, however, the bombs had fallen on the field itself and well over 100 craters were counted inside the airfield boundary.

My first enquiries when I slid down from the cockpit were as to whether anybody had seen Snipe. There was no sign of him running out to meet me in the usual way. Somebody told me that he had been spotted going like a scalded cat across an adjacent field soon after the bombs had started to fall so, at any rate, it sounded as if he was still alive.

EGO was still in one piece, unlike a number of other cars which had not been so lucky, and picking my way through the shambles, I drove off to the Mess. Walking into the cloak-room to wash my hands I saw Al Deere, subsequently to become one of Britain's highest-scoring fighter aces, splashing water on his face from a basin. He was in his shirt sleeves but I could see that he had scratches on his face and his uniform trousers were torn. "Hey, Al!" I said, "What the hell has happened to you?"

"I'm bloody lucky to be alive, Tim. I was hit by a bomb just as I was airborne and my aircraft broke into three pieces. The engine went one way and the tail unit another. The middle of the fuselage, with me in it, rolled across that ploughed field and ended up in a ditch upside down."

"My God," I said, "I saw it happen! I didn't know it was you and I didn't give one small hope in hell to whoever was the pilot. What happened?"

"Well, the bugger was that I couldn't get out," said Al. "I was there for about half an hour. Then I heard somebody passing but I think I would still be there now if I hadn't shouted like hell."

I asked Al what had happened to the aircraft that the bomb had blown into the ploughed field. "The pilot's alright. He slithered across the field and ended in another ditch with his aircraft standing on its nose. I haven't heard of anybody yet who was killed on the ground."

"What a bloody miracle," I replied. After I'd had a pint of beer and some lunch I set about the task of trying to find Snipe. I asked Johnny Hill if I could be excused for a couple of hours and drove all round the station enquiring if anybody had seen Snipe. Another person thought they had caught a glimpse of him disappearing over the same field but there was no sign of him having returned. I left the station and drove off down the road into the local town in the direction of where he had last been seen. After my many enquiries had proved negative, I approached a policeman. "Have you by any chance seen a large white dog with a rough coat and brown ears running through town?" I asked.

"Yes, Sir. Just after the bombs dropped on the airfield I saw a dog like you describe runnin' like 'ell up the road there." I looked in the direction he had pointed out and after more enquires was delighted to hear that Snipe had been caught and taken by a kind lady to the local dogs' home. I drove off to find the street in which it was situated. I was about 200 yards from the building when Snipe himself came galloping down the street towards me.

I stopped the car and he tried to jump through the window. I quietened him down and, letting him sit on the seat beside me, drove the short distance to the dogs' home. The lady in charge told me how Snipe had started getting excited about five minutes before my arrival and had then jumped the substantial wall that surrounded the home and disappeared.

At the time Snipe seemed to be unaffected by the Hornchurch incident but, later, it was almost certainly a contributor to his death. He was never quite the same again; any violent noise, even a car door banging or a thunderstorm, would start him shivering and running for the nearest shelter. Later in the year when I was posted overseas, I had to leave Snipe at Tullamaine with my parents. It was a very sad parting.

And the battle went on. We were now suffering serious casualties. My good friend Dave Davies failed to get out of his burning aircraft and was killed. Sergeant Baxter, one of the best pilots we had in the squadron, suffered the same fate. Matty Mathieson, on whom I had played the dirty trick whilst flying back after the cocktail party at Duxford, crashed and suffered wounds from which he never was to properly recover.

On the last day of August I came close to getting killed myself. We were diving from 25,000 feet on to a big formation of bombers. There was a lot of cloud and we suddenly found ourselves in the middle of them. I blazed away at a Dornier and then, like a fool, pulled up into a sharp left-hand turn without checking what was behind me. Suddenly there was a crash as a cannon shell fired by a 109 tore broadside into my engine. The next one struck just behind the cockpit and exploded with a bang, sending most of its particles whistling round the armour plating at my back. My instrument panel disintegrated in front of my eyes. The control column was nearly torn from my hands as a third shell hit the tail unit. Smoke and glycol poured from the engine and for a moment I was sure that I was on fire. I was just reaching for the harness release when I found myself in thick cloud. There were no flames so, protected from the enemy for the moment by the enshrouding cloud, I decided to stay put until I could better assess the damage. My blind flying instruments had all shattered so I had no way of telling whether I was flying upwards or downwards or if I was the right way up or on my back. A moment later I slithered into clear air once more to find that I was diving straight at the centre of London.

I started to pull out of the dive. The controls felt funny which was not surprising as more than half of the control surfaces on my tail unit had been shot away and most of my port aileron was missing. But the aircraft was still controllable and although there was a lot of smoke there was no flame.

My immediate reaction was to bail out. Two things stopped me. First, the ground was still about 7,000 feet below me and, whilst there was no reason to believe that the parachute wouldn't open, it did look an awful long way to fall. Second, and more important, I was

217

still smack over the middle of London. My aircraft would almost certainly crash on to a populated area which might easily kill a lot of people and I could end up maiming myself if my parachute landed me amongst buildings.

I decided to sit tight and try and land the aircraft in one piece. I started to glide in an easterly direction and, whilst losing height, searched desperately for a suitable landing site. I had already turned off the petrol and, although there was still a lot of white smoke coming from the broken glycol leads, I assessed the danger of fire as reasonably remote. The controls, particularly the fore and aft reactions, felt very sloppy. Also, in order to see in front of me, I had to crab the aircraft to make the smoke fly off to one side. When I was down to about 2,000 feet I spotted a large field about 300 yards square, surrounded by small suburban houses. Other than vegetables and some bushes, the area seemed clear of obstructions although some high-tension cables ran across the centre of the field.

Although the field was certainly not an easy place to land a Spitfire under the very best of conditions, by now I had no alternative and was too low to bail out. But I was going to need a lot of luck to pull it off. As I glided down towards the field I tried to judge my speed. Once before I had found myself landing a Spitfire without the aid of the airspeed indicator when, for some reason, the instrument had broken. On that occasion I had a 1,000 yard grass airfield in front of me and could get a good idea of the speed I was travelling at from the feel of the controls. But this time I only had, at the most, 300 yards of landing area and, because of the damage done to my elevators and port aileron, it was virtually impossible to get any guidance from the stick and rudder. If I allowed the speed to drop too low I would stall, dive into the ground, and almost certainly be killed. On the other hand, if I came in too fast, I would not be able to get the aircraft to stall when I levelled out and would fly straight into the houses at the far end. The only way I had of making that vital assessment was visually, by watching the ground passing beneath me.

In my life, before and since, I have had hairy experiences in aircraft when extreme skill and a lot of luck were needed to survive. None of those experiences compare with the circumstances of that particular landing.

Crabbing my way along to keep the smoke away from my forward line of sight, I glided down towards the houses which lined the near side of my landing area. Passing a few feet over their roofs, I flung the Spitfire into a steep sideslip to drop off height. In order to cut down my landing run, I had of course left the wheels retracted in the wings. Now, levelling off a few feet above the vegetables, I started to kick the rudder right and left so as to drop off speed again. About two-thirds of the way across the field I realised I was going too fast and wasn't going to make it. Emergency action was needed otherwise I was going to end up in the drawing room of the red brick house which was rushing towards me. I muttered a quick prayer and took the only course open. Flinging over the stick to the

219

left I drove the port wing tip into the ground. There was a grinding noise as the wing dug into the soil and then I was cartwheeling. Landing on its belly, facing back the way we had come, the aircraft was now slithering backwards. The tail struck the hedge dividing the field from the small garden of the house. In a cloud of dirt and branches, we came to a juddering halt. There was a sudden and complete silence, one of the most welcome I have ever known.

As I heaved myself from the cockpit, a lady appeared through the gate from the garden. In her hand she bore a mug. "Are you alright, dear?" she cried. "I thought you might like a cup of tea to steady your nerves."

"Thank you Madam," I replied, taking the proffered mug. "But do you suppose your husband would have a drop of whisky to put in it? That might help to make my nerves even steadier."

"Of course he has," she said. "Come on into the house and I'll get it for you." I followed the lady back into the house. She took a bottle of whisky from the cupboard and poured a generous measure into my tea. It tasted good.

"You boys are so brave," said the lady. "I don't know what we'd be doing without you. Every day I watch the fights above me in the sky here, and me and my neighbours all cheer and clap every time we see one of that horrible Hitler's planes coming down. But there's always so many more of them than you lads and I don't know how you manage to beat them."

"We've got good aeroplanes," I told her. "And we've had a lot of luck. But an awful lot of the boys are getting killed and I just hope we can hold on."

"Well God bless you all!" exclaimed my new friend. "Here, have some more whisky."

I declined her kind offer but asked her if she could help me get to the local railway station. She said she had a car in the garage and would be proud to take me there herself. It was only a mile down the road.

I walked out to take a last look at my Spitfire. She looked a bit sad lying amongst the vegetables with her crumpled propeller and bullet-spattered body and wings. There was a gaping hole in the side of the fuselage behind the cockpit. If the shell had struck a couple of feet further forward I would have been a very dead man. Looking at the damaged tail unit I was amazed how well the controls had reacted, considering how much of them had been shot away. I pulled my parachute out of the cockpit and rejoined the lady in her house.

We got into her small car and she drove me the short distance to the station. I had landed, if it can be called a "landing", in the south-eastern outskirts of London and therefore had to return through the middle of the city to get back to Hornchurch. Whilst waiting for my train I went to a phone box and, on the off chance, called Jill. It was by now after 5.00p.m. and I hoped Jill had got back from work. I was lucky and she answered the phone herself. I gave her a quick run down on the events of the last couple of hours.

221

"As I've got to come through London," I continued, "and as it's too late to get back to Hornchurch to do any more fighting, I feel like a night on the town. Any chance of you meeting me for dinner?"

Jill said she would love to but would have to catch the last train home afterwards as she had to get to her work early the next morning. We agreed to meet at the Berkeley Hotel.

"See you soon," Jill laughed and rang off. As I emerged from the phone box I could see that people on the platform were looking at me curiously. With my parachute slung over my shoulder and my flying helmet in my hand I must have presented a slightly odd picture, even in those troubled times. I didn't want to become the centre of attention so I walked to the end of the platform until the train came in.

As soon as I got to London I called up my Aunt Kathleen who had a flat in Tite Street and asked her if I could have a bed for the night. She was delighted to see me and listened with amazement as I told her of the afternoon's events. After a quick wash I made my way to the Berkeley. I sat in the lobby and waited for Jill to arrive. She was one of those girls who stopped conversations. Everybody in the lobby looked at her when she walked through the door. I jumped up and greeted her and she gave me an extra warm hug to make up for the events of the day. I could see people staring and thinking what a lucky young man I was. I had no reason to disagree with their sentiment, in more ways than one.

We went out to a nearby restaurant and had a gay dinner. She asked after Snipe and suddenly I realised that I hadn't let anybody on the station know what had happened. And Snipe would still be waiting down at dispersal. I dashed to the telephone and was lucky to get through to Johnny Hill who was in the Mess. I brought him up to date and asked him to get somebody to go and collect Snipe from dispersal.

"Why the devil didn't you let us know before?" he asked, with a degree of annoyance in his voice. "We thought you were a gonner."

"Sorry Johnny," I replied. "I've been on the run since I crash-landed and I completely forgot."

"OK," he said, "but do make sure to be back early in the morning. We need you to make up our full strength at readiness."

After dinner we nipped down to Leicester Square for a quick dance in the 400 Club, our favourite night spot and one that we had been to several times over the past six months. The doorman recognised me and asked how the war was going for me. "Long hours of boredom interspersed with short periods of intense fear," I replied. "But as you can see, I'm still in one piece."

As Jill and I stepped onto the darkened dance floor I could not help but marvel at the contrasts of the past few hours. Could it really be such a very short time ago that I was wrestling to get my badly damaged aircraft into that confined vegetable patch, thinking that almost certainly I was going to be dead in the next minute. And here I was with a beautiful girl in my arms smooching round the floor of the smartest nightclub in England. After an hour we dragged ourselves away and took a taxi to the station so Jill could catch her train home.

As I made my way back to Tite Street the air raid sirens were wailing. Searchlights were lighting up the sky over the East End and I could hear the thud of exploding anti-aircraft shells blending ominously with the screech of sirens. The drone of bombers could be heard above the racket and then bombs started to rain down. They fell in sticks of three or four and I could judge from the explosions of the first two in each stick where the subsequent ones were going to fall. Thankfully, from my point of view, the raid seemed to be concentrated elsewhere in the city, at least three miles away.

I climbed the stairs to my aunt's flat. She was watching, fascinated, from her window. The Germans had only just started to switch their attacks from daytime to night time and this was one of the first raids that London had been subjected to.

"The last time I saw anything like this was when the Zeppelins came over London during the first war," said Aunt Kathleen. "It all seems such a short time ago."

"I know. One just wonders why in the hell we let them get so strong again. Those damned politicians should be put up against a wall and shot for being so incredibly stupid."

"Your father always said that if we ever gave them any chance they would do it again." Aunt Kathleen was interrupted then by an ear piercing whistle and crash as a bomb landed unpleasantly close to us. The whole building shook.

"My father was right," I replied, "and they're doing it again a bit too close for comfort! I think you'd better move away from that window." The raid was dying away and about twenty minutes later the all clear sounded.

"Let's get some sleep," I said to my aunt, one of those ladies who liked to sit up talking all night. "I'm kind of tired."

"Of course you are dear Timmy," she smiled apologetically, "how naughty of me to keep you up."

"Look Aunt K," I said, "I've got to get going at five o'clock so I probably won't see you in the morning. Thanks a lot for the bed and all the best to all my cousins when you are talking to them."

It only seemed a couple of minutes after I had gone to sleep that the alarm by my bed sounded and I dragged myself back into consciousness. Making my way quietly downstairs I started on foot towards Fenchurch Street Station. After a while, I flagged down a passing cab, giving him the necessary instructions.

"You'll be lucky if we get there mate," he replied. "That end of town is in one 'ell of a mess since last night."

As we approached the station I could see what the taxi driver meant. Debris littered the streets and many buildings were still on fire. Firemen and air-raid wardens were trying to dowse the fires and clear up the shambles. Several roads were blocked but, by taking a roundabout route, we managed eventually to get to the entrance of the station.

There were no trains to Hornchurch that morning, though the ticket clerk said there might be a bus. I left the station and, hoisting my parachute onto my shoulder once more, walked where the clerk had indicated. I asked two policemen for directions to the bus stop, adding that I was in a hurry to get back to join my squadron. "We'll give you a hand, Sir," one of them said, "and take you to the bus queue."

We walked through to the road and there, sure enough, was a queue of about 100 people lined up by the bus stop. As we approached a number of people started looking at us curiously. Then a murmur arose and some people in the crowd surged towards us. The blue/grey colour of my RAF uniform was not dissimilar to that worn by pilots of the Luftwaffe. In those days my head was covered by a crop of light blond hair. My parachute, helmet and flying boots made me look like somebody who had just got out of an aircraft. With a policeman on each side of me they had taken me for a captured German.

It all started to look nasty. "Quick Sir!" one of the policemen cried, realising what had happened, "get against the wall." We all three of us backed against the station wall but the leaders were on us. "RAF, RAF," one of the policemen yelled. But some were beginning to claw at me. "Can't you see," said the other policeman, "he's RAF, you bloody fools!" I was scared. These wretched people, who had seen their homes going up in flames, meant business. Thankfully, the policemen's words had had an effect and those people at the front of the crowd realised what they were doing. The ferocious hatred in their eyes turned to horror.

"He's RAF!" they yelled and started to try to push back the crowd behind them. But those at the back of the mob pressed on, determined to reek their share of revenge and it was getting unpleasantly crowded up against the wall by the time they realised their mistake. Then the reaction set in. I was quickly hoisted onto the shoulders of a few of the front division and carried through the crowd with everybody cheering and trying to clap me on the back. If anything, this part of the whole incident was more uncomfortable, though less frightening, than the few moments when it appeared certain that I was going to be lynched.

So far as getting me back to my station in a hurry went the bus was a non-starter as it was going in the wrong direction. The two policemen, realising the urgency to return one of the dwindling force of Fighter Command to his base as quickly as possible, found a police car and I was driven home in style.

Hilary had returned from hospital the evening before, only to hear that I was missing. After I had called Johnny he had collected Snipe from dispersal and they both gave me a warm greeting when I got out of the police car. Apart from some scars on his forehead, where the flames had penetrated between his helmet and the top of his oxygen mask, he seemed none the worse for wear and was anxious to get back into the air to get his own back.

Johnny told me to go off to the Mess and get some breakfast but to get back as quickly as possible. I gobbled a large plate of eggs and bacon and was back on the airfield again 45 minutes later. I was allocated a new Spitfire and gave it a quick once over to make sure that everything was to my liking. I had, some weeks ago, decided to fly my own colours on my aircraft as well as those of His Majesty the King and designed a crest to be painted on the nose, just in front of the cockpit. It consisted of a green shamrock with crossed swords over it and the Irish Tricolour underneath it. There was no doubt that, so far, this emblem had brought me luck so I quickly asked my rigger, who was an artist in his spare time, to paint a similar insignia on the front of my new Spitfire.

He had hardly started the job when the telephone jangled and we were ordered off once more. I was leading a flight by this time and, as we passed through 15,000 feet, I was told to detach my flight from the rest of the squadron to intercept a small raid approaching Southend. As I swung away with my six aircraft and headed due east my mind flashed over recent events.

I remembered pulling up after my attack on the bombers, the juddering crash of the cannon shells as they struck my aircraft. The wavering indecision as to whether to jump or not. The hurried search for a possible landing place. I recalled the desperate juggling with the controls to achieve what appeared to be a virtually impossible landing. The crunch as I dug my wing tip into the vegetables, the blessed silence as the dust died down. My lady friend with the welcome tea, and the even more welcome whisky. I thought with happiness of the dinner with Jill and the lulling strains of the band in the 400 Club. I remembered the bombs falling as I chatted with my aunt. The drive through the bombed houses to Fenchurch Street. The look of crazy desire to kill in the eyes of the crowd determined to get their hands on me. The drive back in the police car and the welcome from Snipe and Hilary. Now, climbing up to try to get above the enemy one more time, I was back where I had started from.

Twenty-four hours later, here we were once more in amongst the enemy. Once more the sky was full of tracers. Yet another burst of smoke and flame as an aircraft exploded. Yet another sensation of the blood rushing down from one's head as the turns were tightened in desperate attempts to bring the sights to bear or to escape the hail of bullets from behind. And, suddenly, once again that curious feeling of being alone where, only seconds before, the sky had been full of milling aircraft spitting death and destruction.

Back at Hornchurch, once again we had that anxious wait to find out whether friends were dead or alive. Yet again that sinking in the stomach as some young man, with whom one might have been playing poker only an hour before, failed to put in an appearance. That was the life, and the death, to which we had all grown accustomed. That was the daily routine to which there appeared to be no visible end in sight, unless it came in one's own blazing aircraft. At the time we all took it for granted. In hindsight, it was a draining and nerve-racking existence.

Johnny Hill fell sick for several days and between September 10th and 14th I was ordered to lead the squadron. Although I was still only nineteen years old, I was the pilot with the most battle experience. Then came the day (September 16th) when 222 Squadron, with me at its head, was ordered to join with 603 Squadron. As I led my men into action I could not help thinking of Henry Maudslay. Together we had spent so many of our hours at Eton building and flying model aircraft and fantasising about such situations as the one I now found myself in.

That morning we were lucky and I managed to get the squadron up to 20,000 feet before the familiar cry of "Bandits at three o'clock!" came over the R/T. Even the escorting 109s were below us. The sun was behind us and, as we dived for the attack, I knew we were in for a good killing. With everybody picking their own targets we dived through the escorting fighters destroying a number of them. Then we were amongst the bombers, who broke formation and scattered in every direction. I can't remember our exact score that morning but I can recall that it was high compared with our losses and, when the final results came in, caused a glow of pride to sweep through me.

It was not long after that memorable morning that I developed a bad cold. Normally I would have declared myself sick and unfit for flying. But we were so short of pilots, particularly experienced ones, that I decided to soldier on and hope for the best. The trouble with flying at high altitudes whilst suffering from a heavy cold was that if you had to come down in a hurry the change of pressure caused intense pain in the ears and, at worst, could fracture an eardrum. Of course, as luck would have it, I found myself in exactly that situation that very morning.

We were preparing to attack a large formation of Heinkels when a bunch of 109s dived on us out of the sun. With very little warning of the impending attack we had no opportunity to take evasive action and I saw cannon shells bursting into the fuselage of a Spitfire beside me. A 109 dived through our formation less than twenty yards from my wing tip and, regardless of what friends he might have behind him, I swung downwards after him. He was going faster than I was and, although I got my sights on him, I knew that I was out of range. I opened my throttle fully in an effort to catch him up. We were diving almost vertically towards the ground 20,000 feet below and it was not long before a blinding pain built up in my head which quickly became unbearable.

Checking to make sure I had no enemies behind me, I eased out of the dive and started to climb back to the height I had started from. The pain was so intense that I was nearly crying out in agony but, as I gained height again, it started to ease. I kept on climbing and soon it had subsided to a bearable level. Realising the cause, I began a very gentle descent towards Hornchurch.

As I gradually lost height I tried to clear my ears by going through the motions of sneezing whilst squeezing my nostrils shut. However, it took me the best part of half an hour to get down to 1,000 feet, at which height I entered the Hornchurch circuit. I still had a nasty pain in my head as I taxied back to dispersal and was not long in going to see the doctor for advice. Apart from the pain, I found that I had gone practically deaf in my right ear and the doctor ordered me not to fly again until my cold had cleared up.

Although the problem was better within a couple of days, from that morning till the present day, I have suffered from very bad hearing on the right side. A spin off from this complaint is that my wife, who can never remember which ear is my bad one, accuses me half the time of not listening to what she is saying!

Some time in early October, Air Vice-Marshal Sir Keith Park, Air Officer Commanding 11 Group, came down to inspect the squadron. We were sitting around at readiness at the time of his arrival and, sensing the arrival of high brass by the flag flying from the pennant on his staff car, we quickly sprung to our feet. He got out of his car and came over to talk to us. He was kind enough to congratulate us on the work we were doing. It so happened that my aircraft was parked very close to where we were standing and his eyes suddenly alighted on the Irish flag painted on its nose.

"Whose is that aircraft?" he demanded fiercely.

"Mine sir," I replied, stepping forward.

"What the devil is that flag doing on one of His Majesty's aircraft?" he queried.

"I'm a proud Irishman, Sir!" I replied. "Although my country has seen fit to remain neutral, I feel entitled to fly under my own colours as well as yours."

"Have them removed immediately," spluttered the Air Vice-Marshal. Snipe was standing beside me and I could sense him stiffening and could see the hackles rising on his neck. I put a restraining hand on his collar.

I was on the point of telling the Air Vice-Marshal that I was a mercenary and that I was sick of the war anyway and was more than happy to catch the next boat back to Ireland when I saw the imploring look in Johnny Hill's eyes, willing me to keep quiet and not make a bloody fool of myself. With difficulty I restrained my feelings and kept silent. I just stood stock still and stared straight ahead.

Sir Keith took one last look of disgust at my aircraft, turned on his heel and stalked off. Snipe relaxed and we all lay down on the grass once more and resumed our game of cards. I never made any attempt to remove my crest and the flag and nobody ever raised the subject again. I had been close to exploding and the incident made me realise my nerves were getting awfully taut.

Gradually the enemy's daylight attacks began to ease off. It appeared that Hitler had had to accept the fact that, despite hammering the Fighter Command airfields and the radar stations, he could not gain command of the skies over England. Instead he told Goering to concentrate on breaking the morale of the British people by bombarding their cities by night.

The immediate danger of invasion also seemed to be receding and, despite the fact that we were scrambled at least once and very often twice a day, there was a slackening of the tension which had existed for the past two months. More replacement aircraft and pilots were arriving and the squadron, after being reduced to its last resources in both men and machines, started to come back to full strength.

Most evenings Hilary and I would make a leisurely tour of the local pubs, consuming a pint or so of beer in each and playing darts with the locals. Once or twice a week we would sortie up to London, sometimes meeting up with friends and taking in a few nightclubs or sometimes just treating ourselves to a good dinner at one of our favourite restaurants. It was on one of these nocturnal sorties to the big city that Snipe and I nearly came to grief at the wrong end of a German bomb.

I had dropped Hilary off to visit an uncle and we had arranged to meet up later in a club off Bond Street. It was about 8.30p.m. and I had just parked the faithful EGO in Albany Street near the entrance to the club. The air-raid sirens had sounded about fifteen minutes before but I had got so used to the searchlights criss-crossing the night sky and the occasional crash of bombs falling that I took very little notice of the Luftwaffe's nightly efforts to break London's morale. As I got out of the car I heard a loud whistle and a bang as a bomb dropped about a quarter of a mile away. I was just about to cross the road when another bomb dropped much closer to me. Then I suddenly realised that the explosions were in a straight line towards me and the next one in the stick was going to be unpleasantly close. I grabbed Snipe by the collar and dived back underneath EGO dragging him with me.

The scream of the falling bomb was loud in my ears and I clawed my way further under the car. Then there was an almighty bang as the building across the street took the full impact of the bomb. The ground shook. I heard the rattle of glass as the car windows shattered

234

and the debris started to fall on the bonnet and roof. Gradually silence returned and, with caution, I pulled myself out from under my shelter and scrambled to my feet. The road between the car and the other side of the street was filled with rubble. Smoke and dust filled the air and the sound of falling masonry interrupted the drone of aircraft and the crash of anti-aircraft fire. Snipe, affected by the sudden noise which he hated so much, was standing beside me shivering. I started to survey the damage.

Apart from a tear on the sleeve of my uniform I, personally, had come to no harm. Snipe also appeared to be unhurt. EGO's two right-hand windows were shattered and most of the glass was scattered over the seats. Piles of stone and bricks lay on her roof and bonnet, both of which had been severely dented but not broken. The windscreen and near side windows were all intact. I could hear no crying or moans from the rubble across the street and I was pretty certain that the building which had been destroyed consisted of shops and offices which were unlikely to have been occupied at this time of night. I decided the best thing for my health was a strong drink.

The club where I had agreed to meet Hilary was not far from where I had parked the car and, with Snipe beside me, I made my way through the rubble. I was quite well known by the owner who greeted me warmly. He was standing at the door surveying the damage down the street. "Where were you when the bomb dropped?" he asked me. When I told him how close I had been, he said, "You were bloody lucky not to have been killed."

"The luck of the Irish!" I laughed. "But this Irishman also has a thirst. Be a good man and lead me to the bar and give me a large whisky!" We went on inside and he asked me what was wrong with Snipe and added, "It looks as if he needs a large whisky as well."

"He's been like that since we got bombed at Hornchurch," I replied. "Now, every time he hears a bang he shakes for the next half hour."

Warmed by the whisky I waited for Hilary to arrive. "Hope you didn't get too close to that bomb down the street," he remarked as he joined me at the bar. I told him how close I had been and warned him that we had quite a lot of work to do getting the rubble off EGO before we could go home.

We agreed on a reasonably early night and, after a quick dinner, we made our way back to the scene of the crime. We swept the debris off the roof and bonnet and then, with great care, removed the glass from the seats. Even with the aid of the torch which I always carried in the car, it was difficult to make sure that the seats were cleared of splinters. We kicked away the rocks and bricks which were lying in our path down the street and gingerly got on board and drove off. With no windows on the right-hand side it was a cold old journey home to Hornchurch. As we bade each other goodnight, I did not know that it was the last time I was ever to do so.

The next morning we attacked a large bunch of bombers just north of Dover. We had another squadron from the wing above us who had agreed to look after the escorting fighters. All guns blazing, we dived on the Dorniers as tracers started to tear through us from behind. A cloud of smoke engulfed a Spitfire on my right. "My God," I thought, "that's Hilary!"

I had no time to look round to see if the pilot was able to get out. My hands were full taking evasive action to shake off the 109 who was on my tail. But, back at Hornchurch, I waited in dread of what might be. No sign of Hilary. All the squadron's aircraft were home safe and I knew that the aircraft I had seen in flames must have been Hilary's. "He must have got out. He must have got out," I repeated to nobody in particular.

An hour passed and still no news. I had no appetite for lunch and waited by the telephone at dispersal. At about 2.00p.m. the news came through from Group Headquarters. The wreckage of a Spitfire bearing Hilary's markings had been found in a field near Sevenoaks. The pilot was dead.

A wave of misery swept over me. Up till now I had been able to shrug off the deaths of even my closest friends. But this was different. Hilary had been like a brother to me. For the past nine months, we had pooled all our thoughts, hopes and fears and had somehow managed to support each other through the trauma of those times. Now he was gone. I just couldn't get my mind to accept it. I just could not believe that Hilary, who I had laughed with last night after my near miss with the bomb, who I had shared the draughty ride home with so few hours before, was never to be laughed with again. That he was dead.

I called Snipe and, together, we walked. I tried to explain to him what had happened but he just wagged his tail and didn't seem to understand. Then something occurred which had not happened in years. I started to cry. Snipe realised there was something wrong. I sat down on the grass and he nuzzled up to me. I pulled myself together, wiped my eyes and suddenly a different emotion took hold of me, an emotion which I had not experienced before in my life and was impossible to control. Cold hatred.

I got to my feet and started walking back. As I got near to the hut I could hear the telephone ringing. The operator ran out of the door and shouted, "Scramble!"

I patted Snipe on the head, told him that I would avenge our friend's death, and started running to my aircraft. Soon we were off the ground and climbing, as usual, to get above the enemy. All thoughts for my own safety had vanished. I just had one overpowering motive in mind. That was to kill as many of the enemy as possible. To avenge the death of my friend. During the next half hour I think I shot down three German aircraft; "think", because in the heat of battle amongst the milling aircraft, it was virtually impossible to be certain that an aircraft was destroyed rather than damaged. It was also difficult to be sure that one of one's own side had or had not been shooting at the target at the same time. But, to this day, I like to think that three of them were mine. Mine alone.

From that day on my attitude towards the war changed. I suppose, because of my age, I had treated the whole thing as some dangerous, exciting game, but now it became cold reality. I started thinking of what Hilary had died for. I started thinking of freedom. From all the information which had been fed to us, most of which I subsequently learned was true, freedom of the individual in Germany had been completely destroyed by Hitler. Moreover, that same freedom had been taken away from those individuals who were unlucky enough to live in the countries which he had conquered.

For the first time I realised that, should we allow this monster to conquer us, our beloved freedom would be taken away. And not only from Britain but from my own country as well. Unless we fought as we had been doing, and continued to do so, we ourselves might lose the right to move and speak as we chose. We might be hauled off to a slow painful death in a prisoner-of-war camp or suffer a multitude of varying indignities at the hands of Hitler and his henchmen. It was strange that it was Hilary's death which started me thinking for the first time of what the war was about. From that moment on I lost my mercenary attitude to the job I was doing and, from then on, I fought Hitler's countrymen and also the Japanese with a ferocity and lack of feeling for my own safety, of which I had not realised I was capable.

But the Battle of Britain was nearly over. The Luftwaffe could not gain command of the British skies as Goering had promised Hitler they would. About two weeks after Hilary's death we were given orders to withdraw to Coltishall, about ten miles north of Norwich. Johnny Hill was called to Group Headquarters

239

on the day of our departure and he told me to take the squadron up to our new base. As the sections of aircraft formed up behind me and I started to climb on course for our destination, one thought dawned on me. Of the eighteen pilots who had flown the squadron aircraft to Hornchurch from Kirton-in-Lindsey in August, I was the only one left who was actually flying out of Hornchurch that morning. By no means all of them had been killed. Quite a few had been wounded and had not yet returned to active duty. Others had been wounded mentally and had been unable to carry on under the strain. A few had been posted to other squadrons. But the fact remained that in a period of two and a half months they had all gone their separate ways and I was the only one left.

I was still feeling deeply affected by the death of my friend and I can remember on that flight northwards a sensation of deep sadness and depression sweeping over me. The craziness of human beings who were prepared to massacre each other in the way which we had been doing seemed inexcusable. On one or two occasions during the past weeks we had been able to speak to the crews of German bombers which we had shot down. And before they were carted off to POW camp we had once been able to give two pilots a good dinner in our Mess before handing them over. They had seemed surprisingly normal and pleasant human beings. Very much like ourselves and filled surprisingly with the same desires and emotions. Their participation in the battle had been caused, so it seemed, by the same enthusiasm for flying and excitement which had brought most of us to where we now were. And yet, underneath all these feelings, I had developed a deep conviction that the cause for which we fought was the right one.

The deaths of my friends and companions, and for that matter my own death should it happen, were justified in order to fight for that cause. The sacrifice, no matter how frightful it might be, was worthwhile. By the time the airfield at Coltishall came into view ahead of me I had managed to talk myself out of my depression and face up once more to the job in hand. I ordered the squadron into line astern and joined the circuit for our landing. As I touched down I received directions to the dispersal area which had been allotted to us and led the way over to our new home. The station commander was there to greet us and I explained Johnny Hill's absence. He looked with some surprise at the pilot officer's stripes which still adorned my shoulders. "Where are the two flight commanders?" he asked.

"I am one, Sir," I replied, "and the other flight commander is just pulling up over there. He's also a pilot officer," I added. He eyed me with respect and looked at the ribbon of the Distinguished Flying Cross which was sewn onto my tunic below my wings. Obviously, he remained slightly bewildered that the squadron was being led by a pilot who still only held the lowest officer rank in the RAF.

"We don't have any flight lieutenants or flying officers left, Sir," I explained. "Actually, I was promoted to flying officer last week but I haven't had the time to get the new stripes."

"Alright Vigors," he said, "get all your pilots together and I will arrange for some transport to take you over to the Officers' Mess."

Johnny Hill flew in that evening and the next morning we held a council of war, or maybe more aptly described as "a council of rest from war."

"I see you haven't put up your flying officer's stripes yet," was Johnny's opening remark. "Well it's just as well as they told me at Group Headquarters yesterday that you are being promoted to acting flight lieutenant. Congratulations, you've deserved it!"

"Thank you, Johnny," I replied, "I'll try not to let you down."

"Well don't do anything bloody stupid, like landing with your undercarriage up!" he joked.

"Never have yet," I answered, "and I don't see why I should start now."

The squadron was well below its establishment level of pilots. One of our main tasks during the coming months was to train up to our own high standard those pilots who were being posted in to bring us up to strength. About a week after we had arrived at Coltishall four new pilots were allocated to my flight. They had just completed their training and were all eager to learn the arts of operational flying from people like myself, who had just come out of action. The day after they arrived I brought them all into my office and gave them a pep talk on what A Flight, 222 Squadron, expected from its pilots. They all looked suitably impressed. "One final thing," I concluded, "if any one of you should be so bloody careless as to forget to put your undercarriage down before landing I'll see that you never fly a Spitfire again."

I dismissed them, rose from my chair and picked up my parachute. Out on the field I prepared to test a Spitfire which had just completed an inspection. I took off and, for the next fifteen minutes, went through the normal testing routine without incident. As I rejoined the circuit for my landing I could see the bunch of new pilots standing outside the dispersal hut watching my approach. "I'll show those new boys how a Spitfire should be landed," I thought and commenced a tight 180 degree left-hand turn to bring me into position. Kicking on hard right-hand rudder, and holding the stick back and towards my left thigh, I sideslipped steeply into the final approach. I still was holding the sideslip some twenty feet from the ground with my wings at an angle of about 40 degrees to the grass. At the very last moment I centred the stick and kicked on the right rudder. The aircraft was virtually stalled and, as I eased back on the stick, I waited for the gentle rumble which would denote that all three wheels had touched the grass in a perfect three-point landing.

But there was no rumble!

For one ghastly split second I realised what had happened. I desperately thrust forward the throttle. But it was too late. With a grinding thud the bottom of the fuselage struck the ground and, with the tips of the propeller bending backwards at right angles from the impact, the Spit slithered to a halt. The few seconds of complete silence which followed were broken by the wail of a siren as the crash wagon tore out onto the field.

Wearily, I pulled myself from the cockpit and, by the time the fire engine had arrived, I was standing surveying the damage.

In fact, apart from the bent propeller, there was no visible sign of damage at all. But I was fully conscious of the harm which might have been done to the engine as my propeller struck the ground whilst still turning. I knew only too well the hours of work and testing which would have to take place before this Spitfire took to the air once more. I remembered an occasion a few years before when I had seriously hurt a good hunter by asking him to jump a fence which was unjumpable. Looking at my poor broken Spitfire I felt the same feeling of self-disgust sweep through me. The horrible truth was that, on both occasions, the harm had been caused by my own silly desire to show off. Tim Vigors was not my favourite person at the moment.

Johnny Hill arrived at the scene in his car. "What the bloody hell do you think you are doing?" he spluttered. "Didn't you hear the warning horn sounding?"

"Yes, Johnny I did," I replied, "but I thought someone was trying to pass me."

"Ha, bloody, ha!" said Johnny. "Come and see me in my office in fifteen minutes." I accepted a ride on the crash wagon back to dispersal. The new pilots who had been watching their flight commander perform the perfect landing turned awkwardly away.

I walked into my office and sat down at the wooden table which served as a desk. I was totally mad at myself. My carelessness had not only badly damaged a much needed aircraft but had also made me look the most awful damned fool in my new official position as flight commander. I suddenly remembered Douglas's self-condemnation after he had failed to select fine pitch and crashed his Spitfire into the fence at Kirton. The fact that even such a great pilot as Douglas could make a stupid mistake somehow made me feel a little better.

"You wouldn't be proud of your old friend now Henry," I said to myself as I walked to EGO and headed for my squadron commander's office. I knocked on the door and was told to go in.

"Sit down, Tim," he said. "Tell me what happened."

I removed my cap. "Look, Johnny," I said, "I really am sorry. It was just awful bloody carelessness. I just wanted to show those new guys what a great pilot their flight commander is. I've never felt more of a bloody fool in my whole life. I just can't think what came over me."

"I know how you feel," commiserated Johnny, "and I'm not going to cuss you. Your own feelings are enough punishment. But I'm afraid I shall have to report the matter to Group Headquarters and you're bound to get a severe reprimand for careless flying. I know myself it's the sort of thing which would never have happened to you when we were in action at Hornchurch. But the strain you have been through over the last couple of months has been enormous. When the pressure comes

245

off we can all make silly mistakes. But, for God's sake don't do it again."

I got to my feet, replaced my cap, saluted and left the office. I drove back over to the dispersal hut and entered the room where all the pilots were sitting. They all looked up as Snipe and I walked through the door. "Listen a moment lads," I said. "You have just seen an experienced pilot, through pure carelessness, not only make a bloody fool of himself but also do a lot of unnecessary damage to an aircraft which is in short supply. I don't mind whether you have been with us at Hornchurch or whether you are new here. Remember what you have just seen and let it be a lesson to us all. Don't do the same thing yourselves." I walked over to the new pilots who were bunched together in a corner.

"I still mean what I said this morning. If any one of you is careless enough to forget to put your wheels down I'll see you never fly a Spitfire again. If it wasn't for the fact that my fighting experience is supposed to be of value in training you, I would probably suffer the same fate myself. Now let's go over to the Mess and get some lunch."

In the Mess I ran into an old friend from another squadron who had been at Cranwell with me. Over a pint of beer he commiserated with me over my accident. The story of what I had said to Johnny about thinking somebody was trying to pass me had spread quickly and was causing a good deal of amusement. "Why didn't you put your hand out and wave him on?" queried one wag.

"Knowing the way you drive, I'm surprised you didn't put your foot down and race him," rejoined another. And so it went on.

My Cranwell friend and I went into the dining room. As we sat down he said, "I've found one helluva nice pub about ten miles from here. It's called The Horning Ferry. Kind landlord, who often slips you a free pint, and quite passable pub food. Do you want to join me there this evening?" I agreed readily and so that evening found us heading in EGO for that part of the Norfolk Broads on which "The Ferry" is situated. There were quite a few people at the bar as we walked in and, as usual, Snipe came in for a lot of admiration. My friend was quite right. This pub, which was situated right on the water where the ferry left to take passengers to the other side of the broad, had something a bit extra about it. The moment you walked through the door the atmosphere of warm friendliness swept over you. My friend introduced me to the landlord with whom I straightaway struck up a good relationship. The locals were a friendly lot who did not immediately smother one with well-meaning questions relating to the war, as was so often the case at this time when you entered a pub in RAF uniform.

We spent a pleasant evening, culminating in a fierce game of darts against a couple of locals which we lost in the final game. During those few hours which I spent in The Ferry I had, for the first time for months, completely relaxed. Waking up each morning since I had arrived at Coltishall it had been a pleasant experience not to speculate on the odds against ever

247

waking up again. But somehow the shadow of those days full of danger had lurked over me and the taut strings inside my mind had refused to loosen. Now, at least temporarily, I felt that a weight had slid from my shoulders. I felt once more like a lad of nineteen who had just spent an enjoyable evening in a pub, drinking beer and talking to friends. The desperate need to get the last drop out of every minute had slid away.

"We must do that again," I said to my friend. "That was good medicine." And do it again we did. In fact for the next six weeks The Ferry became the home which I returned to after work. My place of total relaxation. The local inhabitants became good friends and, in fact, one of them lent me a cottage on the river so that I could stay the night if I was tired. It also served as a convenient trysting place with a young lady whose acquaintance I made soon after my first visit. Her husband was in the army and had been posted to the Middle East and I am afraid I had no scruples about taking advantage of the favours which she so willingly offered.

Two months later, and after I had been posted from Coltishall en route for Singapore, a German bomber on a night raid was intercepted by night fighters soon after it crossed the coast. Jettisoning its bomb load it dived for home. The string of bombs fell and exploded across farming land and water in the Norfolk Broads. The last bomb crashed through the roof of The Horning Ferry and exploded in the saloon bar. All its occupants were killed, including my friend the landlord and four pilots from my squadron. Had the bomb fallen twenty yards in any other direction it would have struck only water or fields. Such are the fortunes of war.

The days at Coltishall passed pleasantly enough. Most of the time was taken up with training new pilots interspersed with an occasional convoy patrol. One cold clear morning I got up early to carry out an experiment I had never had time or opportunity to try before.

I wanted to see the sun rise twice on the same day. I climbed into my Spitfire and took off when it was still dark. Hauling up the nose I climbed for the coast. When I reached 30,000 feet the first rays of the sun started shimmering over the horizon. I throttled back and watched the golden rim appear followed gradually by the whole sphere. As soon as the lower rim of the sun separated itself from the horizon, I pushed forward on the stick and dived for the ground. As I roared earthwards I watched the sun gradually disappear below the edge of the earth. I was once more flying in darkness. Levelling out at 10,000 feet I waited for the first rays to appear. Gradually the horizon grew lighter and suddenly the sun's rays were glinting on the wings of my Spitfire. Fascinated, I watched the golden globe creep into the sky and then, strangely moved, I dived for home. You may say that I was wasting the King's petrol, but I reckon he owed an Irishman a few gallons!

Whilst it was nice to wake up in the morning and feel that there was every chance one was going to see darkness fall that evening, a feeling of frustration at being out of action started to creep over me. I started wondering if I couldn't get posted to a squadron which was closer to the action.

At this stage of the war, German U-boats were starting to take a very heavy toll on the convoys of merchant ships bringing badly needed supplies across the Atlantic. The U-boats were helped in this work by long-range Focke-Wulf bombers. The Royal Navy escort ships were doing their best to combat the attacks from enemy submarines, but there was not much they could do to stop the bombers.

The usual tactic employed by the bombers was to appear out of clouds and drop bombs on the unarmoured decks of the merchant ships. Some form of protection against such attacks was needed. One answer to this was large merchant ships fitted with catapults, from which they could launch a Hawker Hurricane into the air as soon as enemy aircraft were picked up on radar. The Hurricane would then do its best to dispose of the enemy bomber. Having done this, the theory was that the pilot would head for land, if there was any in range or, failing this, ditch his aircraft beside one of the ships in the convoy and hope to be picked up. Volunteers were being called for from all squadrons in Fighter Command to fly the Hurricanes on these dangerous missions.

For some reason which I shall never understand I asked Johnny Hill to forward my name for this job. "You're a crazy fool Tim," was his reaction. "If you insist, I will put your name forward. But for God's sake why won't you accept a few months well earned rest?"

"Well Johnny, I really don't know the answer. But I've always been a restless guy and the easy life which I am settling into is starting to irk me." Johnny looked at me wisely. No doubt he had heard of my romance with the married lady who lived near The Ferry and perhaps he recognised quicker than I did my real reason for wanting to get on the road again.

"OK, Tim," he said. "I'll put your name up, but they only want a limited number of pilots and, with your experience they'll probably reckon you're too valuable to throw away on what is virtually a suicide mission." Luckily for me, Johnny was right. Whether they chose the names in alphabetical order and had got sufficient by the time they got to V or whether the reason given by Johnny was correct, I shall never know. One thing for sure is that I was lucky not to be chosen. I've always suffered from chronic seasickness and I'm a rotten swimmer.

But the seed was sown and I started looking out for alternatives. One morning, in the middle of December 1940, Johnny asked me to come over to his office.

"I think I've found something which might interest you," he said as soon as I had sat down opposite him. "They want pilots with solid battle experience to go out to Singapore to form fighter squadrons there to protect Malaya against possible Japanese attack. The squadrons will be flying American Navy fighters which Churchill has borrowed from Roosevelt. The bulk of the pilots will be sent up from New Zealand and Australia. It's a volunteer job but I am pretty sure I can get you accepted if you want to take it. I don't want to lose you but I know you're feeling restless here. Think it over and let me know."

"When would I leave?" I asked.

"Pretty much straight away." I thought quickly. I hated the thought of leaving Snipe but apart from him I had no real ties where I was. All my close friends had been killed and, as yet, I had made no new ones to replace them. I had never been further abroad than a short cruise in the Mediterranean and Malaya sounded an interesting adventure.

"OK, I'll take it Johnny," I said on the spur of the moment. "Do you think you can really get it for me?"

"I'll do my best," said Johnny.

I thanked him and asked if I would get any leave, as I wanted to get Snipe settled in Ireland before I left.

"Yes, I'm sure I can fix that," Johnny said, "and I'll let you know just as soon as I hear anything."

Two days later Johnny drove up to the dispersal hut. I met him outside the door. "You've got the job Tim!" he exclaimed. "I've just heard from Group. You're to go on leave straight away for a week. Then you report to Group Headquarters immediately after Christmas, and they'll tell you where to go."

Several emotions flooded through me. First, the posting meant that I had to leave Snipe. He had been my constant companion for so long that I found it difficult to think of living without him. Second, it meant leaving 222 Squadron with which I had served for nearly a year. So much had happened in that year and the sheet anchor of all those events, happy and sad, had been the squadron itself. I must turn my back on my comfortable life at Coltishall and The Ferry and strike out on new, unknown paths. I must leave behind my beautiful friend Jill. I had kept in constant touch with her over the past year and it was she who had provided, as nobody else could apart from poor Hilary, a gay mind to laugh with and a shoulder to cry on.

"Thank you, Johnny," I said. "I'll start getting packed and making some travelling plans."

I looked with affection and regret at the line of Spitfires drawn up on the grass outside the dispersal hut. What American Navy fighter could possibly possess the qualities of this thoroughbred aircraft?

I called Snipe, walked over to EGO and drove off to the Mess to start packing.

CHAPTER
ELEVEN

Voyage

As is normal during the month of December, the Irish Channel was rough. Every roll and pitch caused a new wave of sickness to sweep over me. Snipe lay at my feet dozing. "How lucky you are to be a dog," I remarked out loud. Snipe opened one eye and regarded me sympathetically. Another enormous wave hit the bows and the whole ship shuddered before wallowing into the following trough.

My mind wandered back over the many uncomfortable journeys I had made on this turbulent stretch of water. "If it wasn't for you Snipe," I groaned, "I would have flown my Spitfire to Belfast and gone down to Dublin by train." This time he didn't even have the courtesy to open an eye. I closed mine and tried, unsuccessfully, to doze.

Once ashore at Dun Laoghaire and on into Dublin things were better. It was good to be home in my own country.

The week's leave passed quickly. Pat, my young brother, was home from school for Christmas. My elder brother, Tel, was in the RAF and learning to fly in far away Canada. I tried to relate my experiences of the last year to my father and mother but somehow it was difficult to convey the excitement and fears of aerial combat to people who had practically never left the ground.

I did manage a couple of days hunting and was welcomed warmly by all my old hunting friends. In Fethard I was given a hero's welcome and it was all I could do to stop some of the locals launching me onto their shoulders and carrying me down the main street. I was left in no doubt as to where the sympathies of the ordinary Irishman lay.

All too soon, the short holiday was over. These six days were so far removed from my life of the past year that it was mind boggling to even try to relate the two, as remote from one another as lives lived on two different planets.

On the morning of my departure I took Snipe for a last walk round the farm. He seemed to sense that something was wrong and, instead of galloping off to search for possible game, he followed closely at my heels. I walked down the yard to say goodbye to the lads who looked after my father's racehorses and hunters.

Amongst them was a staunch friend of mine, Larry Fahy. Many years later, Larry was to become my own stud groom at Coolmore Stud in the days when it had just started to show itself as one of the more important thoroughbred stallion farms in Ireland.

After a poignant farewell to my mother and brother, we were on our way to Fethard where I was to take the local train which connected with the Dublin express at

Thurles. My father drove the trap as usual and Snipe sat beside me on the opposite seat. The short journey to Fethard was soon over and then came the moment I had been dreading.

Snipe knew something was wrong. For a time he steadfastly refused to get out of the trap. When I did finally persuade him he stood beside me awaiting the train with his tail between his legs and his head drooped. The train drew into the station and I shook my father by the hand and thanked him for everything. He wished me luck, patted my shoulder and told me to try to take care. Then I turned to Snipe and took his head in my hands. I kissed his forehead and his long tongue came out and licked me on the chin.

"Now you be a good dog till I get back," I muttered miserably. Then I turned hastily and blundered onto the train. As the train drew out of the station, Snipe stood beside my father gazing at me with sad eyes. I gave one last wave and withdrew into the carriage. People were used to sad farewells in those days and when I took out my handkerchief to dab my eyes, the other occupants of the carriage tactfully looked away.

And that was to be my final parting from my dear and faithful friend. Dogs have always played an important role in my life and I have grown very close to a number of them since that day. But Snipe, who shared with me those hectic days and nights of the year 1940, always held a very special place in my heart.

When I was in Malaya I heard from my mother that he never did seem to recover from being separated from me. He had dug himself a large hole in the wood near the house, and would retreat there when he was particularly sad or when he was scared by a noise. One night, about a year later, there was a severe thunderstorm. Snipe took off out of the house and made for his shelter. Next morning my mother went to look for him and found him dead, curled up in the bottom of his hole. My father and mother could never decide whether he died of a broken heart, fear, or the cold night air. It was probably a combination of all three.

The next morning, somewhat bleary eyed after another rough sea crossing and long train journey to London, I reported to Group Headquarters. I was told that my posting to Singapore had been confirmed and that I was to report to a holding unit nearby to await my embarkation orders.

The first person I ran into when I walked into the Officers' Mess at the holding unit was John Mansel-Lewis. Our paths had crossed a couple of times before in the past year and we had always got on well together. Like me, he had been flying with an 11 Group squadron for the past twelve months and I was delighted to hear that he was also being posted to Singapore. We decided to have dinner in London that night to celebrate our imminent departure.

By this time the Luftwaffe had shifted most of its offensive to night time raids on the capital and there was seldom a night when one part of the city or another was not bombarded. On this night it happened to be the West End which was taking a pounding. Emerging from a nightclub just off Piccadilly in the early hours of

257

the morning the whole city seemed to be on fire and it would have been easy to read a small print newspaper by the light of the flames.

"Well, well," said John looking calmly around him at the fiery desolation, "London's burning down." It was no over-statement.

As we made our way homewards in the faithful EGO, we had to make constant deviations to avoid bombed streets. At one point we stopped to help air-raid wardens drag away the rubble from the door of a house which was burning and then assisted a couple of old ladies to a waiting ambulance. London was certainly burning down.

At the holding unit nobody seemed to know anything about us. After a couple of days I became frustrated with the lack of information as to our future. I happened to know quite well an officer who was working in the Air Ministry and I decided to ask him whether he could find out anything about our future movements. "Come back and see me tomorrow," he said, "and I'll try and dig something out for you." The next day I was back in his office.

"I've got all the gen for you," he said immediately, "but you must understand that it is top secret. I trust you to treat it as such." I gave him my word and he continued.

"You're due to leave from Liverpool in about a week's time. The name of the ship which you will be travelling on is the *Empress of Australia*. If I was you, I'd slip up to Liverpool and see if you can't get yourself a decent cabin. It's likely to be a long journey."

I thanked my friend profusely and reassured him once more that I wouldn't tell a soul what he had told me. As soon as I got back to the holding unit I requested 24 hours leave which rather surprisingly was agreed to. I told John I was going to see a sick aunt and took off in EGO for Liverpool.

Arriving at the docks I asked the guard whether he could direct me to the *Empress of Australia*. Evidently impressed by my flight lieutenant's stripes and my DFC ribbon he acquiesced immediately. I drove on through the gates and was soon halted alongside an enormous liner which a docker confirmed to me was the ship I was looking for.

There was a guard on the gangway but, like the one at the dock gate, he let me on board without any trouble. Well acquainted with passenger ships from my many journeys on the Irish run, I asked the first person I saw for the Purser's Office. I knocked on the door, entered and introduced myself to the purser.

"Look," I said, putting on all the charm I could muster, "I have been told that I am travelling on this ship to Singapore. A friend of mine and myself have been flying Spitfires in the battles around London for the past four months and we are both rather tired. Could you fit us up with a nice quiet cabin where we can get a bit of a rest?"

I felt really bad shooting him this big line but reckoned that anything was justified to avoid being cooped up with five or six other people on the long voyage ahead. The purser was obviously impressed and, asking me to wait a moment, he went off to check the cabin list. After a couple of minutes he came back into the office and said, "I reckon that you and your friend deserve the best. The whole country is in your debt for what you have done. You may not remember, but the King and Queen travelled on this ship a couple of years ago on their state visit to Canada. If you promise not to breathe a word I can give you their cabin. It was supposed to be kept for a general but I reckon you boys deserve it more. I'll give him their sitting room, which is next door, but it is completely soundproofed. Come on down and you can have a look at it."

We entered the cabin. The opulence within was astounding. Two large beds, armchairs, a sofa, private bathroom with separate lavatory, the lot. "I just don't know how to thank you!" I blurted out.

"The King and Queen would be proud to have you and your friend sleeping in their beds!" he replied. "But make sure of one thing. Don't tell a soul where you are or you'll not only get me into trouble but I'll have to turf you out of the cabin. And if I was you, I wouldn't bring any of your friends in here until well into the voyage."

I thanked him again. Immediately I got back to London I gave John the good news. "Some sick aunt," he laughed. Two days later movement control told us to catch a train for Liverpool. A lot of other people, mostly army personnel of all ranks, were boarding the *Empress of Australia*. I checked with the purser and, winking, he handed me the key of the cabin. Although I had prepared him for the luxury, John nearly fell over backwards when he walked through the door.

"Well," he said, "if we do have to spend weeks or months on a boat we couldn't ask to do it in much better style."

The ship sailed the next day. Once away from the harbour we became part of a convoy of about thirty ships of all shapes and sizes. A battle cruiser, four destroyers and a couple of frigates shepherded and guided us out to sea. They were to be our constant companions for the next four weeks.

At the beginning the novelty of the voyage with all its different faces, sounds, tastes and smells kept boredom at bay. Studying the mass of ships in the centre of which we sailed was a novel pastime. Apart from John and myself there were some other RAF fighter pilots on board. Catching up with all their experiences and stories was good temporary entertainment. The occasional scare of a submarine or air attack, too, also helped to relieve the tedium of similar day following similar day. But, by and large, the longer the voyage went on the more frustrating it became.

We could judge from the position of the sun that, for the first week, we were sailing practically due west and we did wonder if we were going to approach Singapore through the Panama Canal. Of course, the speed of the convoy was governed by that of the slowest ship, about half the normal cruising speed of our liner. But after a week we turned south-west and we realised we must be sailing down the American coastline.

A few days later we altered course once more and were now heading south-east towards Africa. The further we returned across the Atlantic the more vulnerable we became to attack both from the air and from beneath the sea.

One morning there was a major scare. Alarm bells rang and everybody was ordered to put on lifebelts. Our escorting ships started zig-zagging about and the sea around the perimeter of the convoy became white with the explosions of depth charges. Standing on deck we saw several torpedo tracks in the water around ships near to us but, miraculously, none of them found their mark. After an hour or so things quietened down and, by lunchtime, everything had returned to normal. Word filtered through from the bridge that the convoy had been attacked by a U-boat wolf pack and that two of them had been sunk by our Royal Navy escort.

That evening we were listening on the radio as usual to the nightly talk by the British traitor, "Lord Haw Haw". His job was to demoralise the British people with false information. To our amazement he opened his speech with news that a convoy of about thirty British ships approaching the coast of Africa had been attacked that morning by a pack of U-boats. Amongst the ships sunk, he went on, was the ex-cruise liner, the *Empress of Australia*. A roar went up from the whole room and the rest of Haw Haw's lecture was lost in cheering and laughter. The "mainbrace" was duly spliced many times that evening in celebration of our "sinking".

One morning, for the first time in three weeks, we woke up in sight of land. We were about to put into Freetown, the capital of what was then the Gold Coast. The convoy formed line astern and gradually we started to snake our way up the estuary on which Freetown lies. The sight of green vegetation after so many days of looking at nothing but grey waves was a sight for sore eyes.

This was a refuelling stop only and we were told the boat would leave after twenty-four hours. However, we RAF pilots managed a trip to the beach before our boat left. The beach was idyllic; white sand, shady palm trees waving in a pleasant breeze, blue ocean and white sand. Only one thing was missing, beautiful girls. We discarded our uniforms and got down to some serious sunbathing.

Later in the morning some army officers came by. One of them came over to us. "Is there a Tim Vigors amongst you by any chance?" he asked. Surprised to say the least, I rose to my feet. "I'm Tim Vigors."

"Good," he replied, "I'm glad I've found you. I believe you were at Eton with your great friend, John Harley." He told me that John was on his ship, which was in our convoy and docked not far from the *Empress of Australia*. Apparently John was confined to the sick bay but had asked him to look out for RAF officers when he was ashore and ask if anybody knew Tim Vigors. "By a stroke of good luck I seem to have found you," he concluded.

"I'm very happy you have," I replied. "I had no idea that John was on this convoy. Where are you all heading for?"

"The Middle East so far as we know," he answered, "but I hear we're going to stop in Cape Town on the way."

"OK," I said, "please will you give John this message from me. Tell him I'm absolutely delighted he is on the convoy but I'm sorry to hear he's sick. Tell him that when we get to Cape Town, or wherever the next stop is, I will wait for him on the quay or he can wait for me if he gets ashore first. Tell him not to make any other plans and we'll paint the town red together!"

The army officer promised he would pass on my message, waved his hand and walked off to rejoin his group. I lay back on the sand and reflected on this chance meeting. I hadn't been able to see much of John since I'd left Eton. We'd had a couple of nights out in London when I was at Cranwell and I had spent a weekend with him and his parents in Shropshire. Since then we'd only been in touch by telephone and not that often. I knew he had joined the army and been commissioned in the Coldstream Guards. And now here we were, by some freak of fate, on the same convoy to different parts of the world.

By nightfall we were back on board as instructed. The next morning the convoy formed up and headed southwards. The battleship had left us and our escort was reduced to two destroyers and a frigate. Earlier in the voyage, part of the convoy had left us for Gibraltar and Malta and we were now reduced to about fifteen ships. The further south we went the hotter the sun became and we spent much of the day sitting, or lying, on deck and soon everybody had a tan. This movement further south also meant that we were less likely to be attacked. After crossing the equator the weather began to cool down again but, as we rounded the southern point of the African continent and headed in for Cape Town, it was still much hotter than anything I had experienced before.

We were told that our stay in Cape Town was likely to be four or five days. Unless we obtained special leave we were to return to the boat each night. Looking forward to my meeting with John Harley I queued early for one of the first boats to go ashore. Reaching the quay, the first thing I saw was the long, thin bespectacled figure of my school friend. I climbed up the steps and we shook hands, surveying each other in uniforms so different from the top hat, white tie and tails in which we had grown up together.

"My God, John, you look like a real bloody officer!"

"And you, Tim," he laughed, "look like a real live fighter boy." We walked off along the quay laughing at the fact that we were so unexpectedly together again. As we passed through the dock gates we were approached by two pretty girls.

"Hello fellows," said one of them, "we've got a car over there and would love to show you Cape Town." John and I looked at each other. I think we were both thinking the same thing. Half of us longed to be in the company of these two nice looking girls. The other half wanted to have time just by ourselves to catch up with all that had happened to us since we had left Eton. We sensed that we were unlikely to see each other again for a very long time, if ever. So, we turned the girls down, if somewhat reluctantly.

The next three days in Cape Town were a complete riot. We ate and drank and laughed our way to a standstill. Each evening we returned to our respective ships to sleep off the day's festivities. And each morning we set off together again to sample the best of Cape Town. We saw the sights, including a trip to the top of Table Mountain from which the view of the city and harbour was something to remember.

But, above everything else, we reminisced and laughed our way through our childhood and school days recalling all those incidents, good and bad and happy and sad, which we had experienced together. On our last evening we stood ourselves a slap-up dinner in one of Cape Town's best hotels, perched on the hillside above the city. We sat at a window table with breathtaking views of the harbour. As we finished dinner John turned to me and said, "Tim, I don't know about you but I'm glad we turned down those two girls."

"Harley my old friend, that makes two of us. Whatever life holds for us in the future you and I will remember these few days in Cape Town." We made our way back to the harbour.

"Look after yourself, John. See you after the war."

"You too, Tim," John said. We shook hands. "I'm already looking forward to that night on the town in London."

Early next morning *Empress of Australia* stood out from Cape Town. But this time we were on our own. The rest of the convoy, including John Harley, headed north up the East African coast, bound for the Suez Canal, and we set our course east for Bombay. Up on deck I thought about my time in the city with John. The night we had planned in London was never to be. Some eighteen months later, during the invasion of Sicily, John led his men onto a beach. He had hardly set foot on the dry sand before a mine exploded and blew him to smithereens.

About four days after we had left Cape Town word got out about the Royal Suite. Probably one of our friends had inadvertently mentioned it in the hearing of some army officers. All hell was let loose. From the start of the voyage there had been a running battle between ourselves and the army, or "pongos" as we called them. They outnumbered us by about 50 to 1 and not all of the studied antagonism was exactly friendly. The long voyage in cramped quarters had set everybody's nerves on edge and the atmosphere was ripe for explosion.

Open rudery and brawling, after a few drinks, now took place and on more than one occasion. The senior army general complained to the senior RAF officer about our accommodation status. It looked odds on that we would be thrown out. In fact, to our great delight, the captain of our ship intervened. He insisted that accommodation arrangements would remain unchanged.

As we drew nearer to Bombay all was peace and quiet once more, at least on the surface. Underneath, a good deal of ill will still rumbled.

About half the army personnel on board were due to disembark for destinations in India and, as a final gesture of goodwill, they invited us RAF officers to their farewell celebrations the night before we docked

267

in Bombay. At the party I played my piano accordion and sang songs to the accompaniment of my ukele. Mansel-Lewis and I fell into our beds at about 4.00a.m. having both consumed more than our fair share of alcohol.

"If I'm not awake by nine Tim, give me a shout," said John as he fell asleep. "I've only got a limited time tomorrow to exert my charms." He had scored well with a hospitable South African lady on the voyage to Cape Town and had for the last few days been talking about the charms of Indian maidens.

"OK, but don't swear at me too much when I wake you!"

Even after impossibly late nights, I have always been an early riser. After about three hours sleep a change in the hum of the ship's motors woke me. I staggered out of bed, and was shaved, bathed and dressed as our ship docked.

It was a beautiful clear morning. I stood entranced by the Bombay skyline, watching the big Indian fishing boats, built on the lines of Chinese junks, plying their way up and down the river beside us. After breakfast I glanced at my watch and saw it was time to wake John. I returned to the cabin and shook him by the shoulder. He groaned. I shook him again.

"Get the hell out of it you sonofabitch!" he grumbled, "let me sleep." I left him be and went to find the others. We only had 24 hours in Bombay so we made our way ashore as soon as we could. One of the other RAF pilots, Colin Pinkney, had been at Eton with me and had been stationed at Hornchurch for a few weeks during my months there. Colin and I grabbed a taxi and made a sightseeing tour of the city.

The impact of one's first arrival in India stays in one's memory for a long time. Above all else the predominant memory is not the architecture, not the noise, not even the smells, but the incredible number of people who jostled and pushed their way through the narrow streets. After a couple of hours of sightseeing we directed our taxi to the world-renowned Taj Mahal Hotel where, under its magnificent domes and arches, we treated ourselves to a real Indian curry.

We returned to the docks and stayed on deck to watch the preparations for departure. A bell rang on the bridge. The engines started and then, with the assistance of two tugs, we were once more leaving a foreign shore. Dusk started to fall as we edged our way out into the river and by the time we reached the open sea it was pitch dark and the twinkling lights of Bombay were receding into the distance. I thanked Colin for spending a pleasant day with me and made my way down below. I entered the cabin and switched on the light. There was an exclamation from the other side of the room and John's head appeared above the blankets on his bed.

"Are we in yet?" he enquired, drowsily rubbing the sleep from his eyes.

"We're not only in but we've also been and now we're gone!" I laughed.

"What the hell do you mean?" John looked at me in bewilderment. "Have you been ashore yet? Hell I must get a move on or I won't have time to make a killing."

Gradually the truth dawned on him. He had slept through the whole day and had missed out on all his chances in Bombay.

"You bastard!" he shouted. "You promised you'd wake me up." Suddenly the funny side of the whole episode struck him and he started to roar with laughter.

"Give me fifteen minutes," he laughed "and we'll go and have a good drink at the bar to make up for it."

Empress of Australia continued her journey southwards to the bottom of India. Having disgorged half her human cargo she was comparatively empty now. The extra elbow room was welcome, the weather was beautiful and the sea calm. We spent long days on deck sunbathing and reading but soon the monotony of day after day at sea became more and more trying. We passed south of Ceylon and headed east once more for Malaya. Now the end of the long journey was in sight we wondered more about what lay in store for us . . .

CHAPTER
TWELVE

Singapore

Few of us knew much about Singapore, apart from what we had read in books and magazines. The prospect of living once more in a country not close enough to any fighting to be affected by the war was a strange one. We had all got so used to austerity, rationing, blackouts and air-raid sirens it was going to be something of a shock to find oneself living once more under virtually peacetime conditions.

For our last night at sea we six RAF pilots decided to have a dinner and party all on our own. We laughed and sang and drank the evening away but with the prospect of arriving at our destination at dawn the following day we were all in bed before midnight. It is sad to relate that only ten months later I was the only one of those six pilots still alive.

Packing my kit the following morning, although I was full of excitement about arriving in Singapore, I still felt a strange sense of sadness at leaving the luxurious cabin which had been my home for the past two months.

By 10.00a.m. our party were ashore. The captain of *Empress of Australia* stood at the gangway to see his passengers off and we saluted him as we left his fine ship. Trucks were lined up to take us to our new home.

In those far off days there were three airfields on Singapore Island; Kallang, Sembawang and Tenghy. We were bound for Kallang which was then, and is still today, the main civil airport of Singapore. In those days it was a roughly circular grass field, about 1,000 yards across, with land on its north and south side and the sea on the other two. It was situated just to the east of Singapore town and on the edge of the main harbour.

At Kallang our truck came to a halt at the Officers' Mess, a bungalow-type building on the southern edge of the airfield. Several white-jacketed Chinese batmen unloaded our bags and carried them to our rooms. I observed with some curiosity the large mosquito net suspended from the ceiling above my bed. My batman noted my interest. "Many mosquitoes here at night, Sah!" he told me. "Every time you go bed you let down net, Sah, or you badly bitten, Sah!" I absorbed this information and was soon to find out how entirely accurate it was.

After lunch we made our way down to the airfield to meet our squadron commander and find out the lie of the land. My new position was flight commander of A Flight, 243 Squadron, RAF. John Mansel-Lewis was given the command of B Flight. Our ground troops had arrived several weeks earlier and were now busily assembling the Brewster Buffalos we were to fly. These aircraft had been delivered to Singapore docks in large wooden crates a few days beforehand and were at

272

varying states of construction. None of them were yet ready for flight testing.

All the squadron pilots, apart from the commanding officer, John and myself, were New Zealanders who had arrived directly from their own country the week before. Most had only just completed their flying training and, although all of them were raring to go, were completely raw material. John and I had ten pilots each allocated to us and it was our job during the coming months to mould them into an effective flying force.

The squadron commander introduced us to our pilots first and then we met the squadron engineer officer and his two flight sergeants. These last three men had the vital job of maintaining the aircraft for both flights. They advised us that the first of the Buffalos could not be ready to take the air for about a week. Meanwhile, the only airworthy machine the squadron possessed was a De Havilland Tiger Moth.

We all stood looking at this old two-seater biplane trainer and I knew that John was thinking what I was thinking. It had been well over two months since either of us had been in the air, a long time considering how much flying we had been used to doing.

"Alright, John," I laughed, "great minds think alike. What say you and I go for a spin together first thing tomorrow morning and case the joint?"

"You've got a deal," replied John. "We'll toss up for who takes the controls first."

Immediately after breakfast the next morning, we collected a couple of parachutes from the squadron store, donned our helmets and goggles and walked out to the Tiger Moth, which had been made ready for us.

I won the toss and climbed into the rear cockpit. John clambered into the front cockpit and an airman swung the prop, the engine kicked into life and we were off. I climbed up over the harbour and then swung in over the centre of the city. Levelling off at 2,000 feet I followed the coastline of Singapore Island, which is separated from the mainland of Malaya by the Johore Straight.

In those days, Singapore Island, apart from the city itself and a few fishing settlements around the coast, was covered by jungle and scrubland. I climbed another 1,000 feet and, just to get it out of my system, did a couple of loops, a roll off the top and a slow roll.

"You haven't lost your touch," John shouted over the intercom. I began a glide down towards the higher ground in the centre of the island and a golf course came into view. On the north side of the course was a small lake surrounded by hills. High trees grew along the edge of the fairway separating the lake from the course. I noticed a gap between two of these trees which I reckoned was just about wide enough to accommodate the wingspan of a Tiger Moth.

"Hold on to your seat John Mansel-Lewis," I shouted "we're going to play golf!" I dived down towards the jungle-covered hillside keeping just above the tree tops. Levelling out over the lake with my wheels nearly skimming the water, I headed for the gap in the trees through which I could see the fairway rising to the clubhouse in the centre of the course. There was

274

about ten feet to spare on each side of the wing tips as the Tiger Moth roared through the gap and then I eased back on the stick to climb just above the rising fairway. Halfway up the hill I intentionally touched the grass with my wheels and then lifted the aircraft over the green which lay ahead. As we shot over the road at the end of the course I could see a collection of huts separated by dirt roads. I was now flying twenty feet above the ground and the huts were rapidly approaching. I throttled back and glided down onto one of the roads that separated the lines of huts. As my wheels touched the surface of the road I opened the throttle and climbed steeply away.

"Hey," yelled John from the front cockpit, "that was great! Come on, hand over to me, I want some action."

"You've got her," I shouted back.

John climbed the aircraft up to 500 feet and swung back over the golf course. Then he dived down the hillside and over the lake repeating exactly what I had done. This time, however, there were four golfers with their caddies walking up the fairway. They scattered like a flock of frightened teal as we hurtled up the hill towards them. As we crossed the road and approached the huts khaki-uniformed figures could be seen at the hut windows. The first premonition of disaster crept over me. This was obviously an RAF or army settlement of one kind or another where our antics might not be entirely appreciated. However, there was no time to pass my fears on to John, who was now gliding down onto the road as I had done a couple of minutes earlier. Dirt spurted from the road as our wheels touched the surface and then we were climbing away once more.

I shouted through the intercom, "That must have been a service camp of some kind or another. I hope it wasn't full of air marshals or generals." We flew around a little longer and then headed back for Kallang.

As we taxied back to the hangar, our squadron commander was advancing across the tarmac. The look on his face was not a good omen. "You know what you two silly young buggers have just done?" he roared. We had got out of the Tiger Moth and now stood before him looking innocent. "Well, I'll tell you what you've done. You've just beaten up Air Headquarters. The AOC wants to see you immediately. Please God, why have I been landed with you two bloody irresponsible imbeciles as flight commanders? Why the hell didn't you two stay in England?"

John and I looked at each other. I thought it incumbent on me to bear the brunt of the attack and provide an explanation. "We are sorry, Sir," I began, "of course we'd no idea it was Air Headquarters or we wouldn't have done it. I'm afraid the whole thing was just an attack of high spirits. We've been cooped up on that boat for so long it was just great to get in the air again. We were just letting off steam."

"One hell of a place to find to let off steam. Now, get into that truck immediately. I've given the driver instructions to take you to Air Headquarters. You are to report to the personal assistant to the Air Chief Marshal."

We dumped our flying gear, donned our caps and climbed into the truck. Soon our driver stopped outside a building halfway down the road where, less than an hour ago, we had touched our wheels down. "Good luck, Sirs," said the driver as we got out. "From what I have heard, you're going to need lots of it."

We entered the door of the personal assistant's office and told him who we were. "Wait a moment," he said. He didn't need to ask us to sit down. His secretary, a pretty fair-haired WAAF, sneaked us a half smile full of admiration.

Air Chief Marshal Sir Richard Peirse was sitting behind a large desk when we entered his office. We saluted and remained standing at attention. He eyed us balefully and said nothing for a long time. Then, rising to his feet, he walked round the desk and stopped in front of us. "Which of you is which?"

Always the spokesman, I said, "I'm Vigors, Sir, and this is Mansel-Lewis."

"Well, the two of you have certainly started your stay in Singapore on a high, or rather I should say, low note," he said severely. "There are a lot of things I could do to you now for what you have just done," he continued, "my first inclination was to ground you both for a month. However, that would be counter-productive as we need your experience to train the New Zealand pilots. Then I thought of confining you to your station or even taking away your flight lieutenant's stripes. In the end I have decided against all these alternatives and I am going to trust to your own common sense.

"In a fit of boyish over-exuberance which was no doubt brought on by your long voyage from England, you have not only played a dangerous stunt right in front of my nose but you have also severely frightened some elderly golfers. All of whom unfortunately happen to be prominent Singapore businessmen. These acts were not only breaking all the rules but were also dangerous and completely irresponsible. You have also set a very bad example to those who you are supposed to be about to train. Instead of punishing you I have decided to ask you to consider what you have done and the damage which you might have caused. Finally, stop behaving like schoolboys and don't think for one moment that just because you happen to have seen some hard action that I am, in future, going to treat you better or worse than any other officers under my command. Now go away and consider what I have said."

With that the AOC turned on his heel and strode out of the office. The whole of his lecture had been delivered in a quiet, serious voice and John and I were left standing alone in his office feeling like the couple of silly young schoolboys he obviously had thought we were. Had he followed any of the original courses which he had considered we would have both felt resentful and bolshie. As it was we just felt stupid. Air Chief Marshal Peirse was a good leader and also an intelligent man.

On our return to Kallang we reported our good luck to our commanding officer who grunted and said we were bloody lucky not to be court martialled. The tale soon got around the island and, whilst it did cause a good deal of merriment in some quarters, it also helped to fuel a deep-seated rivalry between the old squadrons on the island, who were equipped with the antique Fairy Swordfish, and us fighter boys, about to be equipped with brand new Brewster Buffalos.

One or two of us new boys wore the ribbon of the DFC on our tunics and this was very noticeable when we were seen in public at places like the fashionable Raffles Hotel and the Tanglin Club. Girls tended to look with special attention at the so-called "hardened war veterans". This also helped to put out the noses of the other pilots on the island who, through no fault of their own, had been slogging along at their mundane, more or less peacetime, duties for many months.

When the first of the Buffalos was ready to fly it was my lot to perform the air tests. I had studied the pilot's manual carefully and had no difficulty in handling this tubby little radial-engined fighter. I did notice a slight roughness in the engine just after take-off, which gave me a bit of a scare, but it cleared quickly and the flight was otherwise uneventful. The Buffalo was slow and heavy on the controls when compared with the Spitfire, but otherwise it seemed to be quite a pleasant and workmanlike aircraft.

On landing, I reported the short period of roughness to the engineer officer and thought no more of it. The next day I tested another aircraft. I had reached 2,000 feet when the engine cut out completely. In a sudden deathly silence I stuffed the nose down and turned back towards the airfield. A quick check of fuel controls, switches and instruments revealed nothing was wrong, but there was no sign of the motor starting again so I glided back to the airfield and completed an engineless landing. The engineer officer met me and I told him what had happened. The aircraft was towed back to the hangar. A thorough inspection was carried out and the trouble diagnosed as a blocked air filter.

The next two aircraft I tested were perfect but a couple of days later I had another engine failure. This time I had only reached 1,000 feet, which made it a lot more dicey getting back to the field with a dead prop. Moreover, the same day, John, testing one of the aircraft in his flight, had experienced much the same problem. In his case the motor picked up again after a time so he was able to get back to the airfield without trouble.

Quite obviously something was very wrong. In every case the trouble was narrowed down to inefficient air filters. They had not been designed for the damp, humid climate in which we were operating. About 24 hours later our engineer officer, who was to say the least a resourceful man, came up with a temporary solution. He asked his wife for some sanitary towels and proceeded to fit them at the front of the air filter. When the engine of my aircraft was tested on the ground the result was perfect. Once he was really sure that everything was working well, the engineer officer asked me to test fly the aircraft once more.

Very much on the alert for trouble, I took off on purpose over the harbour so that if anything went wrong I could ditch in the sea. But the engine ran smoothly throughout the flight and I landed without incident. On my return, the engineer officer said, "Well, all we need now is a gross of sanitary towels to see us through until we can come up with a proper modification!"

"Who's going to buy them?" I asked bluntly, as I did not see myself going into a chemist and getting them.

"Well, that's your job!" said the engineer officer. "I'm much too busy here."

I consulted with John who, although less bashful than myself on matters relating to sex, felt very much the same as I did in this case.

"Tell you what," he said. "Let's get all the pilots together and draw lots. Whoever is the unlucky winner will have to do the job."

The lottery was held with great merriment. Inevitably, the unlucky winner was a fresh-faced young man whose mother and sisters had never even told him what a sanitary towel was. The squadron commander armed him with the necessary money drawn from the station fund and John and myself escorted him to a large chemist in the centre of Singapore. We pushed him through the door and wandered around the shelves at the same time remaining within earshot.

He approached the girl behind the counter.

"Can I help you, Sir?" she asked.

"Well," blushing. "Yes please miss. I want some sanitary towels," said our man.

"How many would you like?" asked the girl, looking only slightly surprised.

"One gross please miss," came the hushed reply, accompanied by an even deeper blush.

"What size do you want, Sir?" The girl was now looking definitely amused.

"I don't know miss. They're for Buffalos." At which point we took pity on our man and laughingly told the girl what it was all about. What is amazing is that, thereafter, we never had any further engine failure caused by faulty air filters.

Now the Buffalos started to roll out of the hangar and we commenced serious training. The sky over Singapore reverberated to the roar of Wright-Cyclone engines with which the Buffalos were fitted. Our neighbours over at Sembawang, flying the Swordfishes, became even more jealous. One morning six Swordfish in tight formation appeared over Kallang out of nowhere. As they passed over our hangar at about 100 feet we saw an object dropping from the leading aircraft. It hit the ground near the Buffalo hangar and we ran to see what it was. John reached it first and came walking back holding a message bag in his hand. We all crowded round whilst he took the message from the bag. Clearly written in bold capitals was the following.

Fighter boy, Fighter boy,
Rise and shine
Undo your top button
And shoot us a line

Tell us again
In Cyranos and Raffles
Of flack and ack ack
And the German Jagstaffles

Tell us again
Of that night black as ink
There you were on your back
And climbing like stink

Fighter boy, Fighter boy
Rise and shine
Undo your top button
And shoot us a line.

I seized the message and ran back to the office, at the same time shouting to the flight sergeant to get John's aircraft and my own ready to fly. Grabbing a piece of foolscap I printed the following:

Bomber boy, Bomber boy
We'll teach you to fly
But to shoot you a line
We're much too shy!

"John," I called, still writing, "we'll teach these bastards what flying's all about. We're going to drop this message back outside their hangar door just about whilst they're landing. Tight formation like theirs, but you and I will be inverted!"

We ran to our aircraft. Understanding the urgency, the flight sergeant had already started the engines of both aircraft. In tight formation we tore across the airfield and were hardly off the ground before we went into a steep left-hand climbing turn. It only took us a few minutes to cross the island to Sembawang and, as we approached the Swordfish airfield, we could see the six bombers preparing for their landing. I gave the sign to John and we flipped our aircraft into the inverted position. Hanging from our shoulder harness we dived for the hangar. Judging it to a nicety, I released the message bag and it hurtled to the ground.

"Break!" I yelled to John. We turned the right way up and climbed steeply away in opposite directions. As we turned back for Kallang I saw a single Swordfish flying across the island at about 2,000 feet. "John, do you see that Swordfish at twelve o'clock?" I called over the R/T.

"Roger," came his curt reply.

"Well, let's scare the shit out of him!" I called. "You go up and I'll go down. I'll call when to attack and we'll try to meet under his tail."

"Roger."

We judged our attack perfectly, almost too perfectly. With John diving from above and myself climbing steeply from below our paths crossed not more than twenty feet from the tail of the Swordfish. For one frightful moment I thought I had hit John's aircraft as a shudder passed through my Buffalo but was relieved that it was just the effect of the two slipstreams merging. As I flashed by the "enemy", the look of surprised horror on the face of the unsuspecting airman manning the gun in the rear cockpit of the Swordfish made the whole operation a success. Landing back at Kallang we strolled together back to the office. We agreed that honour had been satisfied.

This silly rivalry between ourselves and the other pilots on the island continued for some time. However, it was to lead to disaster, the scale of which was to bring these childish pranks to an abrupt end.

Also stationed at Kallang was a Blenheim squadron commanded by a pleasant Irishman called Sam Hackett. On March 16th 1941, Sam and myself were enjoying a drink in the Mess, and talking about how we missed "the auld sod". On the spur of the moment we decided to have dinner together the next evening to celebrate St Patrick's Day. We decided on the smart restaurant, Cyranos, and agreed to invite John and one of Sam's flight commanders as our guests.

The evening went well, the wine flowed freely and the conversation drifted naturally enough onto the merits of the different aircraft we were flying. "I've heard about your exploit over at Sembawang the other day," said Sam. "It sounds to me like a pretty nice bit of flying. But you boys needn't think that you're the only ones who can perform tricks in formation. I've never tried inverted formation in a Blenheim but I can tell you that we can do just about everything else."

"Come on Sam," I taunted. "Those old twin-engined tubs of yours aren't fit for anything more than wallowing round the sky dropping an odd bomb and scurrying for home."

"Bloody ignorant fighter boy," laughed Sam. "If you'd like to come flying with me in the morning, I'll show you what our 'twin-engined tubs' can do."

"You've got a deal," I replied. "If I could fit you into a Buffalo, I'd offer you a return trip." We drove home in Sam's car and when we reached the Mess Sam reminded me of our appointment.

"You on for the trip in the morning Tim?"

"Sure I am Sam," I replied. We arranged to meet at 10.00 a.m. in the morning, said goodnight and went off to our rooms.

The next morning, parachute over my shoulder, I walked out on to the tarmac. Sam and two of his pilots, together with their observers, were talking in a group beside the three Blenheims being prepared for flight. "Morning Tim," Sam greeted me. "Ready for action?"

"Sure am!"

"Let's get going then. Come with me Tim."

We climbed up on to the wing of Sam's Blenheim and I clambered through into the right-hand seat. Sam followed and seated himself on my left. I had not been in a Blenheim since I had flown one at Aston Down soon after leaving Cranwell, but the surroundings were familiar and I felt quite at home.

Sam pulled over a lever to turn on the petrol, pressed the start switch and the port engine sprung into life. In a moment the starboard engine was running as well. Looking round to check that the other two aircraft were ready to go, he raised his right hand above his head and waved it from side to side as a signal to the ground crew to pull away the chocks from in front of the wheels. He gently eased forward on his throttles and we started to move.

At that moment an airman, who I quickly recognized as a clerk from my office, came running onto the tarmac in front of us. He was waving his arms in a signal for us to stop. With a gesture of annoyance, Sam braked to a halt. The airman climbed onto the wing and Sam opened his door.

"Sorry, Sir!" shouted the airman above the noise of the engines. "There is a message from Air Headquarters that Flight Lieutenant Vigors is to go to the AOC's office immediately for an operational conference."

"Damn!" I cursed. "Why in the hell does he want me?"

Sam said that I had better go. "You can't keep an air marshal waiting."

"Hell, Sam," I said, "I was really looking forward to this trip."

"We'll do it another day," he shouted. "I can't wait to teach you fighter boys how to fly."

I got out of the Blenheim and, carrying my parachute, set off back to my office. I hadn't gone ten yards when I met John running towards me. "I heard what happened. Give me your parachute and I'll take your place," he laughed.

"OK, enjoy yourself." I turned and signalled to Sam to wait for John to join him.

The squadron commander was outside the office waiting impatiently. "Come on Tim. We're going to be late." In the car I asked him why this high powered conference needed me.

"Well, the AOC decided at the last moment that, as you have got more operational experience than anybody else around, he wanted you to sit in. He wants to discuss general defence tactics in the event of surprise attack."

We went straight into the AOC's office where about eight high-ranking officers were sitting round a table. The moment we were seated the meeting began. The air marshal had been talking for about five minutes, outlining the general tactical situation, when the door opened and his personal assistant, looking pale, hurried into the room.

"Sorry for interrupting, Sir. There is an important call for you coming through."

The air marshal lifted the telephone. He listened and became tense. A worried look came into his eyes.

"How many aircraft did you say?" he asked. Then, "My God, that's awful!" He listened for another couple of minutes. "Keep me informed," he said and replaced the telephone.

"There has been a terrible accident. Apparently three Blenheims, led by Squadron Leader Hackett, were trying to do a loop in formation. They collided on top of the loop. All three aircraft have crashed into the harbour and, at the moment, there don't appear to be any survivors. The air-sea rescue launch has left Kallang to search the area where the aircraft came down."

My heart felt as though it had stopped and I turned stone cold. My squadron commander was looking at me. "Are you alright Tim?" he murmured, breaking the stunned silence in the room.

"Oh, my God," was all I could reply, my mind in turmoil. Almost certainly John was dead, and Sam and his other pilots and their crews. And it was all my fault. It was I who, only last night, had playfully taunted Sam about "twin-engined tubs". Without that conversation this awful accident would never have happened. And it was I who, but for a freak of fate, would have been sitting beside Sam as the three aircraft collided. If the airman had run out ten seconds later we would have been on our way and almost certainly I would now be dead. I lowered my head into my hands and, silently and without tears, I wept.

The conference cancelled, we drove silently back to Kallang. Entering the office the clerk asked, "Have you heard the latest, Sir?"

"No, what's happened now?" asked the commanding officer.

"Well, we all heard a big explosion out in the harbour about 20 minutes ago. They say that the air-sea rescue launch hit a mine and blew up."

We drove down to the harbour and stopped alongside the pier from which the launch had left. Apparently what the clerk had heard was true. The immediate approaches of Singapore harbour had been recently mined against surprise attack from any enemy. In his excitement and hurry to get to the position where the aircraft had been seen to crash, the coxswain of the launch had evidently either forgotten or chosen to disregard this fact. Apparently, eleven people were on board the launch and all but three of them were killed in the explosion.

Of the survivors, none were from the Blenheims. John's body was picked up later that day. Evidently, he had tried to parachute from the aircraft and had hit the tailplane. He was practically decapitated.

In a daze, I made my way back towards the hangar. I could not help feeling largely responsible for the whole horrible disaster. And now I had to face up to John's death. We had grown close together over the long voyage and closer still since we had arrived in Singapore. We knew nearly everything about each other and had laughed a great deal. Now, like so many of my friends, John was dead.

When I got back to my office my New Zealand pilots crowded round me. I thanked them for their kindness and escaped into the privacy of my own office. Pilot Officer Pevreal, one of my New Zealand pilots with whom I had become quite close, came into the office. "What you need Tim," he said, "is a large, stiff drink. Come on over to the Mess with us."

Drinks were a temporary solace. I couldn't face lunch. Later that afternoon I told the flight sergeant to get my aircraft ready. Taking off towards the west I climbed out over the harbour. Below me a number of small boats were still milling around searching for wreckage and bodies. I flew on out to sea, glad to be alone with my thoughts. Sadness lay heavy on my shoulders but gradually as I climbed higher and higher into the clear sky I started to feel better. During the past year I had learned to live with death nearly every day. Nothing was to be gained by mourning too long over this latest tragedy. Suddenly my mother's words came back to me. She used to say whenever disaster struck, "On! On!"

I swung my Buffalo into a tight turn and dived back towards the land.

Thinking of my mother, it suddenly occurred to me that on March 22nd, four days hence, it would be my twentieth birthday.

On! On! It had to be.

CHAPTER
THIRTEEN

Prince of Wales
and Repulse

That summer of 1941 was to pass pleasantly and quickly. The dramatic events of my first weeks in Singapore were replaced by a smooth routine of intensive flying training by day and a busy social life after working hours.

Weekends, still largely spent as in peacetime, were for swimming, playing tennis or, for my part, racing sailing dinghys around the harbour. The Tanglin Club provided both social and sporting activities. The scars of the St Patrick's Day calamity gradually faded and, as so often happened during the war, previous friendships though never forgotten, were replaced by new ones.

The New Zealand pilots under my command quickly showed themselves to be apt pupils in the art of handling a fighter aircraft. One in particular quickly won my highest respect, both in the air and on the ground. His name was Pilot Sergeant Wipiti. He was a Maori and his features, so serious in repose, would quickly break into a smile that could light up any situation, no matter what.

An important part of the early flying training schedule was close formation flying. I liked to teach this art to my pilots individually. By doing so I could observe the qualities of each pilot within moments of being in the air and correct any inherent faults before they became too pronounced.

I viewed my first flight with Wipiti with a certain degree of trepidation. I had never had a black man close to me in the air before but was quickly to learn that the colour of a man's skin in no way affects his ability to fly a high-speed aircraft.

That first morning we took off early in a loose formation, so that our two aircraft were about fifty yards apart. Having reached a height of 1,000 feet I turned along the coast and told Wipiti to close in on me. Within a moment he was tucked in beside me with his wing tip nearly inside my own. Flying straight and level I then started a gentle turn. Wipiti never budged an inch. His position was rock solid. I quickly realised that I had somebody special flying beside me. For half an hour we flew around, climbing and diving gently and executing some easy turns. Wipiti maintained his position throughout these manoeuvres with an accuracy which was exceptional for a pilot undertaking a first exercise of this kind.

Back on the ground I congratulated Wipiti on his flying. "Thank you, Sir," he grinned. "I enjoyed that half hour as much as anything I have done since I started flying."

The following morning we were in the air again. This time Wipiti's wing tip was solidly lodged well within my own and, despite the fact that I tightened up the turns and speeded up changes to our manoeuvres, he stuck beside me like a limpet. We then changed our position into line astern, which meant that his propeller was positioned right under my tailplane. Glancing back I could see the tip of his wing, below and behind me. He continued to hold his position as accurately as he had done when he was flying beside me.

I felt like doing some aerobatics before I landed. I told Wipiti that I wanted to fling my aircraft round a bit and that he could go and do the same if he wanted to. Free of our formation, I dived steeply and completed a couple of quick loops followed by a roll off the top. I was just about to wing into a slow roll when I caught sight of the wing of another Buffalo, and then the penny dropped. My friend Wipiti was still with me! Instead of obeying my order to break away he had stuck with me and followed me through the violent manoeuvres which I had just completed. He had held his position perfectly. No mean feat, even for a pilot with five times his experience.

"What the hell are you doing, Wipiti?," I yelled over the intercom. "I told you to break away and go home!"

"I didn't hear you, Sir," came the reply.

"Well you can go home now," I said and watched as he peeled off and dived back towards Kallang. "That," I said to myself, "is one hell of a pilot and I want him close when the action starts."

Later that day I asked Wipiti why he had not broken away when I told him to. "There must have been a fault in my intercom, Sir," he said. His broad grin split his face from ear to ear. My wish to have him with me never materialised. By the time the Japanese attacked Malaya, I had been posted to Sembawang to take command of an Australian squadron. But Wipiti fought with distinction in 243 Squadron during the Singapore battle and then escaped to Java on a small merchant ship. Halfway there the boat was sunk and Wipiti, along with the other survivors, spent two days on a life raft before being picked up by a destroyer.

I next ran across him in Karachi. "Can you help me, Sir?" he asked me. "I want to get back into action quick." By that time I was a squadron leader and, using my influence, I arranged for Wipiti to join a Hurricane squadron in Burma. At the same time I also recommended him for a commission, which he was subsequently granted.

In Delhi, nine months later, when I was acting staff officer in charge of flying training at Air Headquarters, Wipiti had somehow heard where I was. He had got 48 hours leave from his squadron in Burma and bummed a ride back on a transport aircraft to come and see me. I congratulated him on his pilot officer's stripes.

"Great to see you again, Wipiti. I hear you've been knocking quite a few Japs out of the sky."

"I've been been lucky enough to get three since I've been in Burma. But then it is easier in a Hurricane than it was in a Buffalo."

"What can I do for you?" I asked, "apart from taking you out to lunch."

"Well, I am in an awkward situation." Wipiti looked serious for the first time. "From time to time we get leave in India and I find that, because of the colour of my skin, I am not allowed into half the clubs and restaurants which the other boys like to frequent. This has never happened to me before in New Zealand."

I told him that I was sorry. "It is just bloody ridiculous, but I don't think there's much that I can do to help you."

"Yes there is," he countered. "That's why I have come to see you. You can get me posted back to England. There I won't be treated like I have been here and anyway I wouldn't mind having a stab at some of those Germans."

It was only then that I realised how deeply upset he was by what was happening to him. I took him out and gave him a good lunch and then shook him once more by the hand and bade him goodbye. Later on, by pulling a few strings, his posting to England was arranged. I got word to a good friend of mine in 11 Group telling him what a fine pilot this Maori was and asking him to make sure that Wipiti got to a good squadron.

Wipiti fought the Germans just as well as he had the Japanese. Flying offensive sweeps over France, which were by then the order of the day, he shot down four or five enemy aircraft and was later awarded the DFC for his courage and daring. One morning, about a year after he had arrived in England, he was diving onto some Messerschmitt 109s which were threatening to attack a formation of American bombers carrying out a daylight raid on a target in France. During the ensuing fight a 109, trying to avoid the fire from another

Hurricane, collided with Wipiti's aircraft and the two plunged earthwards locked together. So ended the life of a very brave Maori man.

During my time in Singapore, I was lucky enough to become friendly with the Murray family. Group Captain Murray, a somewhat austere figure who hid a kind heart under a severe facade, was senior RAF accountant officer.

Murray's wife, Rachel, was no more or less than a saint. Seldom have I met anybody who combined sympathy and understanding with so much realism and humour. The Murray home became open house every weekend for all the family's many friends. It was situated on the waterfront around the corner from Singapore harbour. The three daughters, Barbara, Elspeth and Jan, all of whom had found themselves various jobs on the island, lived at home.

The Murray's only son, Thomas, or "Tucker" as the family called him, was away in England busy fighting the war in Bomber Command. He had passed out of Cranwell just before I arrived and was to become one of the bravest and most distinguished bomber pilots of the war. He completed tour after tour of operational flying, on Wellingtons, Hampdens and finally Lancasters, steadfastly refusing to take a rest. By the end of the war he was smothered in decorations which included just about everything except the VC. If truth be told he probably deserved that high accolade as well. His combination of bravery and obstinancy was of the type that usually brought a violent end. But what saved Tucker from death, time and time again, was his incredible natural ability to handle an airplane in all conditions and circumstances.

Some years later, when I was commanding a night-fighter station at Castle Camps in Essex, Tucker was looking after three squadrons of Lancasters at nearby Stradishall in Suffolk. On the day after the Germans finally surrendered, and VE day had been announced, I telephoned Tucker. At that time I was married to his sister, Jan, and wanted him to come over and have dinner with us.

During our conversation I asked, "What do you think of the peace Tucker?"

He paused for some time to consider my question. Then, after a moment, "Well, I really don't know old boy," he replied, "trade is falling off a bit isn't it?" Surely, that has to be one of the classic remarks of the war!

The two younger sisters were both engaged, Jan to a Blenheim pilot, and Elspeth to an army officer. Although I continued to visit the Murray household, I had to look further afield for feminine company. This presented no problem as there were plenty of pretty unattached girls in Singapore. I decided to play the field for a bit and had plenty of fun doing so.

Later that summer my flight was sent on detachment for three weeks to an airfield at Kota Baharu, in those days a little settlement on the bank of a big river where it flowed into the sea. As matters turned out this was the very spot the Japanese chose to make their first landing in Malaya later that year. It was a delightfully quiet and beautiful little place, bordered on one side by wide sandy beaches and on the other by lush green jungle in which exotic birds flitted through the colourful undergrowth.

To begin with Kota Baharu was a pleasant enough change from the bustling life of Singapore but there was not a great deal to do and when the order came to return to Singapore it was welcomed by everybody. Not long after my return, I was called to Air Headquarters for an interview with the AOC. Three months previously, a Buffalo squadron had been formed at Sembawang. In this unit, 453 Squadron, all the pilots and the ground crew were Australians. There had apparently been a certain amount of trouble within the squadron, caused mostly by personality clashes, and the AOC told me he was not happy with the progress which was being made with the training programme. He asked me if I thought I could lick it into shape. I told him I would be honoured to do so. I did not tell him that some sixth sense told me I might be letting myself in for a tough job. I was still only a flight lieutenant and promotions had to be confirmed by the Air Ministry in London. This would take some time. I would therefore be taking on the job holding only the same rank as my two flight commanders. As I was subsequently to learn, I was not only the only non-Australian in the entire squadron but also, as it turned out, the youngest pilot in the squadron.

With regret I said farewell to Pevreal, Wipiti and the rest of my New Zealanders of whom I had grown so fond, packed my bags and headed for Sembawang.

I was greeted in a casual way by my adjutant, who showed me into my new office. I asked him to summon the two flight commanders. After an unnecessarily long delay these two officers, upon whom I would have to rely so much, slouched through the door. No sign of a salute from either of them as, without so much as a by your leave, they collapsed into two chairs. One of them raised his legs and settled his feet on the other side of my desk.

"Well mate," said the one with his feet up, "what brings you here?"

I made a quick decision. "What I'm here for," I began quietly, "is, first, to teach you how to fly. Second, I'm here to teach you how to fight. From your behaviour so far, it would appear that the other job I've got on hand is to teach you buggers some manners. Now, both of you, kindly get your fat arses off those chairs and get out of my office."

"We didn't mean no offence cobber," one of them said.

"I don't mind what you meant," I said. "Just get out." Without further ado they removed themselves.

"My God," I thought to myself. "I hope I'm playing this the right way." I called in the adjutant.

"I want every man in the squadron on parade, on the airfield, in exactly one hour's time." I then added, "Also, I want an aircraft ready for me to fly immediately."

An hour later I was pleased to see that my orders had been obeyed. The whole squadron was drawn up in two lines in front of the hangars and a couple of ground crew were standing beside a Buffalo. I walked over to it and climbed in.

Without further ado I took off and as I started to climb I turned the Buffalo on its back and went into a climbing turn, upside down. For the next ten minutes I put on a show of aerobatics, mostly very low to the ground, which to this day scares me when I think about it. Finally I dived so low over the lines of troops that they all instinctively ducked. I pulled up into a loop and as I reached the inverted position I switched off the engine. Then, in a steep, sideslipping turn I brought the Buffalo back over the airfield boundary with the propeller being turned over only by the wind and touched down heading straight for the parade. As my speed dropped, the propeller stopped turning. About thirty yards from the line of men I stood on the brakes. The tail came up in the air and the aircraft came to a halt not more than ten yards from where the squadron was standing.

Without a word, I got down from the aircraft. Passing the adjutant I said, "You can dismiss the parade." I stalked off to my office and sat down once more behind my desk. Ten minutes later there was a knock on my door.

"Come in." My two flight commanders entered, stood smartly to attention and saluted.

"I'm sorry, Sir," one of them said. "We got you wrong. We thought you were just another pommie bastard who'd been sent here to interfere with us. That was the greatest display of flying any of us have seen. We want to let you know that we're behind you, Sir."

"Well," I laughed, "I'm not a pommie, I'm an Irishman. Now, sit down the two of you and let's start talking about how we're going to turn 453 Squadron into the best fighting force on the island. By the way, my name's Tim."

It had been the most blatant piece of showing off. But it was a calculated gamble and it had paid off. From that moment on, I had every man in the squadron behind me. And what a fine lot of people they turned out to be. The next two months were taken up with intensive flying training, spurred on by rumours that the Japanese were about to enter the war. I was satisfied with the progress which we were making and was confident that when the moment came I would have a well-organised force behind me.

These rumours intensified throughout the autumn. One morning, in the middle of November, when I was testing a new aircraft which had just been assembled, I saw below me, steaming up the Johore Straight, two battleships with their escorting destroyers on either side. We were later to learn that these two great ships were *Prince of Wales* and *Repulse* and would be based at the naval base near Sembawang.

The arrival of these two ships, in particular *Prince of Wales*, had a double effect on the population of Singapore. First, it made everybody realise that the threat of war in their area must now be very real. Why else would the pride of the British Navy have been sent to Malaya? Second, it gave most people's confidence a boost, out of all proportion to what the presence of a couple of battleships could realistically mean. But the feeling that Britannia ruled the waves was still a very real one. With these two battleships to protect Singapore, why would anyone worry about their own security?

A couple of days later I was called to Air Headquarters and told that my squadron had been appointed Fleet Defence Squadron. I was told to work out how to defend the battleships against attack from the air should they be sailing in the vicinity of the Malayan coast. I was to report back with my plan as soon as possible.

I called in my two flight commanders and together we worked out a schedule of patrols which would allow us to keep at least six aircraft over the fleet during all daylight hours, as long as they stayed within sixty miles of the Malayan coastline. To make this plan work, we must have reasonable notice of the battleships' departure as we would have to deploy at least six, and depending on the movement of the fleet possibly more, aircraft to airfields up the coast. These would include Kuantan halfway up the east coast and also Kota Baharu should the fleet move to the far north.

I submitted this plan to Air Headquarters and it met with approval. I was told to go to the naval base and meet the air liaison officer on board *Prince of Wales*. The following day, on board the battleship, I spent an hour discussing my plan with a number of officers. The plan seemed to have the general blessing of Admiral Phillips's staff. Call signs and radio frequencies were exchanged so that there would be no problem with communications between the ships and ourselves. In short, everything seemed satisfactory.

At the squadron, I briefed all my pilots on our new role. I also pointed out that, should the Japanese declare war and the battleships put to sea and come under attack, it was very unlikely that any enemy bombers would have the luxury of a fighter escort. The range involved would be too great. I stressed the extreme importance of the part we must play in defending the fleet and the necessity of pressing home any attack without regard for our own safety.

The Japanese attack on Pearl Harbor in December 1941 was a bombshell. The next morning we heard that Japanese troops were making a landing at Kota Baharu. Suddenly, once more, the war was upon us. Anticipating the departure of the fleet, 453 Squadron was placed on readiness. But no order was received to go ahead with our plans for deploying aircraft to our planned advance bases. Then, without warning, I heard from a Blenheim pilot who happened to land at Sembawang that the fleet had put to sea. He told me that he had seen the ships sailing through the Johore Straights.

It had been agreed earlier, at my meeting on the battleship, that we should be told of any impending departure to enable us to put our deployment plans into action. But, I repeat, no such warning was received.

In the RAF, we had an expression which we used in order to describe any chain of disastrous events. Such unfortunate circumstances were called SABU. These letters stood for Self Adjusting Balls Up. There is surely no expression which could better describe the sinking of *Prince of Wales* and *Repulse*.

Having heard that the ships had left port, I immediately queried with Air Headquarters whether any request had been received from them for air cover. The answer was no. I was told to keep my squadron at readiness during daylight hours and that everybody was to be on half an hour's call at night. I asked whether I should go ahead with sending aircraft to our planned advance bases and was told that the entire squadron was to stay put for the moment. We waited. On the following day nothing happened. We remained at readiness.

"Why the bloody hell haven't we been allowed to send aircraft to Kuantan?" I commented to one of my flight commanders.

Still we waited for yet another day. On the third day after the fleet had put to sea, we got word that we might be told to scramble. I ordered all pilots into their aircraft. We waited for another half an hour. Then, over the radio, came our orders.

"The battleships *Prince of Wales* and *Repulse* are under heavy attack from Japanese torpedo bombers. Their position is about fifty miles off Kuantan. You are to get there as quickly as possible and render whatever assistance you can."

The entire squadron scrambled. Time was obviously of vital importance so, having taken off, I did not wait to get everybody into formation but straightaway headed for the north with throttle wide open.

I issued my orders. "Follow me and catch up if you can. If necessary, we'll get into formation before we reach the scene of the action."

Climbing to 3,000 feet, I set course for a point east of Kuantan and flew northwards at full speed. Looking over my shoulder I could see the rest of my aircraft strung out behind me. After flying for forty minutes, objects in the sea on the horizon could be seen. As I drew closer, the objects gradually became one large ship and several smaller ones. I searched ahead for any sign of enemy aircraft but the sky was empty. I eased back on the throttle to allow the rest of the squadron to catch up. By this time we were only a few miles from the ships and as we drew nearer the full scale of the disaster gradually sunk home.

The first thing that struck me was that there was no sign of *Repulse*. But a large patch of oil spreading over the water suggested where she might have been. *Prince of Wales* listed badly and was down at the stern. A destroyer was lying alongside her bows, obviously trying to take men off her decks. Suddenly her bows rose in the air nearly knocking over the destroyer. Then, like an enormous whale, she started to slide backwards beneath the gentle waves which were lapping at her sides. *Prince of Wales* was gone.

At one moment the great battleship, said to be unsinkable, was there in front of my eyes and the next moment there was nothing on the surface but the accompanying destroyer, which had by now righted itself, and a mass of oil and bubbles.

Whilst watching this dramatic sight I was also keeping my eyes skinned for any sign of the enemy. But apart from ourselves there was not another aircraft in sight. I gave orders to my flight commanders to get their own aircraft into loose formation and for one of them to patrol the area at 3,000 feet and for the other to climb and patrol at double that height. I also gave them instructions to throttle right back to conserve fuel so that we could stay at the scene for as long as possible.

I myself dived down to get a closer look at the devastation. I could now see that the sea was full of struggling bodies. Some people were being picked up by two destroyers and lifeboats. Others just clung to debris. As I flew over many waved their hands at me. I was so moved by this that I subsequently, and rather stupidly, wrote to the admiral in Singapore giving him a first-hand account of the bravery of his men and mentioned the fact that many had waved at me. Apparently I was being a little over enthusiastic about these gestures. I heard later that the waving hands did not denote friendship but were in fact fists clenched in anger at the fact that the RAF had not been there to protect them in the first place. They were not to know that this lack of air support was not the fault of the air force at all.

There was still no sign of the enemy and it gradually became evident that after wreaking their destruction the Japanese bombers had departed the scene. But I was determined to stay there as long as possible in order to protect the helpless survivors in the event of even a few Japanese returning to confirm what damage they had done. I started calculating when the squadron must return to base if we were not to run out of fuel. We were in fact well south of Kuantan and I therefore decided to send them home rather than to divert to another airfield. But I was loathe to leave the scene myself so, having given orders for the rest to go home, I continued to patrol the area just in case the enemy reappeared.

Eventually I had to leave. With a final circle over the carnage I headed west for the coast. I knew of a little airstrip just inland and gingerly headed for it, with my engine turning over only just fast enough to maintain height. My fuel gauge was showing empty long before I crossed the coast and every minute I expected the engine to cut out.

With relief, I saw the airstrip ahead of me as I crossed the coast and at that moment my engine spluttered and stopped. Luckily, I had just enough height to glide down and scrape over the trees at the end of the strip. With a dead prop I rolled to a stop.

A truck drove out to meet me and find out what the devil was going on. I quickly explained and asked to be taken immediately to a telephone. I got through to Air Headquarters and was connected to the AOC. I explained exactly what had happened and what I had seen. He told me to come straight away to see him when I got back to base. My aircraft was refuelled and thirty minutes later I was back at Sembawang and in a car on my way to headquarters.

"Why in the world didn't they ask for continual air cover?" I asked the Air Vice-Marshal.

"Your guess is as good as mine Vigors," he replied, "but I think that certain elements in the navy have still not come to terms with the importance of air cover."

During the next two days, gradually, the story of what had happened came out. Despite the fact that I had guaranteed to maintain a continuous daylight cover of six aircraft, the naval commander seemed to disregard this protection when he left port. On the morning of the second day the two battleships were picked up by a Japanese spotter plane who shadowed them out of gunshot range throughout the daylight hours. One of the reasons which was later given for the failure to call for air cover was the fact that the commander did not want to break radio silence. But as they were already being shadowed, to my mind, his excuse doesn't hold much water.

At this vital time, when the navy knew that an air attack must be imminent, I could not only have had at least six aircraft over them but I could also have called for the assistance of my old friends, 243 Squadron. I had arranged for them to act as a back-up should matters look like hotting up. In other words, by using an advance base I could probably have had at least twelve aircraft covering the fleet at the time they were attacked.

The Japanese attacks employed waves of torpedo bombers. These aircraft were slow and vulnerable and, because of the extreme range from which they were operating, were not escorted by any fighters. Of course, even with twelve aircraft we would have been outnumbered but, with no fighter escort to worry about, we could have completely disrupted the attack. With the Japanese willing to adopt suicide tactics if necessary there is no doubt that both battleships would have suffered damage. *Repulse*, which carried considerably less armour plating round her hull than *Prince of Wales*, might even have been sunk. But the flagship, which was capable of taking terrible punishment before collapsing below the waves, would undoubtedly have been saved and would have been able to have limped back to port.

The presence of those two battleships in the area at that time was probably of more psychological importance than tactical, both to the enemy and to ourselves. Their sinking undoubtedly had a worse effect on the morale of the Allies than any event since the evacuation of Dunkirk. For the Japanese it meant that they had not only destroyed the core of the American Pacific Fleet at Pearl Harbor but had now also sunk the cream of the British Navy. No wonder their tails were high as their troops poured ashore on the beaches around Kota Baharu.

The sinking of *Prince of Wales* and *Repulse* finally brought home to the navy the absolutely vital necessity of support from the air. But the lesson was an expensive one to learn.

I started this sad story by describing the episode as a "SABU". As a footnote there is one final factor, revealed to me later, which makes it tally even more with this description. It appears that Admiral Phillips never called for air support. It was the captain of *Repulse* who broke radio silence as his ship was sinking. That signal, sent to Naval HQ in Singapore, took nearly one hour to reach me sitting at readiness in my Buffalo three miles away!

That evening as I sat looking back on the events of the day, I started reflecting on the blunders which had led up to what must live in history as one of the greatest defeats ever suffered by the Royal Navy. As commanding officer of the squadron whose job it was to defend the fleet I could not but feel a degree of personal responsibility for what had occurred. But what, I asked myself, could I have done, to change the path of those events? Had I failed to attend to some detail? Had I neglected to allow for some unforeseen contingency? No matter how hard I tried I could not, from the facts at my disposal, arrive at any reason to blame myself for the disaster.

As there was no more fleet to protect, the role of 453 Squadron had become superfluous. Obviously, we would now become integrated into the general air defence plan for Malaya itself.

During the next couple of days I had to attend several war conferences at various headquarters. Here information became available that allowed me to form a reasonably clear picture of what had actually occured during the fateful voyage of *Prince of Wales* and *Repulse*. It was then that I resolved to sit down and write, for the record, a full report on what had occurred. What I have written in this chapter about those events is taken from the notes I made at the time.

311

However, the full report was never written as, no sooner had I made that resolution, than orders came through for the squadron to move north the next morning. We were tasked to help defend the army from Japanese air attacks. All thoughts of report writing quickly left my mind.

After making their first beach landings at Kota Baharu the Japanese ground forces quickly advanced down the Malayan peninsula. Expertly trained in jungle warfare, they were able to outflank the British forces with continual pincer movements thereby cutting supply routes. Harrowed by these encircling tactics, and subjected to an increasing number of attacks from the air, the British and their allies had little alternative but to retreat.

Now the squadron moved again, this time some 200 miles north to Kuala Lumpur. I was told that on arrival more orders would be issued. With our ground crew following on by road, we flew our aircraft into Kuala Lumpur during the evening. First thing the next morning I received orders to take six of my aircraft to Butterworth, the airfield which lay on the mainland opposite Penang Island. Little did I know, when I took off that morning, that within an hour I would be hanging from a parachute, looking straight into the blazing guns of two Japanese fighter aircraft.

CHAPTER
FOURTEEN

To Java

The bandages had been removed from my hands and arms. The burnt skin was a livid red but the pain and most of the itching had gone. My fingers were very stiff and I couldn't hold a pen properly but I could extract a cigarette from its packet without assistance and even light it. My fingernails, all of which had been burnt off, had started to grow again.

The evacuation had landed me in Johore Hospital. As I walked up and down the ward I was getting stronger. The hole in my leg had completely healed and the act of walking now gave me no pain. I still weighed less than ten stone, nearly three stone less than my normal weight, but I was very definitely on the mend. News from the war front was very bad. The Japanese had continued their relentless advance down the peninsula. Kuala Lumpur had long since fallen into their hands and their forward troops were now less than 100 miles from Singapore.

One day the medical officer in charge of the hospital entered the ward and asked for silence. "I regret to tell you all that, owing to the proximity of enemy troops, it has been decided that this hospital must be evacuated.

All those of you who are capable of walking and not in need of further immediate medical attention will be asked to make your own way to Singapore where you should report to your headquarters. For those who are unable to do so arrangements have been made for transport to Singapore by ambulance. We are aiming to have everybody away by this time tomorrow. Goodbye to those of you who I will not be seeing again and good luck."

Doctors came through the wards deciding who could be discharged and who would still be treated as invalids. I was pleased when I was told that I could make my own way. Whilst I had been in Singapore I had made good friends with Pim Droogleever, a sophisticated man about town who had an important job in insurance in the city. I had often been to dinner at his house and had on occasions stayed overnight with him. He had come to see me in hospital a week before and had told me that if I wanted a roof over my head when I came out of hospital I could treat his house as my home. I telephoned Pim and told him what the state of play was. He said that he would come and pick me up immediately.

He was as good as his word and, an hour later, I was in his car heading for his home which was situated in the middle of Singapore Island. It was great to be out of hospital and free to move again. I felt a bit weak but otherwise fine.

The next day was Sunday and Pim stayed at home for the day. We discussed the war and watched some Japanese bombers crossing the island to the west of us, heading for the city. Some Buffalos were climbing to attack them. We cheered when the leading fighter opened fire and black smoke poured from the engine of one of the bombers. I wondered who the pilot of the Buffalo was and whether it was one of my friends. The next moment the crunch of bombs reached us and we saw columns of smoke rising from the direction of the city.

After lunch we were sitting drinking our coffee when once again we heard the drone of approaching aircraft. Looking out of the window to the north I saw a formation of about twelve Japs heading straight towards us. This time several Buffalos had managed to climb above them and were diving on them out of the sun. It was clear that the bombers were going to pass straight over us and, with memories of the stray bomb which a German aircraft under attack had jettisoned onto my favourite Norfolk pub, I suggested to Pim that it would be prudent to take cover. He agreed and, for want of anywhere better, we crawled under the dining room table. We heard the enemy aircraft pass overhead amongst the stutter and crackle of machine-gun fire. At that moment a pair of black clad legs appeared close to my nose and started circling the table. Pim's Chinese servant, unperturbed by events, was clearing away lunch. With some embarrassment I stuck my head out and suggested that he take cover.

"No necessary, Sah," said the Chinaman coolly, "Jap aircraft now passed over." Feeling somewhat foolish, Pim and I resumed our coffee.

315

Pim was of the opinion that whilst the Japanese were quite likely to reach the northern shores of the Johore Straight reasonably soon, there was no way that they would be able to invade Singapore Island itself. I told him that I thought that he was being unduly optimistic. "If you're not doing a job with the defence forces, you better start thinking now of how to get off this damned island, Pim" I advised. "I really don't think they'll let me do any more fighting for the moment, but I can tell you one thing for sure, in the next couple of days I've only got one priority and that's to find some way of getting out!"

The next morning I thanked Pim for his hospitality and took a lift with him into town. I patted him on the shoulder; my hands weren't up to a handshake yet. "Remember what I said about looking for an escape route. I don't believe those bloody Japs are going to make very good hosts."

"I'll be OK," Pim reassured me, "you take care of yourself."

I was not to see Pim again for a very long time. Reluctant to make any move to leave his beloved Singapore, he was still sitting there when the city was captured. He spent the next four years in an internment camp. The next time I saw him was in Ireland where he had come to officiate as godfather at the christening of one of my daughters. "Tim, you were damn right about the quality of the Japanese as hosts," he told me. "The bastards killed most of my friends and if I had not been very strong physically and mentally resilient they would have seen the end of me too."

When I left Pim and went into Singapore itself, I reported to Air Headquarters. They advised me to try for one of the numerous boats now evacuating civilian and non-operational service personnel from the island. I was given a pass showing that I was on indefinite sick leave and asking other service personnel to give me assistance.

"Where shall I make for?" I asked the personnel officer.

"You'd better make for Australia," he told me, "and if you manage to get there in one piece make your way to the headquarters of the RAAF in Sydney."

I accepted these rather vague orders with a fair degree of resignation. I went to the guardroom gate and bummed a ride into town. I decided to treat myself to a good lunch at Raffles and then start looking for a boat in the harbour with a spare berth. I sat down at the long bar and ordered a gin and tonic. A man wearing a Quantas Airways uniform sat down beside me. His face was vaguely familiar.

"I know that we have met somewhere," I said, "but I can't think where."

He looked at me for some time. "Are you Tim Vigors?" he queried.

"Yes I am. What's left of Tim Vigors that is!" I laughed.

"I'll tell you where we met. We played squash together at the Tanglin Club about two months ago. We had a good game but you beat me." Now I remembered him. He was the captain of a flying boat that Quantas ran between Singapore and Sydney. I told him briefly

317

what had happened to me and how I had got to Singapore. "I wouldn't have much hope of beating you now," I said.

"You're bloody lucky to be alive," he responded.

"The devil looks after his own. Let's have lunch."

During lunch I asked him if his flying boat was still in service. "Well, yes, it is in a way. It's turned into a straight evacuation run. Instead of Singapore to Sydney we just go to Darwin and then come straight back again. I got in here last night and was supposed to return with a full load first thing this morning. But we had a bit of trouble with one of the motors and the maintenance guys wanted a day to work on it. We're now aiming to leave tomorrow."

"You wouldn't by any chance have a spare seat?" I asked him. "I'm supposed to get to Australia and have been told to try and get on a boat. But I'd a hell of a lot rather go there on a flying boat!" I showed him my leave pass.

He considered for a moment. "I'm afraid we are chockablock Tim, as far as passengers go. But I'll tell you what," he continued, "if you don't mind a bit of discomfort, you can squash in with us on the flight deck."

"Thanks a million," I responded quickly, "you've just got yourself another crew member." We finished our lunch and he told me where his flying boat was moored. "See you tomorrow," he said. "You'd better be there at first light."

"Don't worry, I won't over sleep, I'll be there."

As I left Raffles I ran into Jan Murray. We stopped and chatted for a bit. I enquired after her family and her fiance. For one reason and another they had broken off their engagement. In the meantime her sister Barbara, whom I had been rather keen on, in what now seemed a long time ago, had got herself engaged to a major in the Sappers. Father and mother were both well. Her father, together with a number of other RAF non-operational headquarters staff had been posted to Java and they were all due to leave on an evacuation ship the next day.

I told Jan I had been lucky and had just got myself a ride on a flying boat to Australia. As we parted company and I watched her walk away, I thought her fiance must be a bloody fool. What a lovely girl she was.

That afternoon I got myself to Sembawang to pick up my things. My Quantas friend had told me to travel light as the aircraft would already be taking off heavily overloaded. My room had not been occupied since I had left it six weeks before and I looked with regret at my piano accordion which had been with me since I was a child. Throwing bare essentials into a carrier bag, I sadly said goodbye to the rest of my possessions and headed back for Singapore.

During lunch at Raffles I had booked a room for that evening. As I entered the hotel, the air-raid warning was wailing. Looking up, I saw a formation of Japanese bombers at about 10,000 feet over the harbour. Anti-aircraft shells were bursting around them. Then I saw plumes of water shoot into the air as the bombs dropped in a cluster onto a group of ships. Flames sprung from the deck of one of them.

Six Buffalos now appeared and dived into the attack. Two bombers dropped away from the formation with black smoke pouring from their engines. One Buffalo burst into flames and plunged towards the sea. I watched for any sign of a parachute but none appeared. I wondered which one of my friends was in the aircraft. I was half inclined to make my way out to Kallang to touch base with my New Zealanders and find out how they had been faring. But the day had taken its toll and I was starting to feel shaky and totally exhausted. I decided that a night on the town would do me more harm than good and walked into the hotel.

The evening was just getting going and someone was playing a piano in the bar area. A mixed group of service personnel and civilians were clustered around the bar drinking. Some couples were dancing. The last time I had spent an evening like this in Raffles the war had seemed far away. The environment then had radiated a luxurious and tranquil stateliness like that to be found in the foyers of top-class hotels the world over. Now the mood had changed, to one of devil may care, but contrived, gaiety.

If the penny had dropped as to how serious the situation had become these people were determined not to show their anxiety. I would have liked to join in the fun but felt too tired. I contented myself with one drink at the bar, a quick dinner by myself and then bed.

I had asked to be called at 5.30a.m. and managed to struggle out of bed in the dark when I heard the porter knock on my door. He had brought me a welcome cup of tea and, after a quick bath and shave, I paid my bill and was soon in a taxi on the way to the harbour.

I had no difficulty locating the Quantas flying boat but was disappointed to see that there were still mechanics working on one of the engines. A group of hopeful passengers were waiting on the quayside and we were soon told that the flight would be delayed another three hours. However, we eventually got airborne at 11.00 a.m. and set our course for Sourabaya on the south-east coast of Java.

I sat on the floor of the flight deck for most of the long flight but the second pilot and engineer took pity on me from time to time and swapped places with me. Sitting in the second pilot's seat as the big aircraft lumbered southwards was a delight. To be once more in the cockpit of an aircraft, even such an unfamiliar animal as this enormous flying boat, was wonderful. The captain let me fly the aircraft from time to time. It took me a few moments to get used to the heavy, sluggish controls but it was good to feel an aircraft once more responding to my actions.

We landed outside the harbour at Sourabaya just before darkness fell and passengers and crew were all taken in a bus to a comfortable hotel. I had dinner with the captain and his crew and slipped off early to bed. The next morning whilst I was sitting at breakfast a British army officer came to our table and addressed the captain.

"I hear that you are departing for Darwin in the next couple of hours. It is of utmost importance that I should get to Australia as quickly as possible. I must ask you to offload one of your passengers and allow me to travel in his stead. Here are my orders issued by the Commander-in-Chief." It was then I noticed the badges of rank on the officer's uniform. He was a general.

The captain studied the document the general had handed to him. "Alright, Sir," he said. "I will have to find somebody who is willing to give up his place. The bus will be leaving here for the harbour in one hour's time. I look forward to seeing you on board."

The general thanked him and walked back to his table. The quick decision I then made was to prove one of the luckiest I ever made in my life. "Look," I said to the captain, "don't bother to worry any of the other passengers. I'm in no real rush to get to Australia and am perfectly willing to stay in this pleasant spot for a couple of days. I'd be grateful though if you could leave word for the next of your aircraft which passes through here to give me a lift."

"Thanks a lot, Tim," said my friend, "that's a great help. Of course, I'll give instructions about your onward journey."

Later that evening we heard that the flying boat had been shot down by Japanese carrier-based fighters, one hour out of Sourabaya. There were no survivors. As it happened, I was sharing a table for dinner with some American navy pilots. They told me that their squadron had lost two Catalina flying boats that day in the same area. "I guess life's just too short to cry," said one of them.

Death had come uncomfortably close to me many times during the past year, including my incredibly lucky escape that morning.

"Yes," I agreed with the American pilot, "I believe you're right. Life is too short to cry. Let's have another drink."

While we were finishing our drinks, I thought about my mother and how she probably would have put it another way.

She would have said, "On, on Tim! But hide the tears."

Also available in ISIS Large Print:

Evader

Denys Teare

"Bale out! Bale out!" came the urgent order over the intercom, and I knew that a moment far more dangerous and exciting than anything I had yet experienced was close at hand.

From the moment he landed in Occupied France, after bailing out of his burning Lancaster bomber, Denys Teare was a wanted man — an evader behind enemy lines. He could have chosen to surrender to the occupying forces, and see out the war as a prisoner. Instead he went underground, sheltered by patriots to whom the very presence of this aviateur anglais could be an automatic death sentence. Soon he became an active member of the Resistance and then, as the Allied forces advanced across France, came the greatest danger of all . . .

ISBN 978-0-7531-9450-8 (hb)
ISBN 978-0-7531-9451-5 (pb)

Dangerous Devotion

Christopher Portway

"In silence we watched her go, a slight figure pushing her bicycle. I was convinced, even then, that meeting her had changed the course of my life."

As a prisoner-of-war, 20-year-old Christopher Portway found himself a virtual slave in the mines of Silesia, working for the Nazis in the most inhumane conditions imaginable. A born survivor, Christopher escaped three times, and it was during his second period on the run that he met Anna, the daughter of a Czech family who offered him shelter.

Although determined to be together after the turmoil of the war, Anna and Christopher found their plans thwarted as the Iron Curtain descended to divide Europe. But Christopher refused to give up the thought of being with Anna, and in a show of remarkable resilience, spent the next ten years risking everything in order to reach her.

ISBN 978-0-7531-9434-8 (hb)
ISBN 978-0-7531-9435-5 (pb)

Men of the Bombers

Ralph Barker

"He had no way of knowing that his entire crew had baled out. The awful loneliness he had felt for the last six hours had become reality."

What sustained the morale of the Men of the Bombers in their titanic struggle against the forces arrayed against them? A vastly superior enemy, technological inferiority, policy blunders, target distance and the weather, all brought continual frustration and heavy losses. Was it belief in themselves, or in their leaders? Was it personal pride? How did they manage to sustain their much-maligned campaign?

The secret lay in crew bonding. Once a member of a bomber crew, posted to a squadron, one couldn't let the other blokes down. This is the quality that shines through all these stories, from the 55-year-old gunner lost over Dunkirk to the fierce loyalty of surviving crewmen who championed awards for lost comrades.

ISBN 978-0-7531-9418-8 (hb)
ISBN 978-0-7531-9419-5 (pb)

Lie in the Dark and Listen

Wing Commander Ken Rees
with Karen Arrandale

"If the war hadn't intervened, instead of the stuff of films I suppose my life could have been the stuff of television. Are You Being Served say, rather than The Great Escape."

Often quoted as the model for the Steve McQueen character in The Great Escape, Ken Rees had already had an eventful life by the age of 21. He had trained to be a pilot officer, flown 56 hair-raising bomber missions by night over Germany, taken part in the siege of Malta, got married, been shot down into a remote Nowegian lake and been captured, interrogated and sent to Stalag Luft III. He took part in and survived the Great Escape and the forced march to Bremen. Truly a real-life adventure story, written with accuracy, pace and drama.

ISBN 978-0-7531-9400-3 (hb)
ISBN 978-0-7531-9401-0 (pb)